1987

China
and the
Soviet Union
1949-84

China
and the
Soviet Union
1949-84

Compiled by Peter Jones and Siân Kevill

General editor: Alan J. Day

Facts On File Publications
New York, New York • Oxford, England

CHINA AND THE SOVIET UNION, 1949–84

First published in the United States by
Facts On File, Inc., 460 Park Avenue South,
New York, New York 10016, USA

Library of Congress Cataloging in Publication Data

Jones, Peter, 1953—
   China and the Soviet Union 1949–84.

   Based on reports published in Keesing's contemporary archives.
   Includes index.
   1. China—Foreign relations—Soviet Union. 2. Soviet Union—Foreign relations—China. I. Kevill, Siân. II. Day, Alan J. (Alan John). III. Keesing's contemporary archives. IV. Title.
DS740.5.S65J65   1985   327.51047   85–10209

ISBN 0–8160–1302–0
Printed in Great Britain by
The Eastern Press Limited, London and Reading

CONTENTS

CONTENTS

INTRODUCTION

It is now virtually 30 years since the first rumblings of dissension between the two communist giants of the Asian continent impinged itself on the world's consciousness. Over this period the Sino-Soviet dispute has consistently held attention as one of the more fascinating spectacles of the international scene. After a post–1949 honeymoon relationship in accord with the best principles of international revolutionary solidarity, the People's Republic of China and the Soviet Union began, from about 1956, a descent into increasingly bitter mutual hostility and recrimination. Ideological differences have featured prominently in the propaganda onslaughts of both sides, but the underlying causes are much more to do with realpolitik issues than with competition between Beijing and Moscow to be accepted as the true fount of communist wisdom. These issues are the familiar ones of insecurity in the face of the perceived military threat from the other side and, in the case of China, of unassuaged resentment over territorial encroachments by its neighbour during the era of European colonialist expansion.

Exacerbated by the ideological frictions generated by the Chinese Cultural Revolution of the late 1960s, Sino-Soviet territorial tensions escalated into direct military clashes on the border in 1969, to the extent that some Western observers were confidently positing the inevitability of a fullscale war between the two powers. That particular brink was drawn back from, however, and the past 16 years have been a period of uneasy searching for a modus vivendi, accompanied by periodic resort to the full panoply of state-directed hostile propaganda against the other side. In recent years the ascendancy of the "moderate" faction within the Chinese leadership and the accompanying repudiation of the Cultural Revolution's excesses have taken the ideological heat out of the Sino-Soviet dispute (although it may revive with the boot on the other foot, so to speak, now that the Chinese have officially declared that Marxism-Leninism cannot provide all the answers to present-day problems). This new realism in Beijing has facilitated a degree of rapprochement with Moscow and the resumption during 1984 of high-level ministerial contacts, after a gap of 15 years. Nevertheless, underlying Sino-Soviet tensions—not only over the border issue but also arising from Chinese suspicion of Soviet intentions in Afghanistan and Vietnam—remain eminently unresolved and seem likely to render the search for further normalization of the two countries' relations difficult.

The purpose of the present volume is to describe in detail the course of Sino-Soviet relations from the establishment of the People's Republic of China in 1949 up to the end of 1984. From the select bibliography given on pages 189–90 it will be apparent that modern Sino-Soviet relations have generated a copious literature from academic and other analysts of international relations. The gap which this book seeks to fill is the absence of a reference-style account of the dispute as it has unfolded over the last

30 years—one which concentrates on what has been said and done by the protagonists and does not enter into the realms of analysis or comment. The book is in fact a revised and updated successor to a Keesing's research report called *The Sino-Soviet Dispute* which appeared in 1970 and which was well received at the time as a guide to the intricacies of the subject. Compilation of the new volume was undertaken by two members of the editorial team of *Keesing's Contemporary Archives* (from which most of the source data has been drawn) and every effort has been made to maintain KCA-style thoroughness and objectivity in the presentation of the material.

January 1985   AJD

I: THE PERIOD OF FRIENDSHIP AND CO-OPERATION, 1949–55

The Bolshevik Revolution in Russia in October 1917 inspired the formation nearly four years later of the Communist Party of China, which thereupon received backing from the Soviet Union in its long quest for power. After World War II the Chinese Communists led by Mao Zedong mounted a final push against the Kuomintang (Nationalist) regime of Chiang Kai-shek, whose forces rapidly ceased to offer resistance despite their numerical superiority. The People's Republic of China was formally inaugurated on Oct. 1, 1949, and was officially recognized by the Soviet Union on the following day.

However, the seeds of future conflict between the two Communist super-powers were already germinating, as was indicated by the fact that the Communist seizure of power in China was carried out against the Soviet Government's advice. This was confirmed some years later, when Mao revealed publicly in 1962 that Joseph Stalin had warned the Chinese Communists in 1945 not to resume civil hostilities and had urged them to co-operate with the Kuomintang regime.

Treaty of Friendship and Other Agreements (February 1950)

Mao Zedong, then Chairman (President) of the Chinese People's Republic, arrived in Moscow on an official visit on Dec. 16, 1949, and was joined by Zhou Enlai, the Chinese Prime Minister and Foreign Minister, on Jan. 20, 1950. Negotiations between the two Governments terminated on Feb. 14 with the signature of (i) a treaty of friendship, alliance, and mutual assistance; (ii) an agreement providing that after the signing of a peace treaty with Japan, and in any case not later than the end of 1952, the Soviet Union would transfer free of charge to the Chinese Government all its rights in the joint administration of the Manchurian (Zhangzhun) Railway, together with the property belonging to the railway, and would withdraw its troops from the Port Arthur naval base, whose installations would be handed over to China; (iii) an agreement on the granting of long-term credits to the amount of 300,000,000 US dollars by the USSR to China, to enable China to obtain industrial, mining, and railway equipment from the USSR. The provisions of the treaty of friendship and alliance were as follows:

Art. 1. China and the USSR would take jointly "all the necessary measures at their disposal for the purpose of preventing a repetition of aggression and violation of the peace on the part of Japan or any state uniting with Japan, directly or indirectly, in acts of aggression". Should either China or the USSR be attacked by Japan, or states allied with that country, the other party would immediately render military and other assistance with all the means at its disposal. Both China and the USSR "declare their readiness, in a spirit of sincere co-operation, to participate in all international actions aimed at ensuring peace and security throughout the world,

2CHINA AND THE SOVIET UNION

and will do all in their power to achieve the speediest implementation of these tasks".

Art. 2. China and the USSR undertook "by means of mutual agreement to strive for the earliest conclusion of a peace treaty with Japan, jointly with the other powers which were allies during World War II".

Art. 3. Both parties undertook not to conclude any alliance directed against the other, or to take part in "any coalition or in acts and measures" directed against the other.

Art. 4. Both parties would "consult each other in regard to all important international problems affecting the common interests of the Soviet Union and China, being guided by the interests of the consolidation of peace and universal security".

Art. 5. Both parties undertook "in a spirit of friendship and in conformity with the principles of equality and mutual respect for sovereignty, territorial integrity, and non-interference in the affairs of the other party, to develop and consolidate economic and cultural ties between the Soviet Union and China, to render each other all possible economic assistance, and to carry out the necessary economic co-operation".

Art. 6. The treaty would come into force on exchange of instruments of ratification (to take place in Beijing), and would be valid for 30 years. Should neither party give notice of its intention to denounce the treaty one year before the term of its expiration, it would remain in force for another five years, and would be extended thereafter in conformity with this procedure. The treaty was drawn up in Russian and Chinese, both texts having equal validity.

An official announcement said that the negotiations had "proceeded in an atmosphere of cordiality and friendly mutual agreement", and had "confirmed the desire of both parties to strengthen and develop in every way relations of friendship and co-operation between them". Mao Zedong stated in 1962, however, that Stalin had held up the signing of the treaty of alliance for two months because he feared that the Chinese Communists, like the Yugoslav Communists, would pursue an independent policy, and that he had not begun to trust them until after the Korean War (of 1950–53).

Under the economic aid agreement, 50 Chinese enterprises were built or renovated with the aid of Soviet experts. Joint Sino-Soviet companies were set up for mining certain metals in Xinjiang (Sinkiang), for the extraction and refining of oil in that province, for the construction and repair of naval vessels at Dairen, and for the operation of civil airlines.

Issue of Chinese Membership of the United Nations

The Soviet delegate to the Security Council proposed unsuccessfully on Aug. 1, 1950, that China should be represented in the United Nations by the Communist instead of the Kuomintang regime, which had been transferred to Taiwan (Formosa). The proposal was thereafter repeatedly revived in the General Assembly, although without success until 1971. Despite their differences, the USSR consistently supported Communist China's admission to the United Nations throughout this period.

The Korean War—Soviet Military Aid to China (1950–53)

The Korean War began on June 25, 1950, when Soviet-equipped North Korean forces crossed the 38°N parallel in an attempt to conquer the

South. By October of that year forces of the United Nations deployed to resist the North Koreans were rapidly advancing towards the Chinese frontier, whereupon Chinese troops entered Korea. During the war the USSR supplied China with military aid to the value (according to US estimates) of $2,000 million, including about 1,000 MiG-15 aircraft and aid to war industries in Manchuria and the Chinese transport system. The modernization and mechanization of the Chinese armed forces with Soviet aid continued after the armistice of July 27, 1953, which ended the war. The Chinese produced heavy artillery and tanks copied from Soviet models, and later began producing MiGs under Soviet licence, whilst the small Chinese Navy was equipped with submarines, at first supplied by the USSR and later produced in China.

Transfer of Soviet Rights in Manchurian Railway to China—Extension of Joint Control of Port Arthur (September 1952)

After talks in Moscow lasting nearly a month between Soviet leaders and a Chinese mission led by Zhou Enlai, the official Soviet news agency Tass announced on Sept. 15, 1952, that the transfer of the Manchurian Railway would be completed by the end of the year, as agreed in 1950, but that at the Chinese Government's request the withdrawal of Soviet troops from Port Arthur would be postponed until Japan had concluded peace treaties with China and the USSR.

Increased Soviet Economic Aid to China (September 1953)

When Stalin died on March 5, 1953, he was succeeded as Prime Minister by Georgi Malenkov and as general secretary of the Soviet Communist Party by Nikita Khrushchev. The new Soviet regime greatly increased economic aid to China; a letter from Mao Zedong to Malenkov, published on Sept. 15, revealed that the Soviet Government had promised to "extend systematic economic and technical aid in the construction and renovation of 91 new enterprises in China and to the 50 enterprises now being built or renovated".

Restoration of Port Arthur to China—Further Increases in Soviet Aid (October 1954)

During 1953–55 a struggle for power in the Soviet Union developed between Malenkov and Khrushchev, in which the latter apparently sought and obtained Chinese support. He arrived in Beijing on Sept. 29, 1954, for the celebrations of the fifth anniversary of the establishment of the Chinese People's Republic, at the head of a delegation which also included Marshal Bulganin (then the Soviet Defence Minister). At the conclusion of his visit it was announced on Oct. 12 that the agreements detailed below had been reached.

(1) In view of the changed situation in the Far East caused by the ending of the Korean War, the establishment of peace in Indo-China by the Geneva Agreements, and the strengthening of China's defence potential, all Soviet troops would be evacuated from Port Arthur by May 31, 1955, and the installations would be transferred to China without compensation.

(2) The USSR would grant China a long-term credit of 520,000,000 roubles; the USSR would aid China in building 15 new industrial undertakings, and would

increase deliveries of equipment for the 141 enterprises covered by the earlier agreements; and a joint commission of Soviet and Chinese technicians and scientists would meet at least twice a year to discuss Soviet technical aid to China. The USSR would hand over to China on Jan. 1, 1955, all her shares in the joint Sino-Soviet companies, the value of which would be refunded in goods over a number of years.

(3) Two new railways linking China and the USSR would be built, one running from Alma Ata (in the Soviet Republic of Kazakhstan) via the Chinese province of Xinjiang to Lanzhou (in north-west China), whilst the second would run from Tinmin (in northern China) to Ulan Bator (capital of the Mongolian People's Republic), which was already connected by rail with the Trans-Siberian Railway. The Chinese and Soviet Governments would be responsible for building the sections of the first railway in their respective territories, and Outer Mongolia would co-operate with the USSR in building the second.

Nuclear Co-operation Agreement (May 1955)

Georgi Malenkov resigned the Soviet premiership on March 8, 1955, and was succeeded by Marshal Bulganin, who said in one of his first official statements that "China can count in all circumstances on the aid of the USSR". Moscow Radio announced on May 1 that an agreement with China had been signed on Soviet aid in atomic research for peaceful purposes. It was stated that the agreement provided for (i) the completion of the necessary preparatory work in 1955–56 and the supply of experimental atomic piles and accelerators; (ii) the free supply of scientific and technical information required for the installation of this apparatus, and the loan of Soviet specialists; (iii) the supply of sufficient quantities of fissile material and radioactive isotopes until China was able to keep its atomic piles working without further Soviet aid; (iv) the training of Chinese in nuclear physics.

II: THE BEGINNINGS OF DISAGREEMENT, 1956–59

Sino-Soviet friendship and co-operation reached its highest point during the period from 1953 to 1956, between the death of Stalin and Nikita Khrushchev's announcement of the de-Stalinization policy at the 20th congress of the Soviet Communist Party in February 1956. During the next four years the two countries gradually drifted apart, largely as a result of their differences on foreign policy, although these were not made public at the time.

20th Congress of the Soviet Communist Party (February 1956)

In his report to the 20th congress of the Soviet Communist Party, held on Feb. 14–25, 1956, Khrushchev reaffirmed the Soviet party's support for a policy of peaceful coexistence between countries with different social and political systems; rejected Lenin's theory that war was inevitable so long as capitalism existed; and held that in certain countries the transition to socialism might take place peacefully by parliamentary means.

Principles of Coexistence. "The forces of peace", Khrushchev said, had been "considerably augmented by the emergence in the world of a group of peace-loving European and Asian states which have proclaimed non-participation in blocs as a principle of their foreign policies". As a result, "a vast zone of peace has emerged in the world, including peace-loving states, both socialist and non-socialist, of Europe and Asia. This zone embraces vast areas inhabited by nearly 1,500 million people—that is, the majority of the population of our planet".

"Under the impact of these incontestable facts", Khrushchev continued, "symptoms of a certain sobering-up are appearing among influential Western circles. More and more people in these circles are realizing what a dangerous gamble war against the socialist countries may prove for the development of capitalism. . . . Nor is it a coincidence that prominent leaders of bourgeois countries with increasing frequency frankly admit that 'there will be no victor' in a war in which atomic weapons are used. . . ."

On relations with the USA he said: "The establishment of firm friendly relations between the two biggest powers of the world, the Soviet Union and the USA, would be of great significance for the strengthening of world peace. If the well-known 'five principles of peaceful coexistence' were to underlie the relations between the Soviet Union and the USA, it would be of truly great importance for all mankind. . . . These principles—mutual respect for territorial integrity and sovereignty, non-aggression, non-interference in one another's domestic affairs, equality and mutual advantage, peaceful coexistence and economic co-operation— are now subscribed to by a score of states. . . . We want to be friends with the USA and co-operate with it for peace and international security, and also in the economic and cultural spheres. We propose this with good intentions, without holding a knife behind our back. . . ."

Enlarging on the Soviet attitude to peaceful coexistence, Khrushchev said: "It has been alleged that the Soviet Union puts forward the principle of peaceful coexistence merely out of tactical considerations—considerations of expediency.

But it is common knowledge that we have always, from the very first years of
Soviet power, stood with equal firmness for peaceful coexistence. Hence it is not a
tactical move, but a fundamental principle of Soviet foreign policy. . . . It goes
without saying that among Communists there are no supporters of capitalism. But
this does not mean that we have interfered, or plan to interfere, in the internal
affairs of countries where capitalism exists. . . .

"When we say that the socialist system will win in the competition between the
two systems, the capitalist and the socialist, this by no means signifies that its
victory will be achieved through armed interference by the socialist countries in the
internal affairs of the capitalist countries. Our certainty of the victory of communism
is based on the fact that the socialist mode of production possesses decisive
advantages over the capitalist mode of production. . . . We have always held, and
continue to hold, that the establishment of a new social system in this or that
country is the internal affair of the people of the country concerned. . . . The
principle of peaceful coexistence is gaining ever wider international recognition.
. . . And this is natural, for in present-day conditions there is no other way out.
Indeed, there are only two ways: either peaceful coexistence or the most destructive
war in history. There is no third way."

The "Inevitability of War". Discussing whether a third world war was inevitable,
Khrushchev said: "There is, of course, a Marxist-Leninist precept that wars are
inevitable as long as imperialism exists. This precept was evolved at a time when
imperialism was an all-embracing world system, and the social and political forces
which did not want war were weak, poorly organized, and thus unable to compel
the imperialists to renounce war. . . . At the present time, however, the situation
has radically changed. Now there is a world camp of socialism which has become a
mighty force. In this camp the peace forces find not only the moral but also the
material means to prevent aggression. Moreover, there is a large group of other
countries, with a population running into hundreds of millions, which is actively
working to avert war. The labour movement in the capitalist countries has today
become a tremendous force. The movement of peace supporters has sprung up and
developed into a powerful factor.

"In these circumstances the Leninist precept certainly remains in force that, so
long as imperialism exists, the economic basis giving rise to wars will continue to
exist. That is why we must display the greatest vigilance. As long as capitalism
survives in the world, the reactionary forces representing the interests of the
capitalist monopolies will continue their drive towards military gambles and
aggression, and may try to unleash war. But war is not fatalistically inevitable.
Today there are mighty social and political forces possessing formidable means to
prevent the imperialists from unleashing war, and, if they actually do try to start it,
to deliver a smashing rebuff to the aggressors and frustrate their adventurist plans."

Forms of Transition to Socialism. After declaring that the transition to socialism
might take a number of forms, Khrushchev quoted a saying of Lenin that "All
nations will arrive at socialism, but not all will do so in exactly the same way", and
observed that this saying had been confirmed by the experience of history. "It is
probable that more forms of transition to socialism will appear", he continued.
"Moreover, the implementation of these forms need not be associated with civil
war. The greater or lesser degree of intensity which the struggle may assume, the
use or the non-use of violence in the transition to socialism, depends on the
resistance of the exploiters—on whether the exploiting class itself resorts to violence
rather than on the proletariat.

"In this connexion", Khrushchev went on, "the question arises whether it is
possible to make the transition to socialism by parliamentary means. No such
course was open to the Russian Bolsheviks, who were the first to effect this
transition. . . . Since then, however, the historical situation has undergone radical
changes which make possible a new approach to the question. . . . The present

situation offers the working class in a number of capitalist countries a real opportunity to unite the overwhelming majority of the people under its leadership and to secure the transfer of the basic means of production into the hands of the people. . . . The winning of a stable parliamentary majority backed by a mass revolutionary movement of the proletariat and all the working people could create for the working class of a number of capitalist and former colonial countries the conditions needed to secure fundamental social changes. In the countries where capitalism is still strong and has a huge military and police apparatus at its disposal, the reactionary forces will, of course, inevitably offer serious resistance. There the transition to socialism will be attended by a sharp revolutionary struggle."

At a secret session of the 20th congress Khrushchev made a long speech in which he denounced Stalin's wholesale executions of innocent people, the extraction of confessions by torture, his strategy in World War II, his responsibility for the breach with Yugoslavia in 1948, and the "personality cult" surrounding him.

Khrushchev's advocacy of peaceful coexistence did not mark in any sense a new departure in Soviet policy, nor was it incompatible with the views on international relations put forward by the Chinese Government at that time. At the 19th Soviet Communist Party congress in October 1952, at which Stalin was present, Malenkov had said: "The Soviet policy of peace and security of the nations is based on the premise that the peaceful coexistence and co-operation of capitalism and communism are quite possible, provided there is a mutual desire to co-operate, readiness to carry out commitments, and adherence to the principle of equal rights and non-interference in the internal affairs of other states. The Soviet Union has always stood for, and advocates, the development of trade and co-operation with other countries irrespective of the difference in social systems. . . . We have not the least intention of forcing our ideology or our economic system upon anybody. 'The export of revolution is nonsense. Every country will make its own revolution if it wants to, and if it does not want to there will be no revolution', says Comrade Stalin. . . ."

The five principles of peaceful coexistence, to which Khrushchev referred in his report, were first formulated in an agreement between China and India signed on April 29, 1954. At the Bandung conference of Afro-Asian countries, held in April 1955, Zhou Enlai supported a resolution calling for the total prohibition of the manufacture of nuclear weapons and universal disarmament, and issued the following statement on relations between China and the USA: "The Chinese people are friendly to the American people. They do not want a war with the United States. The Chinese Government is willing to sit down and enter into negotiations with the US Government to discuss the question of relaxing tension in the Far East, especially in the Formosa area."

The new features of Khrushchev's report were his rejection of the theory of the inevitability of war under capitalism and his acceptance of the possibility of a peaceful transition to socialism. Although these theories, together with his denunciation of Stalin, were later to become the subject of bitter controversy between the Soviet and Chinese Communist parties, they were not publicly questioned at the time by the Chinese party, which endorsed his criticisms of Stalin in a statement issued on April 5, 1956.

Chinese Intervention in the Polish and Hungarian Crises
(October–November 1956)

Khrushchev's repudiation of Stalin's policies had profound repercussions throughout Eastern Europe, which in Poland and still more in Hungary assumed the form of open revolt against the Stalinist system. The central committee of the Polish United Worker's Party, at a session on Oct. 19–21, 1956, elected a new politburo from which Stalinists were excluded and chose Wladyslaw Gomulka, who had recently been released from prison, as its first secretary. Khrushchev and other Soviet leaders flew to Warsaw on Oct. 19, and Soviet tank formations began to move on Warsaw; the Polish leadership stood firm, however, and on Oct. 23 Khrushchev gave an assurance that all Soviet troops in Poland would return to their bases. In later official statements the Chinese party revealed that it had intervened in this crisis, and had advised the Soviet leaders against using force, and also against calling an international conference of Communist parties to condemn the Polish party.

An armed revolt in Hungary in the last week of October 1956 was followed by the establishment on Oct. 30 of a four-party Government, which announced the discontinuation of the one-party system. The Soviet Government announced on the same day its readiness to withdraw its forces from Budapest, but on Nov. 4 the Soviet Army attacked Budapest, suppressed the national uprising by force, and installed a new Government headed by János Kádár. Later Chinese statements revealed that this reversal of policy had been carried out on Chinese advice, and alleged that Khrushchev had adopted a vacillating attitude and had only with great difficulty been persuaded by the Chinese Government to "go to the defence of the Hungarian revolution".

Zhou Enlai arrived in Moscow on Jan. 7, 1957, for discussions with the Soviet leaders; he visited Warsaw on Jan. 11–16 and Budapest on Jan. 16–17, and returned to Moscow on Jan. 17 to resume his discussions. A joint statement issued by Marshal Bulganin and Zhou Enlai on Jan. 18 called for the replacement of military alliances by collective security pacts for Europe and Asia and an agreement between the great powers on disarmament, and claimed that attempts by both the USSR and China to establish peaceful coexistence with the USA had been frustrated by "the claims of American monopoly circles for world domination and their policy of aggression and war preparations". The statement condemned the Hungarian uprising as "provoked by imperialist aggressive quarters and Hungarian counter-revolutionary elements" in order to "destroy the socialist system in Hungary, restore fascist dictatorship, and thereby create a hotbed of war in Europe", and described its suppression as "a major victory for the cause of peace and socialism". It affirmed the principle of complete equality between socialist countries, and stated that "it is fully possible in their relations to combine the unity of socialist countries and the independence of each individual country".

Secret Agreement on Nuclear Armament of China (October 1957)

Under a secret agreement signed on Oct. 15, 1957, the USSR undertook to supply the necessary scientific information and technical materials to enable China to manufacture its own nuclear weapons. This agreement was never carried out, and its existence was revealed by China only in 1963.

12-Nation Moscow Declaration (November 1957)

Delegations from all the Communist countries visited Moscow in November 1957 for the celebrations of the 40th anniversary of the Bolshevik Revolution, the Chinese delegation being headed by Mao Zedong. During the celebrations representatives of the ruling parties of all the 13 Communist countries except Yugoslavia met on Nov. 14–16 for discussions, at the conclusion of which they issued a lengthy joint declaration. In a speech to the conference, which later aroused much controversy, Mao said that there was a possibility of preventing another world war, but even if nuclear war broke out at least half the world's population would survive, and "the whole world would become socialist".

The 12-nation Moscow declaration reaffirmed the principle of peaceful coexistence and the possibility of achieving socialism through parliamentary means, and condemned both "revisionism" and "dogmatism." According to later Chinese statements, however, in its final form it incorporated significant amendments on which the Chinese party had insisted.

The declaration stated that the 12 parties adhered to the "Leninist principle of peaceful coexistence . . . which . . . coincides with the five principles put forward jointly by China and India in the programme adopted at the Bandung conference of Afro-Asian countries".

On "dogmatism" and "revisionism" the declaration said: "In condemning dogmatism, the Communist parties believe that the main danger at present is revisionism—in other words, right-wing opportunism as a manifestation of bourgeois ideology paralyzing the revolutionary energy of the working class and demanding the preservation or restoration of capitalism. However, dogmatism and sectarianism can also be the main danger at different phases of development in one party or another. It is for each Communist party to decide what danger threatens it more at a given time. . . . Modern revisionism seeks to smear the teaching of Marxism-Leninism, declares that it is 'outmoded', and alleges that it has lost its significance for social progress. . . . The revisionists deny the historical necessity for a proletarian revolution and the dictatorship of the proletariat during the period of transition from capitalism to socialism; [they] reject the principles of proletarian internationalism; and call for the rejection of the Leninist principles of party organization and democratic centralism. Above all, they call for the transformation of the Communist party from a militant revolutionary party into some kind of debating society. . . .

"The working class and its vanguard—the Marxist-Leninist party—seek to achieve the socialist revolution by peaceful means", the declaration continued. "In a number of capitalist countries the working class today has the opportunity—given a united working class and people's front, or other workable forms of political co-operation between the different parties and organizations—to unite a majority of the people, win power without civil war, and ensure the transfer of the basic means of production to the hands of the people. . . . [The] working class . . . can secure a firm majority in parliament, transform parliament from an instrument serving the class interests of the bourgeoisie into an instrument serving the working people, launch a non-parliamentary mass struggle, smash the resistance of the reactionary forces, and create the necessary conditions for the peaceful realization of the socialist revolution . . . .

"In the event of the ruling classes resorting to violence against the people, the possibility of non-peaceful transition to socialism should be borne in mind. Leninism teaches, and experience confirms, that the ruling classes never relinquish power voluntarily. In this case the degree of bitterness and the forms of the class struggle will depend not so much on the proletariat as on the resistance put up by the reactionary circles. . . ."

[The term "revisionism" was originally applied to the teachings of the German Social Democrat Eduard Bernstein, who in 1898 put forward the view that Marx's theories should be revised in view of subsequent political and economic developments; hence it has been applied by Communists to theories which are considered to depart from the fundamental principles of Marxism. The terms "dogmatism" and "sectarianism" are used of ultra-leftist doctrines and policies which fail to take the practical realities of the existing political situation into account.]

A Peace Manifesto, calling for the complete prohibition of nuclear weapons, the ending of the arms race and military blocs, and support for a policy of peaceful coexistence, was signed by representatives of all the 64 Communist parties taking part in the November 1957 Moscow celebrations, including the Chinese party.

The Yugoslav League of Communists neither participated in the 12-party discussions nor signed the declaration, although it did sign the Peace Manifesto. Edvard Kardelj, who had led the Yugoslav delegation at the celebrations, said on returning to Belgrade that "we did not sign it because we did not agree with it". Relations between the Soviet and Yugoslav Communist parties drastically deteriorated in 1958, when a new programme adopted by the League of Communists was attacked in the Soviet press, and still more violently in the Chinese press, for its "revisionist" character.

The Middle Eastern Crisis of July–August 1958

Fundamental differences between China and the USSR on questions of international policy first became apparent in the summer of 1958. Following the Iraqi revolution of July 14, President Chamoun of Lebanon appealed to President Eisenhower to send US forces to that country, and King Hussein of Jordan made a similar appeal to Britain; in consequence US Marines landed in Lebanon on July 15, and British parachute troops arrived in Jordan two days later. In a letter to President Eisenhower, Khrushchev proposed on July 19 an immediate conference of the heads of government of the USSR, the USA, Britain, France, and India. President Eisenhower in his reply proposed on July 22 that such a meeting should take place within the framework of the UN Security Council, and this suggestion was accepted by Khrushchev on the following day.

Khrushchev visited Beijing from July 31 to Aug. 3, 1958, for talks with the Chinese leaders. The communiqué issued at the conclusion of the talks referred to the "complete identity of views" between the two Governments; condemned the US and British "aggression" in Lebanon and Jordan; and called for an immediate conference of heads of government and the immediate withdrawal of the US and British troops from Lebanon and Jordan. It also said that the two Communist parties would "wage an uncompromising struggle against revisionism—the principal danger in the Communist movement", which had found its clearest manifestation in the programme of the Yugoslav League of Communists.

On the question of war and peace the communiqué said: "The Soviet Union and the Chinese People's Republic will do everything possible to ease international tension and prevent the horrors of a new war. Both parties declare once again that the right of the peoples of all countries to choose their own social and political systems must be respected; that countries with different social systems must co-exist peacefully, in accordance with the well-known 'five principles' which have received wide international recognition; that all controversial international issues must be settled peacefully by negotiation; and that the development of economic and cultural relations between countries on the basis of mutual benefit and peaceful competition . . . must be encouraged.

"The major task in preserving and consolidating peace is the reaching of agreement among states to reduce armaments, to end [nuclear] tests and ban atomic and hydrogen weapons, to abolish all military groupings and bases on foreign territories, and to conclude a pact of peace and collective security. Whether war can be averted does not, however, depend solely on the good intentions of the peace-loving peoples and their unilateral efforts. Right up to the present moment, aggressive circles of the Western powers are refusing to take any genuine measures to preserve peace; on the contrary, they are senselessly aggravating the international tension and putting mankind on the brink of catastrophe. If the sabre-rattling imperialist maniacs dare to force war on the peoples, they should realize that all the peace-loving and freedom-loving countries, closely united in a single unit, will put an end to the imperialist aggressors once and for all and establish everlasting peace the world over."

After returning to Moscow Khrushchev again wrote to President Eisenhower on Aug. 5, 1958, withdrawing his support for the proposed summit meeting on the ground that the Security Council was dominated by the USA and its allies, and demanding the admission of the Chinese People's Republic to the United Nations. His volte-face was believed to be a direct result of his discussions in Beijing.

In his letter Khrushchev said inter alia: "If we glance at the composition of the Security Council as it now stands, we are bound to draw the conclusion that . . . this body has become a kind of committee dominated by member-countries of NATO, the Baghdad Pact and SEATO [South-East Asia Treaty Organization], a committee in which the lawful seat of the great Chinese People's Republic is held by a representative of a political corpse—Chiang Kai-shek.

"The policy of ignoring People's China is sheer madness. This great power exists and is growing stronger, regardless of whether or not it is recognized by certain governments. . . . Without the Chinese People's Republic, the Security Council and the UN cannot be completely effective bodies in safeguarding peace and ensuring security. . . . A situation has thus arisen in which the Security Council has in fact been paralyzed and is unable to take, against the will of the United States, any decision which would effectively promote the safeguarding of world peace. . . ."

The Quemoy Crisis (August–October 1958)

On Aug. 23, 1958, the Chinese Army began an almost daily bombardment of the offshore island of Quemoy, which was held by the Kuomintang forces. John Foster Dulles (then the US Secretary of State) declared on Sept. 4 that US forces would be used for the protection of Quemoy, and by the middle of the month a powerful US air and naval force had been assembled in the Western Pacific. Khrushchev warned President Eisenhower on Sept. 8 that "an attack on the Chinese People's Republic, which is a great friend, ally, and neighbour of our country, is an attack on the Soviet Union", whilst stressing his wish to "find a common language with you" so that the parties concerned might "join their efforts in removing the tension which has arisen in the Far East". President Eisenhower replied on Sept. 13, accusing the Chinese Government of "aggression". In a Note of Sept. 19, which was formally rejected by the US Government, Khrushchev contended that US support for the Kuomintang Government was responsible for the crisis, and that there could be no lasting peace in the Far East until the US armed forces were recalled from Formosa (Taiwan) and the Formosa Straits. Tension in the area relaxed after the Chinese Government temporarily suspended the bombardment of Quemoy on Oct. 6, 1958.

Mao Zedong revealed in September 1962 that Khrushchev had proposed at this time that China and the USSR should form a joint war fleet. This proposal was rejected by the Chinese leaders, who, according to Mao, regarded it as an attempt by the USSR to control the Chinese coast and to facilitate an eventual blockade of China.

The Communes and the "Great Leap Forward" (1958)

Between April and August 1958 the movement for the grouping of agricultural co-operatives into large people's communes combining small-scale industry with agriculture swept China. The Communist Party politburo formally approved the movement in August, and at the same time approved the "Great Leap Forward" policy for the rapid industrialization of China, the target for steel production for 1958 being raised to 10,700,000 tonnes, compared with 5,900,000 tonnes produced in 1957. For this purpose the party abandoned its previous policy of relying for its industrial output primarily on large industrial complexes built with Soviet aid and requiring several years to construct, and instead adopted a policy of constructing hundreds of thousands of small and medium plants all over China.

The Chinese Government's new economic policy was not received with approval by the Communist Party in the USSR, where the press and radio were extremely reticent in their references to it. The *Washington Post* reported on Dec. 17, 1958, that at a recent meeting with Senator Hubert Humphrey Khrushchev had described the commune system as "reactionary" and inappropriate.

The central committee of the Chinese party, meeting from Nov. 28 to Dec. 10, 1958, approved a proposal by Mao that he should resign the post of Chairman of the Republic, while remaining chairman of the party, in order to concentrate on theoretical work. It was widely suggested that he had been forced to resign because of the failure of the communes, the plan to double steel production, and Chinese policy on the offshore islands. A resolution adopted at the same time said that industrialization would take a very long time; that the transition from socialism to communism (i.e. from the principle of "to each according to his work" to that of "to each according to his needs") would take "fifteen, twenty, or more years, counting from now"; and that attempts to distribute supplies "according to need" were "an attempt to enter communism by over-reaching ourselves— undoubtedly a Utopian concept that cannot succeed." Liu Shaoqi succeeded Mao as Chairman of the Republic in April 1959.

21st Soviet Party Congress (January–February 1959)

At the 21st Soviet Communist Party congress, held from Jan. 27 to Feb. 5, 1959, no open signs of tension between the USSR and China appeared. In his report to the congress Khrushchev described "the aggressive policy of the USA towards the Chinese People's Republic and other peace-loving states" as the main source of tension in the Far East, and suggested the creation of a nuclear-free zone in the Far East and the Pacific. He also said that "the Communist Party of China is employing many original forms of socialist construction, but we have no disagreements with it. . . . We are in full and complete agreement with our brother party in China, though in many respects its methods of building socialism do not resemble our own."

Zhou Enlai, addressing the congress, spoke of the "eternal and unbreakable" friendship between the USSR and China, and read a message from Mao praising Khrushchev's "correct leadership", but made no reference to the latter's proposal for a nuclear-free zone in the Far East.

The Peng Dehuai Episode (May–September 1959)

During an official visit to Albania on May 25–June 4, 1959, Khrushchev met the Chinese Defence Minister, Marshal Peng Dehuai. It was later revealed that at this meeting Marshal Peng showed him a memorandum strongly criticizing the Great Leap Forward and the communes, which he afterwards submitted to a meeting of the central committee of the Chinese party held in July and August. It was announced on Sept. 17 that he had been replaced as Defence Minister by Marshal Lin Biao. The new appointment marked a significant change in Chinese military policy, as Marshal Peng favoured close collaboration with the USSR as the only possible source of modern weapons, whereas Marshal Lin was the leading advocate of the Maoist theory that manpower and morale rather than armaments were the decisive factors in war.

Soviet Repudiation of Agreement on Nuclear Weapons (June 1959)

The USSR repudiated on June 20, 1959, the secret agreement of 1957 on the supply of aid to China in manufacturing nuclear weapons. This reversal of policy, which was deeply resented by the Chinese and contributed to bring about the fall of Marshal Peng Dehuai, was apparently motivated by Khrushchev's desire to achieve a rapprochement with the USA, by his plan for a nuclear-free zone in the Far East, and by his distrust of the increasingly bellicose tendencies of China's foreign policy. A Chinese broadcast of Aug. 15, 1963, which first revealed details of the agreement, asserted that its repudiation was intended "as a gift for the Soviet leader to take to Eisenhower when visiting the USA in September".

The Longju Incident (August 1959)

A series of developments in the summer and autumn of 1959, arising from Khrushchev's attempts to improve relations with the USA and China's expansionist policy on the Indian frontier, brought the differences between the USSR and China over foreign policy to a head. On Aug. 25–26 of that year Chinese troops occupied the frontier post of Longju, which the Indian Government claimed was within the North-East Frontier Agency; Zhou

Enlai, however, maintained in a note to India that it was in Chinese territory and had been illegally occupied by Indian troops.

A statement issued on Sept. 9, 1959, by the Tass agency pointed out that the Soviet Union "maintains friendly relations with the Chinese People's Republic and the Republic of India"; that the Chinese and Soviet peoples were "linked by unbreakable bonds of fraternal friendship based on the great principles of socialist internationalism"; and that "friendly co-operation between the USSR and India is developing successfully in keeping with the ideas of peaceful coexistence". It expressed confidence that China and India would settle their misunderstandings arising out of the "deplorable" frontier incidents, and declared that "attempts to exploit the incidents . . . for the purpose of fanning the cold war . . . should be resolutely condemned". At the 1960 Moscow Conference [see below] Deng Xiaoping, general secretary of the Chinese Communist Party, declared that this "tendentious" communiqué first "revealed our differences to the world".

Khrushchev's Visit to USA (September 1959)

Nikita Khrushchev and Andrei Gromyko (the Soviet Foreign Minister) paid an official visit to the USA from Sept. 15–28, 1959, at the conclusion of which the former had three days of private talks with President Eisenhower at Camp David. In his public statements during the visit Khrushchev repeatedly emphasized the dangers of nuclear war, appealed for peaceful coexistence and universal and complete disarmament, and paid high tributes to President Eisenhower. After returning to Moscow he expressed his conviction that the President "sincerely wants to liquidate the cold war and improve relations between our two great countries". His praise of President Eisenhower aroused particular anger in China; at the 1960 Moscow conference Deng Xiaoping said that "no considerations of diplomatic protocol can explain away or excuse Khrushchev's tactless eulogy of Eisenhower and other imperialists".

Khrushchev's Visit to Beijing (September–October 1959)

Immediately after returning from the USA Khrushchev and Gromyko flew to Beijing for the celebrations of the tenth anniversary of the Chinese People's Republic. In their public statements the Chinese leaders abstained from criticism of Khrushchev's visit to the USA. At a banquet on Sept. 30 Zhou Enlai congratulated him on "the success of his mission to the USA as an envoy of peace". In his reply Khrushchev emphasized that war must be precluded as a means of settling international disputes, gave a warning against "testing the capitalist system by force", and declared that "socialism cannot be imposed by force of arms".

"The stronger the forces of the socialist camp become, the more opportunities it will have for successfully upholding the cause of peace," Khrushchev said. "The forces of socialism are already so great that concrete possibilities are developing of precluding war as a means of settling international disputes. In our times the heads of government of some capitalist countries are beginning to show a certain tendency towards a realistic understanding of the situation existing in the world today. When I talked to President Eisenhower, my impression was that the President of the United States—and he has the support of many people—is aware of the need to relax international tension. . . . We, for our part, must do everything possible to preclude war as a means of settling outstanding questions. These questions must be solved through negotiations. . . . There is only one way to maintain peace—the way of peaceful coexistence of states with different social systems. . . .

"The socialist countries", Khrushchev continued, "have the means of defence against the imperialist aggressors should the latter attempt to force them to leave the socialist road by interference in their affairs. . . . That time has gone for ever. But . . . this certainly does not mean that since we are so strong we should test the stability of the capitalist system by force. That would be wrong; the peoples would never understand and would never support those who took it into their heads to act in this way. . . . Even such a noble and progressive system as socialism cannot be imposed by force of arms against the will of the people. That is why socialist countries, pursuing their consistent peace policy, concentrate on peaceful construction. . . . The question of when this or that country will embark on the socialist road must be decided by the people themselves. This principle is sacrosanct for us. . . ."

While in Beijing Khrushchev had a series of meetings with the Chinese leaders, but no communiqué was issued, suggesting that they had failed to reach agreement. Before leaving Beijing on Oct. 4, 1959, Khrushchev made a short speech at the airport in which he reaffirmed his belief that it was possible to "rule out war for all time as a means of solving international disputes", and said that the Soviet Union would "take advantage of any possibilities in order to end the cold war".

The Ladakh Incident (October 1959)

A second serious incident on the Indian border occurred on Oct. 20–21, 1959, when nine members of an Indian police patrol were killed and 10 captured in a clash with Chinese troops. The Indian Government claimed that the incident took place 40 miles inside Ladakh (the northern region of Kashmir); the Chinese Government maintained that the Indians had intruded into Chinese territory.

Khrushchev said on Nov. 7, 1959, that the Soviet Government would "do everything to help" in finding a solution to the Sino-Indian frontier dispute, which should be settled amicably; as regards the Ladakh incident, he said that the area was "uninhabited and not of any particular significance". The Soviet press adopted a completely neutral attitude towards the incident, printing the Indian and Chinese versions side by side without comment.

Continued Soviet Economic Aid to China (1956–59)

Soviet economic and technical aid to China was continued throughout this period, the main agreements being as follows:

(1) An agreement signed on April 7, 1956, provided that 55 new factories and plants would be built in China with Soviet assistance, in addition to the 156 industrial enterprises stipulated under earlier Sino-Soviet agreements. The new installations to be built would include metallurgical, engineering, and chemical plants, factories to produce plastics and artificial fibres, electro-technical and radio plants, power stations, an artificial liquid fuel plant, and aviation industry research institutes. The total cost of these installations would amount to about 2,500 million roubles [approx. $636,000,000 then at nominal rates], which the Chinese Government would defray by supplying goods of various kinds to the Soviet Union.

(2) An agreement for the joint development of the Amur-Argun river basin, which forms the boundary between Manchuria and the Soviet Far East, was announced on Aug. 19, 1956. The plan provided for the building of a series of hydro-electric power stations, the industrial development of the area, and a new outlet for the Amur River, which is not deep enough for large ships and is frozen at its mouth for much of the year.

(3) An agreement signed on Aug. 8, 1958, provided for the construction or expansion of 47 metallurgical, chemical, coal-mining, machine-building, woodworking, and building materials enterprises and power stations.

(4) An agreement providing for additional Soviet financial and technical aid during the eight-year period 1959–67, which was signed on Feb. 7, 1959, envisaged the construction of 78 large enterprises, 31 more than in the previous agreement, which it superseded. The total amount of Soviet assistance under the agreement was given as 5,000 million roubles (about $1,250 million), which China would repay by deliveries of goods.

(5) A protocol on scientific and technical co-operation was signed on Oct. 12, 1959, under which Soviet and Chinese institutions were to exchange specialists and technical information on metallurgy, machine-building, the coal and chemical industries, and other aspects of scientific research.

In a survey of this subject published on March 20, 1969, *Le Monde* stated: "The 141 'units' created with Russian aid [i.e. those announced in 1953]—factories, enterprises, dams, laboratories, development projects, etc.—gradually became 156 in 1954, then 211 in 1956, and finally about 250 in 1959. In many cases the Chinese merely built the factories from Russian plans, and the Russians supplied all the machinery, directed its installation, set it going, and left only when production had begun. Zhou Enlai has said that between 1949 and 1959 the USSR supplied 10,800 technicians, in addition to whom 1,500 came from Central Europe. Between 1951 and 1957 the Russians claim to have trained 13,600 Chinese specialists, students, and workers in the USSR. The total amount of Soviet loans to China has never been revealed, but American experts have estimated it at $2,200 million, of which a little over $400,000,000 went to military aid and the rest to industrialization."

III: THE BEGINNING OF OPEN CONTROVERSY, 1960–62

In April 1960 the Chinese Communist Party made public for the first time its ideological differences with the Soviet party, although until the end of 1962 both sides refrained from attacking each other directly. The Chinese directed their attacks ostensibly against "revisionists" in general and the Yugoslavs in particular, often using criticism of the positions taken by the Italian Communist Party (then led by the pro-Soviet Palmiro Togliatti) as an oblique way of attacking the Soviet leadership. The Soviet Communists directed their polemics against "dogmatists" in general and (after the breach with the Albanian party in 1961) the Albanians in particular. The main issues in debate in the earlier stages of the controversy were as follows:

(1) The Chinese rejected as a "naïve illusion" Khrushchev's view that war was no longer inevitable under capitalism, that disarmament was possible, and that certain Western political leaders recognized the necessity of peaceful coexistence, and held that Khrushchev's foreign policy involved not only rejection of the class struggle but also "peace at any price".

(2) As an argument in favour of peaceful coexistence, the Soviet party emphasized that nuclear war would prove equally disastrous to all concerned. The Chinese party upheld Mao Zedong's view, as expressed at the 1957 Moscow conference, that a third world war would result in further victories for communism.

(3) The USSR was more cautious than China in assisting nationalist movements in colonial and underdeveloped countries, in view of their possible repercussions on the international situation. Whereas, for example, the Chinese recognized the Provisional Government set up by the Algerian nationalists immediately after its formation in 1958, the Soviet Government did not do so, apparently in order to avoid complications in its relations with France, and granted de facto recognition only in October 1960.

(4) Soviet theoreticians contended that in underdeveloped countries Communists should ally themselves with the "national bourgeoisie" in the struggle for national independence, which would prepare the way for the transition to socialism; an example of this theory in practice was Stalin's advice to the Chinese Communists in 1945 to collaborate with the Kuomintang. The Soviet Communist daily newspaper *Pravda* emphasized on Aug. 26, 1960, that "high-handed treatment of anti-imperialist actions" not led by Communists constituted "a very dangerous form of sectarianism", and condemned the idea of "exporting revolution" and imposing on other countries social systems not developing from their internal conditions. In reply, the Beijing *People's Daily* declared on Aug. 30 that "if we view the movement led by the bourgeoisie in colonial countries as the mainstream of the national liberation movement, and give full support to it while ignoring or expressing contempt for the anti-imperialist struggle waged by the revolutionary masses, it will in fact mean the adoption of bourgeois viewpoints".

(5) The Chinese party adopted a sceptical attitude towards Khrushchev's view that in certain circumstances it was possible for Communist parties to attain power by parliamentary means without violent revolution.

(6) The Soviet party held that China's nationalist foreign policy, as exemplified in its relations with India, seriously harmed the international Communist movement.

(7) The Chinese did not support the Soviet repudiation of the "personality cult" surrounding Stalin—largely, Soviet sources suggested, because Mao had himself become the centre of a similar cult in China.

(8) The Chinese accused the Soviet party of seeking to impose its will on the world Communist movement; in 1956, for example, the party had condemned Stalin and put forward the theories of the non-inevitability of war and the possibility of a peaceful transition to socialism without previously consulting other Communist parties. The Soviet party retaliated by accusing the Chinese of splitting the movement by their "fractionalist" activities.

(9) The Soviet party upheld the accepted Marxist theory that intensive industrialization was an essential prerequisite for the transition from socialism to communism, and regarded the Chinese communes [see above] as an attempt to "by-pass certain historical stages". Chinese theoreticians, on the other hand, contended that agricultural expansion was "the one essential base".

(10) The Soviet press laid increasing emphasis on the dangers of dogmatism and sectarianism, and since 1959 had relaxed its campaign against the Yugoslavs' alleged revisionism. The Chinese party, however, continued to uphold the assertion of the 1957 Moscow declaration that revisionism was "the main danger" to the international Communist movement.

The Beginning of the Controversy (April–June 1960)

The Chinese party journal *Red Flag* published on April 16, 1960, the first of a series of substantial articles entitled *Long Live Leninism*, which forcefully stated the Chinese view on many of the issues in dispute. While accepting the principle of peaceful coexistence and holding that Communists must seek to avoid a major war, it maintained that the danger of such a war would remain as long as capitalism existed. It rejected the view that a nuclear war would destroy civilization, and declared that "on the ruins of destroyed imperialism the victorious peoples will create with tremendous speed a civilization a thousand times higher than the capitalist system, and will build their bright future". The articles also distinguished between major wars and local wars arising from revolutionary movements, which could only assist the progress of the revolution. Quoting Lenin in support of the view that the transition to socialism was impossible without revolutionary violence, the articles advocated that all revolutionary movements should be supported "resolutely and without the least reservation".

Soviet spokesmen speedily replied to this challenge. Otto Kuusinen (a member of the party presidium) said in a speech on April 22, 1960, that there existed "a division in the ruling quarters of the imperialist states", and that "side by side with the hardened enemies of peace there appear sober-thinking statesmen who realize that a war fought with the new means of mass destruction would be madness". He went on to criticize those who held dogmatically to the view that imperialism was aggressive, and who failed to realize the need to make use of this new factor to save mankind from another war.

A number of pointed references to the controversy appeared in the Soviet press in 1960 in articles commemorating the 40th anniversary of the publication of Lenin's *Left-Wing Communism: An Infantile Disorder*, in which he criticized ultra-leftist Communists who refused to work in "reactionary" trade unions or to participate in "bourgeois" parliaments, and emphasized the necessity of accepting compromises in certain circumstances. *Sovietskaya Rossiya* said on June 10 that "present-day leftists regard the policy of achieving peaceful coexistence, stopping the arms race, and friendship between the peoples of capitalist and socialist countries as a retreat from Marxism-Leninism. They take the slightest deterioration in the international situation as proof of the correctness of their sectarian views." *Pravda* stated two days later that "we consider erroneous and incorrect the statements of leftists in the international Communist movement to the effect that, since we have taken power into our own hands, we can at once introduce communism, by-passing certain historical stages in its development". *Kommunist* declared on June 23 that "the tendency of some political leaders to see the policy of peaceful coexistence and the struggle for disarmament as a retreat from Marxist-Leninist positions . . . and the desire to show distrust for the decision of the 20th and 21st party congresses regarding the policy of averting a new war in present circumstances cannot be described otherwise than as being mistaken, dogmatic, and left-sectarian".

The Chinese press in turn replied vigorously to these criticisms. *Red Flag* denounced on June 15, 1960, the "Yugoslav revisionists" who contended that "sober" and "sensible" imperialist politicians had "orientated themselves in the positive direction," and that this constituted "a new factor in the situation". The *People's Daily* asserted on June 25 that "so long as the monopoly capitalist clique continues its rule in the USA and American imperialism exists, the threat of war will not be eliminated and world peace will not be guaranteed". It also denounced the "revisionists" who, "frightened out of their wits by imperialist blackmail of nuclear war, have exaggerated the consequences of such a war and have begged imperialism for peace at any cost".

The Bucharest Conference (June 1960)

In a letter of June 2, 1960, to the Chinese party, the Soviet party proposed an international meeting to resolve differences. The Chinese party agreed, but asked for time to prepare for it. The Soviet party suggested on June 7 that the forthcoming congress of the Romanian Workers' Party would provide the opportunity for a preliminary conference, to which the Chinese agreed.

Delegations from all the Communist countries of Europe and Asia except Yugoslavia attended the Romanian party congress, which was held in Bucharest from June 20 to June 25, 1960, the Soviet delegation being headed by Khrushchev and the Chinese delegation by Peng Zhen, a member of the party's politburo and secretariat. Addressing the congress on June 21, Khrushchev reaffirmed the view that war was no longer inevitable, and defended his conduct at the abortive summit conference held in Paris on May 16–17 of that year.

"In present conditions", he said, "when there are two world systems, it is imperative to build mutual relations between them in such a way as to preclude the possibility of war breaking out. . . . One must bear in mind that the attitude to the question of peaceful coexistence is not everywhere the same in the imperialist countries. During the conversations I had in Paris with President de Gaulle and Prime Minister Macmillan (of the United Kingdom), it seemed to me that they showed a certain understanding of the necessity for peaceful coexistence, and were even persuading themselves that the policy of coexistence must be the guiding principle in the future relations between states with different social systems. . . .

"We do not intend to yield to provocation and to deviate from the general line of our foreign policy, which . . . is one of coexistence, consolidating peace, easing international tension, and doing away with the cold war. The thesis that war is not inevitable in our time has a direct bearing on the policy of peaceful coexistence . . . Lenin's propositions about imperialism remain in force, and are still a lodestar for us in our theory and practice. But it should not be forgotten that Lenin's propositions on imperialism were advanced and developed decades ago. . . ."

Developing this latter point, Khrushchev continued: "The Soviet Union, with its enormous economic and military potential, is growing and gaining in strength. The great socialist camp, which now numbers over 1,000 million people, is growing and gaining in strength. The organization and political consciousness of the working class have grown, and even in the capitalist countries it is actively fighting for peace. . . . One cannot mechanically repeat now on this question what Lenin said many decades ago on imperialism, and go on asserting that imperialist wars are inevitable until socialism triumphs throughout the world. . . . History will possibly witness a time when capitalism is preserved only in a small number of states. . . . Even in such conditions, would one have to look up in a book what Lenin said, quite correctly for his time? Would one have to repeat that wars are inevitable since capitalist countries exist? . . . One cannot ignore the . . . changes in the correlation of forces in the world, and repeat what the great Lenin said in quite different historical conditions. . . ."

The speech of Peng Zhen, who addressed the congress on June 22, 1960, was in striking contrast to that of Khrushchev. Whilst endorsing the 1957 Moscow declaration, he declared that "as long as imperialism exists there will always be a danger of aggressive war", adding that war could be prevented only if the "socialist camp" and the Afro-Asian and Latin American countries united. This, he declared, made it necessary to fight against the "revisionism" of "the Tito group, who are playing the imperialist game".

Private discussions meanwhile took place between the delegations. The Soviet delegation circulated on June 21, 1960, a letter containing a detailed criticism of the Chinese party's positions, which contended inter alia that the Chinese, after accepting that peaceful coexistence and a peaceful transition to socialism were possible, had reversed their attitude; that to regard war as inevitable "paralyzed the revolutionary struggle" by inducing a spirit of despair; that coexistence did not involve the renunciation of national liberation movements; and that the Soviet party did not regard the "peaceful way" to socialism as the only way, as the Chinese party had suggested. In the course of the discussions, which were often heated, Khrushchev was reported to have attacked Mao by name, calling him "an ultra-leftist, an ultra-dogmatist, indeed, a left revisionist", and to have accused China of "great-nation chauvinism" in its dealings with India.

A communiqué approved on June 24, 1960, reaffirmed the 12 parties' support for the 1957 declaration, including its statements on peaceful coexistence, the possibility of preventing wars, and the possibility of a peaceful transition to socialism. It also reaffirmed their support for the Peace Manifesto, and emphasized the need to strengthen "the unity of the countries of the world socialist system". It was also agreed to convene a world Communist conference in Moscow. The central committee of the Soviet party, meeting on July 13–16, 1960, adopted a resolution approving the Soviet delegation's line at the Bucharest conference, and condemning "dogmatic and left-wing sectarian deviations".

The Chinese party replied in detail to the Soviet letter of June 21 in a letter of Sept. 10, 1960, which contended inter alia that the conflict of views went back to the Soviet party congress of 1956, when the Soviet party had ignored Stalin's "positive role" and had put forward a false theory of "peaceful transition" without previously consulting the other Communist parties.

Withdrawal of Soviet Technical Aid to China (July–August 1960)

The Soviet Government informed the Chinese Government on July 16, 1960, of its decision to withdraw the following month all Soviet technicians working in China. This unilateral decision, which aroused greater resentment in China than any other action of the Soviet Government, with the possible exception of the repudiation of the agreement on nuclear weapons, struck a crushing blow at China's economy at a time when the country was suffering from a series of natural disasters described by Beijing Radio as "without parallel in the past century," including drought, typhoons, floods, and plagues of locusts and other insects. According to later Chinese statements, 1,390 experts were withdrawn, 343 contracts concerning technical aid cancelled, and 257 projects of scientific and technical co-operation ended, with the result that many projects in progress had to be suspended and some factories and mines which were conducting trial production could not go into production according to schedule.

The Moscow Conference (November 1960)

A commission of representatives of 26 Communist parties met in Moscow in September 1960 to prepare a draft policy statement for the forthcoming conference. According to Chinese sources, the Soviet delegation agreed to important changes in the draft which it had submitted, but withdrew its consent after Khrushchev returned on Oct. 14 from New York, where he had been attending the UN General Assembly. On Nov. 5 the Soviet party issued its reply to the Chinese letter of Sept. 10, which strongly criticized Mao Zedong and the Chinese party leadership.

The conference opened on Nov. 11, 1960, and was attended by representatives of 81 Communist parties; the Yugoslav League of Communists was not invited. Although it took place in conditions of strict secrecy, many details of the proceedings have since become known from material published by a number of the parties taking part.

The Chinese position was stated on Nov. 14 by Deng Xiaoping, who protested against the Soviet letter of Nov. 5 and maintained that it misrepresented the Chinese viewpoint. He denied that the Chinese party considered a world war inevitable, although it regarded one as probable while capitalism existed. Reaffirming that "just" local wars must be supported and counter-revolutionary local wars resisted, he pointed out that such local wars as the Suez campaign of 1956 had not led to world war. The Chinese party wanted world peace, but this could not be built on the goodwill of imperialist politicians, and talk of total disarmament was dishonest and misleading.

In colonial countries, he continued, the workers and peasants must ally themselves with the bourgeoisie in the struggle against imperialism, but after independence a struggle against the bourgeoisie was inevitable. In India, he alleged, the Government was manufacturing frontier incidents in order to postpone its own overthrow, but instead of supporting China in this situation the USSR had taken the Indian Government's side. After accusing the Soviet party of over-estimating the possibility of a peaceful transition to socialism and defending the Chinese party's economic policy, Deng dealt in conclusion with the question of relations between Communist parties. Although the Soviet party was the "leading party", he said, there were no "superior" or "inferior" parties; all Communist parties were independent and equal, and the Soviet party therefore could not claim to bind others by the resolutions passed by its congresses.

Deng was strongly supported by Enver Hoxha, leader of the Albanian Party of Labour, who alleged that at the Bucharest conference the Soviet leaders had tried to rush through a condemnation of the Chinese party, and that they had exercised "unbearable pressures" to force Albania to join a bloc against China; when in August, as a result of floods and drought, Albania had had only 15 days' supply of wheat in stock, the USSR had promised after 45 days' delay to supply 10,000 tonnes, or 15 days' supply, instead of the 50,000 needed, with delivery to be spread over two months. The only other parties which consistently supported the Chinese, however, were the Burmese, Malayan, and Australian parties.

The conference concluded on Nov. 25, 1960, and a 20,000-word statement summarizing its conclusions was published on Dec. 5. In general it represented a victory for Soviet views, although in the wording some concessions were made to the Chinese viewpoint. Its main points were as follows:

War and Peace. "The aggressive nature of imperialism has not changed", the statement said, "but real forces have appeared that are capable of foiling its plans of aggression. War is not fatally inevitable. . . . World war can be prevented by the joint efforts of the world socialist camp, the international working class, the national liberation movement, all the countries opposing war, and all peace-loving forces. . . . The policy of peaceful co-existence is also favoured by a definite section of the bourgeoisie of the developed capitalist countries, which takes a sober view of the relationship of forces and of the dire consequences of a modern war. . . . But should the imperialist maniacs start war, the peoples will sweep capitalism out of existence and bury it. . . .

"The near future will bring the forces of peace and socialism new successes. The USSR will become the leading industrial power of the world. China will become a mighty industrial state. The socialist system will be turning out more than half the world industrial product. The peace zone will expand. . . . In these conditions a real possibility will have arisen of excluding world war from the life of society even before socialism achieves complete victory on earth, with capitalism still existing in a part of the world. . . .

"Peaceful co-existence of countries with different social systems does not mean conciliation of the socialist and bourgeois ideologies. On the contrary, it implies intensification of the struggle of the working class, of all the Communist parties, for the triumph of socialist ideas. But ideological and political disputes between states must not be settled through war. . . ."

Colonial and Under-developed Countries. "Communists have always recognized the progressive, revolutionary significance of national liberation wars", the statement continued. "The peoples of the colonial countries win their independence both through armed struggle and by non-military methods, depending on the specific conditions in the country concerned. . . .

"The urgent tasks of national rebirth facing the countries that have shaken off the colonial yoke cannot be effectively accomplished unless a determined struggle is waged against imperialism and the remnants of feudalism by all the patriotic forces of the nation, united in a single national democratic front. . . . The alliance of the working class and the peasantry is the most important force in winning and defending national independence, accomplishing far-reaching democratic transformations, and ensuring social progress. . . . The extent to which the national bourgeoisie participates in the liberation struggle depends to no small degree upon its strength and stability. . . . In present conditions the national bourgeoisie of the colonial and dependent countries unconnected with imperialist circles is objectively interested in the accomplishment of the principal tasks of the anti-imperialist, anti-feudal revolution, and therefore retains the capacity of participating in the revolutionary struggle against imperialism and feudalism. In that sense it is progressive. But it is unstable, and is inclined to compromise with imperialism and feudalism. . . .

"After winning political independence the peoples seek solutions to the social problems raised by life and to the problems of reinforcing national independence. Different classes and parties offer different solutions. Which course of development to choose is the internal affair of the peoples themselves. As social contradictions grow, the national bourgeoisie inclines more and more to compromise with domestic reaction and imperialism. The people, however, begin to see that the best way to abolish age-long backwardness and improve their living standard is that of non-capitalist development. . . . The Communist parties are working actively for a consistent completion of the anti-imperialist, anti-feudal democratic revolution. . . . They support those actions of national governments leading to the consolidation of the gains achieved and undermining the imperialists' positions. At the same time they firmly oppose anti-democratic, anti-popular acts and those measures of the ruling circles which endanger national independence. . . ."

Forms of Transition to Socialism. The statement repeated verbatim the section of the 1957 Moscow declaration dealing with the possibility of a peaceful transition to socialism.

Revisionism and Dogmatism. After condemning "the personality cult, which shackles creative thought and initiative", the statement repeated the 1957 declaration's formula that "revisionism . . . remains the main danger", but that "dogmatism and sectarianism . . . can also become the main danger at some stage of development of individual parties". In conclusion, it referred to the Soviet party as "the universally recognized vanguard of the world Communist movement", and described the decisions of its 20th congress as initiating "a new stage in the world Communist movement".

Soviet and Chinese Relations with Albania and Yugoslavia (1961)

After the Moscow conference both the USSR and China temporarily refrained from public polemics, and the signing of agreements on economic, scientific, and technical co-operation on June 19, 1961 (of which no details were given), suggested that the USSR was prepared to resume economic aid to China. The continued difference in their positions, however, was made clear by their contrasting attitudes towards Albania and Yugoslavia. The signing of agreements providing for increased trade between China and Albania and a Chinese loan to Albania were announced on Feb. 3, 1961, in a communiqué which emphasized the two Governments' complete agreement on ideological questions. Relations between the USSR and Albania, on the other hand, deteriorated in 1961, and eight Soviet submarines which had been stationed at a base off the Albanian coast were withdrawn in May. Whereas the Chinese press continued its violent attacks on "the Tito clique", Soviet relations with Yugoslavia showed a steady improvement during the same period; a five-year trade agreement was signed in March, and the Yugoslav Foreign Minister visited Moscow in July 1961.

22nd Soviet Party Congress (October 1961)

The 22nd congress of the Soviet Communist Party, held on Oct. 17–31, 1961, widened the breach between the USSR and China. Stalin and the "personality cult" were strongly criticized by Khrushchev and other speakers, and it was decided to remove his body from the Lenin Mausoleum. The congress also adopted a new party programme, which stated inter alia that "the dictatorship of the proletariat has fulfilled its historic mission, and has ceased to be indispensable to the USSR from the point of view of the tasks of internal development. . . . The dictatorship of the proletariat will cease to be necessary before the state withers away. The state as an organization embracing the entire population will survive until the final victory of communism. . . . As a result of the victory of socialism in the USSR and the consolidation of the unity of Soviet society, the Communist Party of the working class has become the vanguard of the Soviet people, a party of the entire people." These formulations were strongly criticized in later Chinese statements.

The congress resulted in an open break between the USSR and Albania. In his report Khrushchev said on Oct. 17, 1961, that the Albanian leaders "have begun to depart from the common agreed line of the Communist movement of the whole world on major issues. . . . They are themselves using the same methods as were current in our country at the time of the personality cult." Zhou Enlai, addressing the congress on Oct. 19, commented that "if a dispute or differences unfortunately arise between fraternal parties or fraternal countries, they should be patiently resolved in the spirit of proletarian internationalism and on the principles of equality and unanimity, through consultation. Any public, one-sided censure of any fraternal party does not help unity, nor is it helpful in resolving problems. To lay bare a dispute between fraternal parties or fraternal countries, openly in the face of the enemy, cannot be regarded as a serious Marxist-Leninist attitude." This statement was welcomed on the following day by the central committee of the Albanian Party of Labour, which accused Khrushchev of "anti-Marxist lies". Zhou Enlai left for Beijing on Oct. 23, without waiting for the end of the congress.

In a speech on Oct. 27, 1961, Khrushchev accused the Albanian leaders of "bloody atrocities", and declared that "all that was bad in our country at the time of the personality cult manifests itself in even worse form in the Albanian Party of Labour". On Zhou Enlai's speech he commented: "We share the anxiety expressed by our Chinese friends, and appreciate their concern for greater unity. If the Chinese comrades wish to make efforts towards normalizing the relations between the Albanian Party of Labour and the fraternal parties, there is hardly anyone who could contribute more to the solution of this problem."

Diplomatic relations between the USSR and Albania were broken off in December. The Chinese party, while nominally remaining neutral, made its support for Albania obvious. The *People's Daily*, for example, gave great praise in November to Hoxha's "correct leadership" and "uncompromising struggle against modern revisionists".

Proposals for New International Conference (February–April 1962)

Proposals for a new international Communist conference were put forward at the beginning of 1962 by the Communist parties of Indonesia, North Vietnam, Great Britain, Sweden, and New Zealand. The central committee of the Soviet party expressed its support for this proposal in a letter to the Chinese party on Feb. 22, 1962, and suggested that "public statements liable to sharpen and not to smooth out our differences be given up". The Chinese party's reply (April 7) proposed as preliminary steps towards such a conference the ending of public attacks; bilateral or multilateral talks between parties; and the restoration of normal relations between the Soviet and Albanian Governments and Communist parties, with the USSR taking the initiative. Although no further steps were taken at the time, a virtual truce from public polemics was in fact observed throughout the spring and summer.

IV: INTENSIFICATION OF THE CONFLICT, 1962–63

Three events in the autumn of 1962—the re-establishment of friendly relations between the USSR and Yugoslavia, the Cuban crisis and the Sino-Indian War—led to a renewal of polemics, in which both sides soon abandoned the pretence that their attacks were directed against Yugoslavia or against Albania.

Soviet-Yugoslav Rapprochement (May–October 1962)

During a visit to Bulgaria Nikita Khrushchev said in a speech at Varna on May 16, 1962, that the USSR must do everything to co-operate with Yugoslavia and thus help her to consolidate her socialist position; thereafter anti-Yugoslav polemics disappeared from the Soviet press. When Leonid Brezhnev (then holding the post of head of state) paid an official visit to Yugoslavia from Sept. 24 to Oct. 4, 1962, he said on his arrival that Soviet policy towards Yugoslavia was based on the principles laid down in Khrushchev's Varna speech.

In China Brezhnev's visit provoked an intensification of anti-Yugoslav propaganda, and on Sept. 28 the Chinese Communist Party's central committee issued a statement violently attacking "the Tito clique", which, it declared, had "become still more despicable in betraying the cause of communism and meeting the needs of imperialism." At this session of the committee Mao Zedong, who since 1958 had played a subordinate role in the leadership to Liu Shaoqi, Deng Xiaoping and Zhou Enlai, began his struggle to regain supreme power—a process which was accompanied by an intensification of the ideological conflict with the USSR, and culminated in the Cultural Revolution of 1966–68.

The Cuban Crisis (October 1962)

President Kennedy stated on Oct. 22, 1962, that the US Government had unmistakable evidence of the installation in Cuba of Soviet missile sites capable of delivering nuclear warheads to large areas of the USA and Central America, and that "a strict quarantine on all offensive military equipment under shipment to Cuba" would be imposed until the missile bases had been removed under UN supervision. The crisis ended when President Kennedy gave an assurance on Oct. 27 that the USA would not invade Cuba, and in return Khrushchev agreed on the following day to the dismantling of the Soviet bases on the island. The Chinese Government showed its disapproval of this compromise by organizing mass anti-American demonstrations; a telegram sent to the Cuban Government on Oct. 29 by a demonstration in Beijing declared that "650,000,000 Chinese will always remain the most faithful and reliable comrades-in-arms of the Cuban people and stand by them through thick and thin".

Soviet Military Aid to India—The Sino-Indian War (October–November 1962)

An agreement for the delivery of Soviet MiG fighters for the Indian Air Force and the building of a factory under licence in India to make these aircraft was concluded in the summer of 1962. Although the first Soviet warplanes did not reach India until Feb. 11, 1963, after the Sino-Indian War, the agreement caused great offence in China, in view of her strained relations with India.

Fighting between the Chinese and Indian forces broke out on Oct. 20, 1962, both on India's north-east frontier and in Ladakh. In the North-East Frontier Agency the Chinese advanced over 100 miles south, threatening the plains of Assam, but in Ladakh they did not advance beyond the line claimed as Chinese territory. On Nov. 21, 1962, the Chinese announced a unilateral cease-fire and the withdrawal of their troops.

The Soviet Government adopted a reserved attitude towards the crisis, expressing overt support for neither side. *Pravda* called on Nov. 5 for a cease-fire and immediate talks between India and China "without any conditions attached".

Communist Party Congresses (November–December 1962)

The deepening of the crisis inside the world Communist movement was illustrated by developments at the Bulgarian, Hungarian, Italian, and Czechoslovak Communist party congresses which took place in November and December 1962. At the Bulgarian congress, held on Nov. 5–14, Todor Zhivkov (the party's first secretary) denounced the Albanian leaders in terms which were clearly intended to apply to the Chinese also.

"The Albanian leaders", he said, "stop at nothing. They invent the vilest lies and spread them all over the world. . . . They have proclaimed nearly all the fraternal Marxist-Leninist parties as being bogged down by 'contemporary' or 'modern' revisionism. To keep silent about the sectarian and adventurist actions of the Albanian leaders and their hypocritical splitting activities has never been and cannot be a serious Marxist-Leninist attitude"—the last phrase being a deliberate quotation from Zhou Enlai's speech at the 22nd Soviet party congress.

Disputes between the Chinese delegation and those from the European parties occurred at the congress of the Hungarian Socialist Workers' Party, held on Nov. 20–24, 1962, but János Kádár (the party's first secretary) adopted a conciliatory attitude, appealing to the Chinese delegation to take into account the views expressed at the congress, just as, he assured them, the Hungarian party would take note of the Chinese position. At the Italian party congress, however, held on Dec. 2–8, the dispute was at last brought into the open, when party leaders directly criticized the Chinese position and commented that "a party like ours does not need to say Albania when it means China".

Palmiro Togliatti (the Italian party's general secretary), emphasizing that a nuclear war would mean the destruction of civilization, defended Soviet policy during the Cuban crisis as having safeguarded Cuban independence; he condemned the conflict between China and India as "irrational and absurd"; and deplored the Albanians' "campaign of calumnies and insults" and the Chinese party's "unacceptable solidarity" with them. He also warned the Chinese delegation that "when you say capitalism has been restored in Yugoslavia—and everybody knows that is not true—nobody believes the rest of what you say".

The same issues were openly debated at the Czechoslovak party congress, held on Dec. 4–8, 1962, The Chinese delegation submitted a letter to the congress proposing "an international consultation of all Communist parties" to discuss the differences between them.

Khrushchev's Foreign Policy Speech (December 1962)

In a speech to the Supreme Soviet on Dec. 12, 1962, Khrushchev defended his policy during the Cuban crisis. Commenting on the Sino-Indian conflict and relations with Albania and Yugoslavia, he implied that Albanian attacks on the USSR had been instigated by China.

"During the peaceful adjustment of the conflict in the Caribbean", he said, "shrill voices of discontent could be heard from people who call themselves Marxist-Leninists, even though their actions have nothing in common with Marxism-Leninism. I mean specifically the Albanian leaders. Their criticism of the Soviet Union in effect echoed that coming from the most reactionary, bellicose circles of the West. Why is it that the loudest shouts today come precisely from the Albanian leaders? I should like to recount an incident from my life to explain this. . . .

"I remember that in mining settlements foul-mouthed people sometimes used to find a small boy who had barely begun to articulate words without yet understanding what they meant and teach him the most foul language. They would tell him: 'Go to that house and say this to the people there.' Sometimes they did even worse. 'Go to your mother', they would say, 'and repeat these words to her. Here are three kopecks for you. Afterwards we'll give you five.' And the child would run to the window, or to his mother, and repeat the foul words. . . . The Albanian leaders are like those unreasoning boys. Someone has taught them foul language, and they go about and use it against the Soviet Communist Party. And yet it is their mother! And for using this foul language they get the promised three kopecks. And if they use stronger and cruder language they get another five kopecks . . . ."

On the Sino-Indian conflict he said: "For the first time a situation has arisen in which a serious armed clash has resulted from a frontier dispute between a socialist country and a country which has started on the road of independent development and is pursuing a policy of non-alignment. . . .

"We regard as reasonable the steps taken by the Government of China when it announced that it had unilaterally ceased fire and started to withdraw its troops. We are most happy about that, and welcome such actions on the part of the Chinese comrades.

"Some might say: 'How is it that you claim this is a reasonable step, if it was taken after so many lives had been lost and after so much blood had been shed? Would it not have been better if both sides had refrained from resorting to arms?' Yes, of course that would have been better. . . . But if it was not possible to prevent such a course of events, it is better to display courage now and to end the clash. . . .

"But there are some people who try to put a different interpretation on the decision taken by the Government of China. They ask: 'Isn't this a retreat?' They also ask: 'Isn't this a concession on the part of the Chinese comrades?' Of course, such questions are asked by those who love to cavil."

Commenting on the rapprochement with Yugoslavia Khrushchev said: "Some people contend that Yugoslavia is not a socialist country. It is then permissible to ask: what sort of a country is it? . . . There have been no landlords or capitalists in

Yugoslavia for a long time now, and no private capital, no private enterprises or private estates, no private banks. . . . Therefore . . . it is impossible to deny that Yugoslavia is a socialist country. And it is from this that we proceed in our policy, on this that we base our relations with Yugoslavia. . . ."

Khrushchev referred to the 1960 Moscow conference's statement, and remarked: "The conference of fraternal parties warned that, unless a consistent struggle was waged against sectarianism and dogmatism, they might become the main danger at some particular stage in the development of individual parties. Events which have since taken place in the Communist movement show how far-sighted that conclusion was.

"Some people . . . place a lop-sided emphasis only on the danger from revisionism, mentioning Yugoslav revisionism in and out of context. But one must take a concrete view of things. In the crisis over Cuba, the Yugoslav Communists took a correct stand, while the dogmatists who pose as true Marxist-Leninists took a provocative one. . . . The crisis over Cuba showed specifically that it was those who took and are taking their stand on dogmatic positions who presented the main danger. . . ."

Chinese Replies to Foreign Criticism (December 1962–January 1963)

The *People's Daily* replied to Khrushchev's speech on Dec. 15, and to Signor Togliatti on Dec. 31, 1962. Defending Mao Zedong's slogan "imperialism is only a paper tiger", which Khrushchev had ridiculed in his speech, the *People's Daily* of Dec. 15 maintained that Communists should "despise the enemy on the strategic level while taking him seriously on the tactical level". Accusing Khrushchev of "defeatism" and "adventurism", it said: "If you dare not make the enemy feel your strength and contempt, that is defeatism. But if you pursue rash tactics, you fall irredeemably into adventurism. By acting in this way without daring to use your strength, you commit both mistakes at once. . . . We neither requested the introduction of offensive weapons into Cuba nor obstructed their withdrawal. No one can reproach us with adventurism, still less with plunging the whole world into a nuclear war."

The article went on to accuse "those who criticize us" over the Sino-Indian hostilities of being more sympathetic to the "Indian reactionaries" than to the Chinese Communists. Denouncing the use of party congresses as a platform for attacking other Communist parties, it said that this "monstrous practice" had originated at the Soviet party's 1961 congress—the only direct reference to the USSR in the article. In conclusion, it repeated the proposal for an international Communist conference.

The *People's Daily* repeated many of these arguments on Dec. 31, 1962, in another long article entitled *The Differences between Comrade Togliatti and Us*. This maintained that the Chinese party's views on the question of war were those expressed in the 1960 Moscow statement, and accused Togliatti of "bourgeois pacifism". On the Cuban crisis it commented: "We have never considered it a Marxist-Leninist attitude to brandish nuclear weapons as a way of settling international disputes. Nor have we ever considered that the avoidance of nuclear war in the Caribbean crisis was a 'Munich'. What we did strongly oppose . . . is the sacrifice of another country's sovereignty as a means of reaching a compromise with imperialism." Asserting that "the extent to which Comrade Togliatti and other comrades [an obvious reference to Khrushchev] have departed from Marxism-Leninism . . . is clearly revealed by their ardent flirtation with the Yugoslav revisionist group", the *People's Daily* contended that the condemnation of Yugoslav policy contained in the Moscow statement was still binding on all Communist parties.

The Soviet leadership gave its fullest exposition of its case to date in a 10,000-word article published in *Pravda* on Jan. 7, 1963. *Pravda* defended Soviet foreign policy along similar lines to Khrushchev's speech of Dec. 12 and again condemned the description of imperialism as a "paper tiger," on the ground that "such phrases can only sow complacency among the people and blunt their vigilance."

Maintaining that the Soviet party still supported the Moscow statement, the article commented that "some people lay a one-sided emphasis on the struggle against revisionism only, and at times decry creative Marxism-Leninism as revisionism". It went on to accuse the Albanian leaders "and those who support them" of themselves departing from the letter and spirit of the Moscow statement by launching "an unceremonious attack on the unity of the Communist movement", whereas the rapprochement between the Soviet Union and Yugoslavia was intended to promote such unity. The article continued: "The steps taken recently by the Yugoslav Communists and their leaders in their home and foreign policy have removed much of what was erroneous and damaging to the cause of building socialism in Yugoslavia. Those who allege that 'capitalism has been restored in Yugoslavia' . . . lie deliberately. . . . The Soviet Communist Party openly declares that there still exist differences with the League of Communists of Yugoslavia on a number of ideological questions. But the rapprochement between Yugoslavia and the country building communism can undoubtedly help in overcoming the differences on a number of ideological questions much quicker. . . ."

The *People's Daily*, replying on Jan. 27, 1963, quoted earlier attacks on Yugoslavia by Khrushchev, and commented that "we cannot understand why some comrades who formerly took a correct stand on Yugoslav revisionism have now made an about turn of 180 degrees".

Soviet Proposal for Talks Accepted by Chinese Party (January–May 1963)

At the congress of the East German Socialist Unity Party, held on Jan. 15–21, 1963, Khrushchev defended the Soviet viewpoint without directly mentioning China. He called for "a halt to polemics between Communist parties" and opposed the holding of an immediate international conference on the ground that it would lead to the danger of a split. The Chinese delegate, Wu Xiuzhuan, welcomed the proposal for ending polemics but supported the holding of a conference at an early date. His speech was several times drowned by booing, whereas the Yugoslav delegate was loudly applauded.

On Feb. 21, 1963, the central committee of the Soviet party, in a letter to the Chinese party, expressed concern that "open, ever-sharpening polemics are shaking the unity of fraternal parties", and suggested a meeting between representatives of the two parties in preparation for an international conference. Before replying, the Chinese party intensified its polemics against its opponents.

The *People's Daily* on Feb. 26, 1963, criticized the Soviet party's 20th congress, declaring that it had "both positive and negative aspects". The differences inside the international movement, it stated, had been brought into the open in September

1959 by the Camp David talks and the Tass statement on the Indian border dispute, when "for the first time in history a socialist country condemned a fraternal socialist country instead of condemning the armed provocations of the reactionaries of a capitalist country". "Certain comrades" had attacked the Chinese party for "its general line of socialist construction, its Great Leap Forward, and its people's communes, and spread the slander that the Chinese party was carrying out an adventurist policy". After the Bucharest conference "some comrades" had applied "economic and political pressure against China, perfidiously and unilaterally tearing up hundreds of agreements and contracts with a fraternal country".

Despite China's attempts at conciliation (the *People's Daily* went on) the Soviet Union had ceased its economic aid to Albania and interfered in Albania's internal affairs. An "unprincipled compromise" had been reached on the Cuban question and "a fraternal socialist country" had "not only supported politically the anti-Chinese policy of the Nehru Government but supplied it with military aid". The climax of the attacks on the Chinese party had been reached at the East German congress, which had created "a serious danger of a split". Necessary pre-conditions for an international conference, it concluded, would be the ending of attacks on the Chinese and Albanian parties, coupled with condemnation of the Yugoslavs as "traitors to the Communist cause".

A 100,000-word article entitled *More on the Differences between Comrade Togliatti and Us*, published in instalments in the *People's Daily* from Feb. 28 to March 3, 1963, taunted the Soviet leaders with being afraid to publish Chinese articles in the Soviet press and with jamming Beijing broadcasts. It accused Togliatti of "revisionism" and "bourgeois socialism", and in particular of rejecting revolution and the dictatorship of the proletariat in favour of parliamentary methods.

The central committee of the Chinese party, replying to the Soviet letter on March 9, 1963, repeated the proposals put forward in its letter of April 7, 1962, and said that it would suspend polemics, while reserving the right to reply to public attacks. The Soviet party replied on March 30, suggesting that talks might take place in Moscow later that year.

The Soviet letter, which was conciliatory in tone, condemned "the splitting activities of the Albanian leaders" but said that the Soviet party had offered in February to enter into discussions with them, and was still prepared to do so. On Yugoslavia it stated: "We maintain . . . that it is a socialist country, and in our relations with it we strive to establish closer relations between Yugoslavia and the socialist commonwealth, in accordance with the policy pursued by the fraternal parties for the cementing together of all the anti-imperialist forces of the world. We also take into consideration the definite positive tendencies shown of late in Yugoslavia's economic and socio-political life. Meanwhile the Communist Party of the Soviet Union (CPSU) is aware of the serious differences that exist with the League of Communists of Yugoslavia on several ideological questions, and considers it necessary to tell the Yugoslav comrades so frankly." Appealing for an end to polemics, the letter said: "We could have found much to say in defence of the Leninist policy of the CPSU, in defence of the common line of the international Communist movement, in reply to groundless attacks made in articles recently carried by the Chinese press. If we are not doing it now, it is only because we do not want to gladden the foes of the Communist movement. . . ."

Chinese Party's "25 Points" (June 1963)

The central committee of the Chinese party approved on June 14, 1963, a 60,000-word reply to the Soviet letter of March 30, which was delivered in Moscow on the following day and immediately published in the *People's Daily*. This letter, which put forward 25 points for discussion at the Moscow talks, was the fullest statement of the Chinese case yet issued. Although it nowhere mentioned Khrushchev or other Soviet leaders, directing its criticisms against "certain persons" without giving names, it contained a comprehensive indictment of his policy and theoretical statements since 1956. The 25 points set out in the Chinese letter are summarized below.

(1) "For several years there have been differences within the international Communist movement. . . . The central issue is . . . whether or not to accept the fact that the people still living under the imperialist and capitalist system . . . need to make revolution, and whether or not to accept the fact that the people already on the socialist road . . . need to carry their revolution forward to the end. . . .

(2) "The revolutionary principles of the 1957 declaration and the 1960 statement [see pages 9 and 22–23 above] . . . may be summarized as follows: . . . Workers of the world, unite with the oppressed peoples; . . . bring the proletarian world revolution step by step to complete victory; and establish a new world without imperialism, without capitalism, and without the exploitation of man by man. . . .

(3) "If the general line of the international Communist movement is one-sidedly reduced to 'peaceful coexistence', 'peaceful competition', and 'peaceful transition', this is to violate the revolutionary principles of the 1957 declaration and the 1960 statement. . . .

(4) "The fundamental contradictions in the contemporary world . . . are: the contradiction between the socialist camp and the imperialist camp; the contradiction between the proletariat and the bourgeoisie in the capitalist countries; the contradiction between the oppressed nations and imperialism; and the contradictions among imperialist countries and among monopoly capitalist groups. . . .

(5) "The following erroneous views should be repudiated . . . : (i) the view which blots out the class content of the contradiction between the socialist and imperialist camps . . . ; (ii) the view which recognizes only the contradiction between the socialist and imperialist camps . . . ; (iii) the view which maintains . . . that the contradiction between the proletariat and the bourgeoisie can be resolved without a proletarian revolution in each country and that the contradiction between the oppressed nations and imperialism can be resolved without revolution . . . ; (iv) the view which denies that the development of the inherent contradictions in the contemporary capitalist world inevitably leads to a new situation in which the imperialist countries are locked in an intense struggle, and asserts that the contradictions among the imperialist countries can be reconciled or even eliminated by 'international agreements among the big monopolies'; and (v) the view which maintains that the contradiction between the two world systems of socialism and capitalism will automatically disappear in the course of 'economic competition', . . . and that a 'world without wars', a new world of 'all-round co-operation', will appear. . . .

(6) "Now that there is a socialist camp consisting of 13 countries—Albania, Bulgaria, China, Cuba, Czechoslovakia, the German Democratic Republic, Hungary, the Democratic People's Republic of Korea, Mongolia, Poland, Romania, the Soviet Union, and the Democratic Republic of Vietnam— . . . the touchstone of proletarian internationalism is whether or not it resolutely defends the whole of the socialist camp. . . ." [The formula "a socialist camp of 13 countries", including Albania and Cuba but not Yugoslavia, had only recently come into use; the *People's Daily* in December 1961 had referred to the "12 fraternal countries", Cuba not being regarded as socialist at that time.]

"If anybody . . . does not defend the unity of the socialist camp but on the contrary creates tension and splits within it, or even follows the policies of the Yugoslav revisionists, tries to liquidate the socialist camp, or helps capitalist countries to attack fraternal socialist countries, he is betraying the interests of the entire international proletariat. . . ." [This passage was obviously directed against the Soviet Union and particularly against Soviet military aid to India.]

"If anybody, following in the footsteps of others, defends the erroneous opportunist line and policies pursued by a certain socialist country instead of upholding the correct Marxist-Leninist line . . . he is departing from Marxism-Leninism and proletarian internationalism.

(7) "The 1960 statement points out: . . . 'US imperialism is the main force of aggression and war.' . . . To make no distinction between enemies, friends and ourselves, and to entrust the fate of the people and of mankind to collaboration with US imperialism, is to lead people astray. . . .

(8) "Certain persons in the international Communist movement are now taking a passive or scornful or negative attitude towards the struggles of the oppressed nations for liberation. . . . The attitude taken towards the revolutionary struggles of the people in the Asian, African, and Latin American countries is an important criterion for differentiating those who want revolution from those who do not. . . .

(9) "The oppressed nations and peoples of Asia, Africa, and Latin America are faced with the urgent task of fighting imperialism and its lackeys. . . . In these areas extremely broad sections of the population refuse to be slaves of imperialism. They include not only the workers, peasants, intellectuals, and petty bourgeoisie, but also the patriotic national bourgeoisie and even certain kings, princes, and aristocrats. . . . The proletariat and its party must . . . organize a broad united front against imperialism. . . . The proletarian party should maintain its ideological, political, and organizational independence and insist on the leadership of the revolution. The proletarian party and the revolutionary people must learn to master all forms of struggle, including armed struggle. . . . The policy of the proletarian party should be . . . to unite with the bourgeoisie, in so far as they tend to be progressive, anti-imperialist, and anti-feudal, but to struggle against their reactionary tendencies to compromise and collaborate with imperialism and the forces of feudalism. . . .

(10) "In the imperialist and capitalist countries the proletarian revolution and the dictatorship of the proletariat are essential. . . . It is wrong to refuse to use parliamentary and other legal forms of struggle when they can and should be used. However, if a Marxist-Leninist party falls into legalism or parliamentary cretinism, confining the struggle within the limits permitted by the bourgeoisie, this will inevitably lead to renouncing the proletarian revolution and the dictatorship of the proletariat.

(11) "Marx and Lenin did raise the possibility that revolutions may develop peacefully. But, as Lenin pointed out, the peaceful development of revolution is an opportunity 'very seldom to be met with in the history of revolution'. As a matter of fact, there is no historical precedent for peaceful transition from capitalism to socialism. . . . The proletarian party must never base its thinking, its policies for revolution, and its entire work on the assumption that the imperialists and reactionaries will accept peaceful transformation. . . .

(12) "If the leading group in any party adopts a non-revolutionary line and converts it into a reformist party, then Marxist-Leninists inside and outside the party will replace them and lead the people in making revolution. . . . There are certain persons who assert that they have made the greatest creative contributions to revolutionary theory since Lenin and that they alone are correct. But it is very dubious . . . whether they really have a general line for the international Communist movement which conforms with Marxism-Leninism. . . .

(13) "Certain persons have one-sidedly exaggerated the role of peaceful competition between socialist and imperialist countries in their attempt to substitute peaceful competition for the revolutionary struggles of the oppressed peoples. According to their preaching, it would seem that imperialism will automatically collapse in the course of this peaceful competition, and that the only thing the oppressed peoples have to do is to wait quietly for the advent of this day. What does this have in common with Marxist-Leninist views?

"Moreover, certain persons have concocted the strange tale that China and some other socialist countries want to 'unleash wars' and to spread socialism by 'wars between states'. As the statement of 1960 points out, such tales are nothing but imperialist and reactionary slanders. To put it bluntly, the purpose of those who repeat these slanders is to hide the fact that they are opposed to revolutions by the oppressed peoples and nations of the world and opposed to others supporting such revolutions.

(14) "Certain persons say that revolutions are entirely possible without war. . . . If they are referring to a war of national liberation or a revolutionary civil war, then this formulation is, in effect, opposed to revolutionary wars and to revolution. If they are referring to a world war, then they are shooting at a non-existent target. Although Marxist-Leninists have pointed out, on the basis of the history of the two world wars, that world wars inevitably lead to revolution, no Marxist-Leninist ever has held or ever will hold that revolution must be made through world war.

"Marxist-Leninists take the abolition of war as their ideal and believe that war can be abolished. But how can war be abolished? . . . Certain persons now actually hold that it is possible to bring about 'a world without weapons, without armed forces, and without wars' through 'general and complete disarmament' while the system of imperialism and of the exploitation of man by man still exists. This is sheer illusion. . . .

"If one regards general and complete disarmament as the fundamental road to world peace, spreads the illusion that imperialism will automatically lay down its arms, and tries to liquidate the revolutionary struggles of the oppressed peoples and nations on the pretext of disarmament, then this is deliberately to deceive the people of the world and help the imperialists in their policies of aggression and war. . . . World peace can be won only by the struggles of the people in all countries and not by begging the imperialists for it. . . .

(15) "The complete banning and destruction of nuclear weapons is an important task in the struggle to defend world peace. We must do our utmost to this end. . . . However, if the imperialists are forced to accept an agreement to ban nuclear weapons, it decidedly will not be because of their 'love for humanity', but because of the pressure of the people of all countries and for the sake of their own vital interests. . . .

"The emergence of nuclear weapons does not and cannot resolve the fundamental contradictions in the contemporary world, does not and cannot alter the law of class struggle, and does not and cannot change the nature of imperialism and reaction. It cannot, therefore, be said that with the emergence of nuclear weapons the possibility and the necessity of social and national revolutions have disappeared, or that the basic principles of Marxism-Leninism, and especially the theories of proletarian revolution and the dictatorship of the proletariat . . . have become outmoded. . . .

(16) "It was Lenin who advanced the thesis that it is possible for the socialist countries to practice peaceful coexistence with the capitalist countries. . . . The People's Republic of China, too, has consistently pursued the policy of peaceful coexistence with countries having different social systems, and it is China which initiated the five principles of peaceful coexistence.

"However, a few years ago certain persons suddenly claimed Lenin's policy of peaceful coexistence as their own 'great discovery'. They maintain that they have a monopoly in the interpretation of this policy. They treat 'peaceful co-existence' as if it were an all-inclusive, mystical book from heaven, and attribute to it every success the people of the world achieve by struggle. What is more, they label all who disagree with their distortions of Lenin's views as opponents of peaceful co-existence. . . .

"Lenin's principle of peaceful co-existence . . . designates a relationship between countries with different social systems. . . . It should never be extended to apply to the relations between oppressed and oppressor nations, between oppressed and oppressor countries, or between oppressed and oppressor classes, and never be described as the main content of the transition from capitalism to socialism. Still less should it be asserted that peaceful co-existence is mankind's road to socialism. . . .

"The general line of the foreign policy of the socialist countries should have the following content: to develop relations of friendship, mutual assistance, and co-operation among the countries of the socialist camp in accordance with the principle of proletarian internationalism: to strive for peaceful co-existence on the basis of the five principles with countries having different social systems, and oppose the imperialist policies of aggression and war; and to support and assist the revolutionary struggles of all the oppressed peoples and nations. These three aspects are inter-related and indivisible, and not a single one can be omitted.

(17) "For a very long historical period after the proletariat takes power class struggle continues. . . . To deny the existence of class struggle in the period of the dictatorship of the proletariat and the necessity of thoroughly completing the socialist revolution on the economic, political, and ideological fronts . . . violates Marxism-Leninism.

(18) "The fundamental thesis of Marx and Lenin is that the dictatorship of the proletariat will inevitably continue for the entire historical period of the transition from capitalism to communism. . . . If it is announced, half-way through, that the dictatorship of the proletariat is no longer necessary . . . this would lead to extremely grave consequences and make any transition to communism out of the question. . . .

"Is it possible to replace the state of the dictatorship of the proletariat by a 'state of the whole people'? This is not a question of the internal affairs of any particular country, but a fundamental problem involving the universal truth of Marxism-Leninism. . . . In calling a socialist state the 'state of the whole people', is one trying to replace the Marxist-Leninist theory of the state by the bourgeois theory of the state? Is one trying to replace the state of the dictatorship of the proletariat by a state of a different character? . . .

(19) "Is it possible to replace the party which is the vanguard of the proletariat by a 'party of the entire people'? This, too, is not a question of the internal affairs of any particular party, but a fundamental problem involving the universal truth of Marxism-Leninism. . . . What will happen if it is announced half-way before entering the higher stage of Communist society that the party of the proletariat has become a 'party of the entire people' and if its proletarian class character is repudiated? . . . Does this not disarm the proletariat and all the working people, organizationally and ideologically, and is it not tantamount to helping to restore capitalism? . . .

(20) "Over the past few years certain persons have violated Lenin's integral teachings about the inter-relationship of leaders, party, class, and masses, and raised the issue of 'combating the personality cult'; that is erroneous and harmful. . . . To raise the question of 'combating the personality cult' is actually to counterpose the leaders to the masses, undermine the party's unified leadership, which is based on democratic centralism, dissipate its fighting strength, and disintegrate its ranks. . . .

"While loudly combating the so-called personality cult, certain persons are in reality doing their best to defame the proletarian party and the dictatorship of the proletariat. At the same time, they are enormously exaggerating the role of certain individuals, shifting all errors on to others, and claiming all credit for themselves. What is more serious is that, under the pretext of 'combating the personality cult', certain persons are crudely interfering in the internal affairs of other fraternal parties and fraternal countries, and forcing other fraternal parties to change their leadership in order to impose their own wrong line on these parties. What is this if not great-power chauvinism, sectarianism, and splittism? . . .

(21) "Relations between socialist countries, whether large or small, and whether more developed or less developed economically, must be based on the principles of complete equality. . . . Every socialist country must rely mainly on itself for its construction. . . . If, proceeding only from its own partial interests, any socialist country unilaterally demands that other fraternal countries submit to its needs, and uses the pretext of opposing what they call 'going it alone' and 'nationalism' to prevent other fraternal countries from applying the principle of relying mainly on their own efforts in their construction and from developing their economies on the basis of independence, or even goes to the length of putting economic pressure on other fraternal countries—then these are pure manifestations of national egoism. . . . In relations among socialist countries it would be preposterous to follow the practice of gaining profit for oneself at the expense of others . . . or go so far as to take the 'economic integration' and the 'Common Market', which monopoly capitalist groups have instituted for the purpose of seizing markets and grabbing profits, as examples which socialist countries ought to follow in their economic co-operation and mutual assistance."

[This section apparently referred to differences which had arisen between the Soviet Union and Romania at a Comecon meeting in February, when the Romanian delegate objected to proposals for co-ordination of economic plans which would have involved cuts in Romania's industrial development programme.]

(22) "If the principle of independence and equality is accepted in relations among fraternal parties, then it is impermissible for any party to place itself above others, to interfere in their internal affairs, and to adopt patriarchal ways in relations with them. If it is accepted that there are no 'superiors' and 'subordinates' in relations among fraternal parties, then it is impermissible to impose the programme, resolutions, and line of one's own party on other fraternal parties as the 'common programme' of the international Communist movement.

"If the principle of reaching unanimity through consultation is accepted in relations between fraternal parties, then one should not emphasize 'who is in the majority' or 'who is in the minority', and bank on a so-called majority in order to force through one's own erroneous line and carry out sectarian and splitting policies. If it is agreed that differences between fraternal parties should be settled through inter-party consultation, then other fraternal parties should not be attacked publicly and by name at one's own party congress or other party congresses, in speeches by party leaders, resolutions, statements, etc.; and still less should the ideological differences among fraternal parties be extended into the sphere of state relations. . . .

"In the sphere of relations among fraternal parties and countries, the question of Soviet-Albanian relations is an outstanding one at present. . . . How to treat the Marxist-Leninist fraternal Albanian Party of Labour is one question. How to treat the Yugoslav revisionist clique of traitors to Marxism-Leninism is quite another question. These two essentially different questions must on no account be placed on a par.

"Your letter says that you 'do not relinquish the hope that the relations between the CPSU and the Albanian Party of Labour may be improved', but at the same time you continue to attack the Albanian comrades for what you call 'splitting activities'. Clearly this is self-contradictory and in no way contributes to resolving the problem of Soviet-Albanian relations.

"Who is it that has taken splitting actions in Soviet-Albanian relations? Who is it that has extended the ideological differences between the Soviet and Albanian parties to state relations? Who is it that has brought the divergences between the Soviet and Albanian parties and between the two countries into the open before the enemy? Who is it that has openly called for a change in the Albanian party and state leadership? All this is plain and clear to the whole world. . . . We once again express our sincere hope that the leading comrades of the CPSU will observe the principles guiding relations among fraternal parties and countries and take the initiative in seeking an effective way to improve Soviet-Albanian relations. . . .

"The comrades of the CPSU state in their letter that 'the Communist Party of the Soviet Union has never taken and will never take a single step that could show hostility among the peoples of our country toward the fraternal Chinese people or other peoples'. Here we do not desire to enumerate the many unpleasant events that have occurred in the past; we only wish that the comrades of the CPSU will strictly abide by this statement in their future actions. During the past few years our party members and our people have exercised the greatest restraint in the face of a series of grave incidents which were in violation of the principles guiding relations among fraternal parties and countries. . . . The spirit of proletarian internationalism of the Chinese Communists and the Chinese people has stood a severe test. . . .

(23) "Certain persons are now attempting to introduce the Yugoslav revisionist clique into the socialist community and the international Communist ranks. This is openly to tear up the agreement unanimously reached at the 1960 meeting of the fraternal parties and is absolutely impermissible.

"Over the past few years . . . the many experiences and lessons of the international Communist movement have fully confirmed the correctness of the conclusion in the [Moscow] declaration and the statement that revisionism is at present the main danger in the international Communist movement. However, certain persons are openly saying that dogmatism and not revisionism is the main danger, or that dogmatism is no less dangerous than revisionism. . . . Genuine Marxist-Leninist parties . . . must not barter away principles, approving one thing today and another tomorrow. . . .

"It is necessary at all times to adhere to the universal truth of Marxism-Leninism. Failure to do so will lead to right opportunist or revisionist errors. On the other hand, it is always necessary to proceed from reality . . . and independently work out and apply policies and tactics suited to the conditions of one's own country. Errors of dogmatism will be committed if one fails to do so, if one mechanically copies the policies and tactics of another Communist Party, submits blindly to the will of others, or accepts without analysis the programme and resolutions of another Communist Party as one's own line. Some people are now violating this basic principle. . . . On the pretext of 'creatively developing Marxism-Leninism' they cast aside the universal truth of Marxism-Leninism. Moreover, they describe as 'universal Marxist-Leninist truths' their own prescriptions, which are based on nothing but subjective conjecture . . . and they force others to accept these prescriptions unconditionally. That is why so many grave phenomena have come to pass in the international Communist movement. . . .

(24) "If a party is not a proletarian revolutionary party but a bourgeois reformist party; if it is not a Marxist-Leninist party but a revisionist party; . . . if it is not a party that can use its brains to think for itself . . . but instead is a party that parrots the words of others, copies foreign experience without analysis, runs hither and thither in response to the baton of certain persons abroad, and has become a hodgepodge of revisionism, dogmatism, and everything but Marxist-Leninist

principle; then such a party is absolutely incapable of leading the proletariat and the masses in revolutionary struggle. . . .

(25) "The public polemics in the international Communist movement have been provoked by certain fraternal party leaders and forced on us. Since a public debate has been provoked, it ought to be conducted on the basis of equality among fraternal parties . . . and by presenting the facts and reasoning things out. . . . Since certain party leaders have published innumerable articles attacking other fraternal parties, why do they not publish in their own press the articles those parties have written in reply?

"Latterly, the Communist Party of China has been subjected to preposterous attacks. . . . We have published these articles and speeches attacking us in our own press. . . . Between Dec. 15, 1962, and March 8, 1963, we wrote seven articles in reply to our attackers. . . . Presumably you are referring to these articles when towards the end of your letter of March 30 you accuse the Chinese press of making 'groundless attacks' on the CPSU. It is turning things upside down to describe articles replying to our attackers as 'attacks'.

"Since you describe our articles as 'groundless' and as so very bad, why do you not publish all seven of these 'groundless attacks' in the same way as we have published your articles, and let all the Soviet comrades and Soviet people think for themselves and judge who is right and who wrong? You are of course entitled to make a point-by-point refutation of these articles you consider 'groundless attacks'. Although you call our articles 'groundless' and our arguments wrong, you do not tell the Soviet people what our arguments actually are. This practice can hardly be described as showing a serious attitude towards the discussion of problems by fraternal parties, towards the truth, or towards the masses. . . ."

The letter ended by saying that "there are other questions of common concern, such as the criticism of Stalin and some important matters of principle regarding the international Communist movement which were raised at the 20th and 22nd congresses of the CPSU, and we hope that on these questions, too, there will be a frank exchange of opinion in the [Moscow] talks".

Chinese Embassy Officials Expelled from USSR (June 1963)

The central committee of the Soviet party, a plenary session of which opened on June 18, 1963, announced on the same day that the Chinese letter would not be published in the Soviet Union "at the present time", as its "unwarranted attacks" on the Soviet and other Communist parties would call for "a public reply which would lead to a further sharpening of polemics". A communiqué issued by the committee on June 21 rejected the Chinese attacks on the Soviet party, on the decisions of its 20th, 21st, and 22nd congresses, and on its programme as "groundless and slanderous".

The Soviet Government demanded on June 27, 1963, the recall of three Chinese embassy officials who had distributed copies of the Chinese letter in the USSR, this demand being described by the Chinese Foreign Ministry as "unreasonable and unfriendly". A Soviet Foreign Ministry statement of July 4 said that members of the Chinese embassy staff had disseminated a specially printed mass edition of the letter in the Russian language in Moscow and other cities, despite two protests from the Soviet Foreign Ministry. A Chinese Note protesting against the expulsions, published on July 5, maintained that "it is perfectly normal for the official organs and personnel of one socialist country in another socialist country to distribute the published documents of their own Government and party".

Talks in Moscow (July 1963)

Talks between the two parties began in Moscow on July 5, 1963, under conditions of strict secrecy, the Chinese party being represented by Deng Xiaoping, Peng Zhen, and Wu Xiuzhuan, and the Soviet party by Mikhail Suslov, Yury Andropov, Boris Ponomaryov, Leonid Ilyichev, and Stepan Chervonenko (the Soviet ambassador in Beijing). They ended on July 20 without agreement being reached; a communiqué issued on the following day said that at the Chinese delegation's suggestion it had been decided "to have an interval in the work of the delegations and to continue the meeting some time later, at a place and time to be agreed upon".

Soviet Reply to the "25 Points" (July 1963)

The Chinese letter of June 14 was published in *Pravda* on July 14, together with an 18,000-word reply which took the form of an open letter from the Soviet central committee to the party membership. This accused the Chinese leaders of being prepared to sacrifice hundreds of millions of lives in a nuclear war, of advocating the revival of Stalin's methods of government, and of organizing disruptive activities inside other Communist parties, and suggested that they were inspired by nationalist and racialist rather than by Communist principles. The Soviet letter is summarized below.

Introduction. "The frankly hostile actions of the CPC [Chinese Communist Party] leaders, their persistent striving to sharpen polemics in the international Communist movement, the deliberate distortion of the positions of our party, and the incorrect interpretation of the motives for which we refrained temporarily from publishing the letter", the letter said, "impel us to publish the letter of the CPC central committee of June 14, 1963, and to give our appraisal of this document. All who read the letter of the CPC central committee will see, behind the bombastic phrases about unity and cohesion, unfriendly and slanderous attacks on our party and our country. . . .

"The document is crammed with charges—overt and covert—against the CPSU and the Soviet Union. The authors of the letter permit themselves unworthy fabrications, insulting to Communists, about 'the betrayal of the interests of the whole international proletariat and all the peoples of the world' and 'a departure from Marxism-Leninism and proletarian internationalism'. They hint at 'cowardice in face of the imperialists', at 'a step back in the course of historic development', and even at 'the organizational and moral disarming of the proletariat and all working people', which is tantamount to 'helping to restore capitalism' in our country. . . ."

Soviet Aid to China. Commenting that the Chinese leaders had "recently sought to belittle the significance of Soviet aid", the letter recalled that the Soviet Union had helped China to build 198 industrial enterprises and other projects, and to establish such new branches of industry as automobile, tractor, and aircraft manufacturing; had supplied China with over 1,400 blueprints of big enterprises; had trained thousands of specialists and workers; and was still providing technical assistance in the construction of 88 enterprises.

Development of the Controversy. The letter stated that at the 1960 Moscow conference, when the majority of Communist parties rejected the CPC's views, the Chinese delegation had "stubbornly upheld its own particular views, and signed the statement only when the danger arose of its complete isolation". Shortly afterwards they had resumed their propaganda, "using the leadership of the Albanian Party of

Labour as a mouthpiece". A series of subsequent appeals aimed at improving relations had found no response in Beijing.

The Chinese leaders, the letter claimed, had carried their ideological differences into international relations by curtailing their economic and trade relations with the USSR and other socialist countries. "On the initiative of the Chinese Government, the volume of China's trade with the Soviet Union has been cut almost 67 per cent in the past three years, and deliveries of industrial plant have dropped to one-fortieth."

From the end of 1961 the Chinese representatives in international organizations had begun openly to demand the exclusion of Soviet delegates and those of other European Communist countries from conferences in Africa and Asia.

War and Peace. "At a first glance", the Soviet letter commented, "many theses in the [Chinese] letter may seem puzzling. Whom are the Chinese comrades actually arguing with? Are there Communists who, for instance, object to socialist revolution or who do not regard it as their duty to fight against imperialism and to support the national liberation movement? . . . The Chinese comrades first ascribe to the CPSU and other Marxist-Leninist parties views which they have never expressed and which are alien to them; secondly, by paying lip-service to formulae and positions borrowed from the documents of the Communist movement, they try to camouflage their erroneous views. . . .

"In point of fact, however, the questions which bear on vital interests of the peoples are in the centre of the dispute. These are the questions of war and peace, the role and development of the world socialist system, the struggle against the ideology and practice of the personality cult, the strategy and tactics of the world labour movement, and the national liberation struggle. . . .

"The world Communist movement, in the declaration and statement, set before Communists as a task of extreme importance that of struggling for peace and averting a nuclear world catastrophe. . . . Though the nature of imperialism has not changed and the danger of the outbreak of war has not been averted, in modern conditions the forces of peace, of which the mighty community of socialist states is the main bulwark, can by their joint efforts avert a new world war. . . .

"The nuclear rocket weapons which have been created . . . possess an unprecedented devastating force. . . . Have Communists the right to ignore this danger? Must we tell the people the whole truth about the consequences of nuclear war? We believe that, without question, we must. This cannot have a 'paralyzing' effect on the masses, as the Chinese comrades assert. On the contrary, the truth about modern war will mobilize the will and energy of the masses in the struggle for peace and against imperialism. . . .

"What is the position of the CPC leadership? What do the theses that they propagate mean—that an end cannot be put to war so long as imperialism exists? That peaceful co-existence is an illusion? That it is not the general line of the foreign policy of socialist countries? That the peace struggle hinders the revolutionary struggle? . . . They do not believe in the possibility of preventing a new world war; they underestimate the forces of peace and socialism and overestimate the forces of imperialism; in fact, they ignore the mobilization of the masses for the struggle against the war danger. . . .

Nuclear War. "The Chinese comrades obviously underestimate the whole danger of nuclear war", the letter continued. "'The atomic bomb is a paper tiger, it is not terrible at all', they contend. The main thing is to put an end to imperialism as quickly as possible, but how and with what losses this will be achieved seems to be a secondary question. To whom, it is right to ask, is it secondary? To the hundreds of millions of people who are doomed to death in the event of the unleashing of a nuclear war? To the states that will be erased from the face of the earth in the very first hours of such a war? . . .

"Some responsible Chinese leaders have also declared that it is possible to sacrifice hundreds of millions of peoples in war." [This referred to a statement made by Mao at the 1957 Moscow conference.] "'On the ruins of destroyed imperialism', asserts *Long Live Leninism*, which was approved by the CPC central committee, 'the victorious peoples will create with tremendous speed a civilization a thousand times higher than the capitalist system, and will build their bright future'. Is it permissible to ask the Chinese comrades if they realize what sort of ruins a nuclear world war would leave behind? . . . They say frankly, 'On the ruins of a destroyed imperialism'—in other words, as a result of the unleashing of war— 'a bright future will be built'. If we agree to this, then indeed there is no need for the principle of peaceful co-existence. . . .

"We ourselves produce the nuclear weapon and have manufactured it in sufficient quantity. We know its destructive force full well. If imperialism starts a war against us we shall not hesitate to use this formidable weapon against the aggressor; but if we are not attacked we shall not be the first to use this weapon. . . .

"We would like to ask the Chinese comrades who suggest building a 'bright future' on the ruins of the old world destroyed by a nuclear war whether they have consulted the working class of the countries where imperialism dominates. . . . The nuclear bomb does not distinguish between the imperialists and working people. . . .

"The posing of the question in this way by the Chinese comrades may give rise to the well-justified suspicion that this is no longer a class approach in the struggle for the abolition of capitalism, but has entirely different aims. If both the exploiters and the exploited are buried under the ruins of the old world, who will build the 'bright future'? In this connexion it is impossible not to note the fact that instead of the internationalist class approach expressed in the call 'Workers of the world, unite', the Chinese comrades propagate the slogan, which is devoid of any class meaning, 'The wind from the east prevails over the wind from the west.' . . ."

The Cuban Crisis. The letter went on: "The Chinese comrades allege that in the period of the Caribbean crisis we made an 'adventurist' mistake by introducing rockets into Cuba and then 'capitulated' to American imperialism when we removed the rockets from Cuba. Such assertions utterly contradict the facts. What was the actual state of affairs? The CPSU central committee and the Soviet Government possessed trustworthy information that an armed aggression by US imperialism against Cuba was about to take place. . . . Proceeding from the need to defend the Cuban revolution, the Soviet Government and the Cuban Government reached agreement on the delivery of missiles to Cuba. . . . Such a resolute step on the part of the Soviet Union and Cuba was a shock to the American imperialists, who felt for the first time in their history that if they were to undertake an armed invasion of Cuba, a shattering retaliatory blow would be dealt against their own territory.

"Inasmuch as the point in question was not simply a conflict between the United States and Cuba, but a clash between the two major nuclear powers, the crisis in the Caribbean area would have turned from a local into a world one. A real danger of nuclear war arose. There was one alternative in the prevailing situation: either to . . . embark upon a course of unleashing a world nuclear war, or, profiting from the opportunity offered by the delivery of missiles, to take all steps to reach an agreement on a peaceful solution of the crisis and to prevent aggression against Cuba. As is known, we chose the second path. . . . Agreement to remove the missile weapons in return for the US Government's commitment not to invade Cuba . . . made it possible to frustrate the plans of the extreme adventurist circles of American imperialism. . . .

"The Chinese comrades regard our statement that the Kennedy Government also displayed a certain reasonableness and a realistic approach in the Cuban crisis as 'prettifying imperialism'. Do they really think that all bourgeois governments lack all reason in everything they do? . . . The Chinese comrades argue that the imperialists cannot be trusted in anything, that they are bound to cheat. But this is not a case of good faith, but rather one of sober calculation. Eight months have passed since the elimination of the Caribbean crisis, and the US Government is keeping its word—there has been no invasion of Cuba. We also assumed a commitment to remove our missiles from Cuba, and we have fulfilled it. It should not, however, be forgotten that we have given a commitment to the Cuban people: if the US imperialists do not keep their promise but invade Cuba, we shall come to the assistance of the Cuban people. . . .

"What are the Chinese leaders dissatisfied with? Is it perhaps the fact that it was possible to prevent the invasion of Cuba and the unleashing of a world war? . . .

Disarmament. "The true position of the CPC leadership is demonstrated very clearly . . . in its complete underestimation and, what is more, deliberate ignoring of the struggle for disarmament", the Soviet letter went on. "They try to prove that general disarmament is possible only when socialism triumphs all over the world. Must the Marxists sit on their hands, waiting for the victory of socialism all over the world, while mankind suffocates in the clutches of the arms race? . . . One can repeat ad infinitum that war is inevitable, claiming that such a viewpoint is evidence of one's 'revolutionary spirit'. In fact, this approach merely indicates lack of faith in one's strength and fear of imperialism. . . .

Peaceful Co-existence. "The CPC central committee accuses the Communist parties of extending peaceful co-existence between states with different social systems to relations between the exploiters and the exploited, between the oppressed and the oppressing classes, between the working masses and the imperialists. This is a truly monstrous fabrication. . . . When we speak of peaceful co-existence we mean the inter-state relations of the socialist countries with the countries of capitalism. The principle of peaceful coexistence, naturally, can in no way be applied to relations between the antagonistic classes inside the capitalist states. . . .

The Personality Cult and the Dictatorship of the Proletariat. "The CPC leaders have taken on themselves the role of defenders of the personality cult, of propagators of Stalin's wrong ideas. They are trying to thrust upon other parties the practices, ideology, ethics, and forms and methods of leadership which flourished in the period of the personality cult." The letter went on to quote statements made in 1956 by Mao Zedong, Liu Shaoqi, and Deng Xiaoping fully supporting the decisions of the 20th congress of the CPSU, including its condemnation of the "personality cult", and commented that "they have made a turn of 180 degrees in evaluating the 20th congress of our party".

Describing the results of "the restoration of Leninist principles and standards in party life", the letter said: "The atmosphere of fear, suspicion and uncertainty which poisoned the life of the people in the period of the personality cult has gone. . . . Ask the people whose fathers and mothers were victims of the reprisals in the period of the personality cult what it means for them to obtain recognition that their fathers, mothers, and brothers were honest people, and that they themselves are not outcasts in our society. . . .

"Soviet people find it strange and outrageous that the Chinese comrades should be trying to smear the CPSU programme", the letter continued. "Alluding to the fact that our party proclaims as its task the struggle for a better life for the people, the CPC leaders hint at some sort of 'bourgeoisification' and 'degeneration' of Soviet society. To follow their line of thinking, it seems that if a people walks in rope sandals and eats watery soup out of a common bowl, that is communism, and if a working man lives well and wants to live even better tomorrow, that is almost tantamount to the restoration of capitalism! . . .

Methods of Revolutionary Struggle. "The next important question on which we differ is that of ways and methods of the revolutionary struggle of the working class. As depicted by the Chinese comrades, the differences on this question appear as follows: one side—they themselves—stands for world revolution, while the other—the CPSU, the Marxist-Leninist parties—have forgotten the revolution and even fear it, and instead of revolutionary struggle are concerned with things unworthy of a real revolutionary, such as peace, the economic development of the socialist countries, the improvement of the living standards of their peoples, and the struggle for the democratic rights and vital interests of the working people of the capitalist countries. . . .

"Lenin taught that 'we exert our main influence on the international revolution by our economic policy'. . . . But now it turns out that there are comrades who have decided that Lenin was wrong. What is this—lack of faith in the ability of the socialist countries to defeat capitalism in economic competition? Or is it the attitude of persons who, on meeting with difficulties in building socialism, have become disappointed and do not see the possibility of exerting the main influence on the international revolutionary movement by their economic successes? . . . They want to achieve the revolution sooner, by other and what seem to them shorter ways. But the victorious revolution can consolidate its successes and prove the superiority of socialism over capitalism by the work, and only by the work of the people. . . .

"The Chinese comrades, in a haughty and abusive way, accuse the Communist parties of France, Italy, the United States and other countries of nothing less than opportunism and reformism, of 'parliamentary cretinism', even of slipping down to 'bourgeois socialism'. On what grounds do they do this? On the grounds that these Communist parties do not put forward the slogan of an immediate proletarian revolution, although even the Chinese leaders must realize that this cannot be done without the existence of a revolutionary situation. . . .

"The Chinese comrades have also disagreed with the world Communist movement on the forms of the transition of different countries to socialism. . . . The Chinese comrades regard as the main criterion of revolutionary spirit recognition of the armed uprising. . . . [They] are thereby in fact denying the possibility of using peaceful forms of struggle for the victory of the socialist revolution, whereas Marxism-Leninism teaches that Communists must master all forms of revolutionary class struggle, both violent and non-violent."

National Liberation Movements. The letter continued: "Yet another important question is that of the relationship between the struggle of the international working class and the national liberation movement of the peoples of Asia, Africa, and Latin America. . . . These are the great forces of our epoch. Correct co-ordination between them constitutes one of the main prerequisites for victory over imperialism.

"How do the Chinese comrades solve this problem? This is seen from their new theory, according to which the main contradiction of our time is not between socialism and imperialism, but between the national liberation movement and imperialism. The decisive force in the struggle against imperialism, the Chinese comrades maintain, is not the world system of socialism, not the struggle of the international working class, but the national liberation movement.

"In this way the Chinese comrades apparently want to win popularity among the peoples of Asia, Africa, and Latin America by the easiest possible means. But let no one be deceived by this theory. Whether the Chinese theoreticians want it or not, this theory in essence means isolating the national liberation movement from the international working class and its creation, the world system of socialism. . . . The Chinese comrades . . . want to amend Lenin and prove that it is not the working class but the petty bourgeoisie or the national bourgeoisie, or even 'certain patriotically minded kings, princes, and aristocrats', who must be the leaders of the world struggle against imperialism. . . .

"The question arises, what is the explanation for the incorrect propositions of the CPC leadership on the basic problems of our time? It is either the complete divorcement of the Chinese comrades from actual reality—a dogmatic, bookish approach to problems of war, peace, and revolution; their lack of understanding of the concrete conditions of the present epoch—or the fact that behind the rumpus about the 'world revolution' raised by the Chinese comrades there are other goals, which have nothing in common with revolution. . . ."

Relations between Socialist Countries. Accusing the Chinese of "activities aimed at undermining the unity of the world socialist camp and the international Communist movement", the letter stated that in the past three years China had reduced the volume of her trade with other socialist countries by over 50 per cent, and by breaking its agreements had seriously harmed the economies of some of them. It went on: "The formula of 'building socialism mainly by our own forces' [see point (21) of the Chinese letter] conceals the concept of creating self-sufficient national economies for which economic contacts with other countries are restricted to trade alone. The Chinese comrades are trying to impose this approach on other socialist countries. . . . It cannot be regarded otherwise than as an attempt to undermine the unity of the socialist commonwealth. . . ."

The International Communist Movement. The letter also accused the Chinese leadership of "organizing and supporting various anti-party groups of renegades", including dissident Communist groups in Belgium, the USA, Brazil, Australia, Italy, India and Ceylon; it alleged that the Trotskyist Fourth International was trying to use the Chinese party's position to further its own ends; and said that the Chinese leaders had published in many languages abusive attacks on the Soviet, French, Italian, Indian, and US Communist parties, and were "trying to subordinate other fraternal parties to their influence and control".

Albania and Yugoslavia. The letter stated that the Chinese leaders had done "everything in their power to use the Albanian leaders as their mouthpiece, and had "openly pushed them on to the road of open struggle against the Soviet Union".

Rejecting the Chinese view that Yugoslavia was not a socialist country, the letter quoted a statement made by the *People's Daily* in 1955 that "Yugoslavia has achieved notable successes in the building of socialism." The Soviet letter asked: "Why then have the Chinese leaders so drastically changed their attitude on the Yugoslav question? It is hard to find an explanation other than that they saw in this one of the pretexts advantageous, in their opinion, for discrediting the policy of the CPSU and other Marxist-Leninist parties.

The letter continued: "Differences on a number of ideological questions of principle continue to remain between the CPSU and the League of Communists of Yugoslavia. But it would be wrong to 'excommunicate' Yugoslavia from socialism on these grounds. . . . At the present time there are 14 socialist countries in the world. . . . The range of questions encountered by the fraternal parties which stand at the helm of state is increasing, and besides this each of the fraternal parties is working in different conditions. It is not surprising that in these circumstances the fraternal parties may develop different approaches to the solution of this or that problem. . . .

"If we were to follow the example of the Chinese leaders, because of our serious differences with the leaders of the Albanian Party of Labour we should long since have proclaimed Albania to be a non-socialist country. But that would be a wrong and subjective approach. In spite of our differences with the Albanian leaders, the Soviet Communists regard Albania as a socialist country, and for their part do everything in their power to prevent Albania from being split away from the socialist community. . . ."

Chinese Comments on Soviet Statement (July 1963)

The first public Chinese comment on the Soviet letter was made on July 19, 1963, by a spokesman of the CPC central committee, who said that its contents "do not accord with the facts, and we cannot agree with the views it expresses". The spokesman's statement, which was ironic in tone, announced that the Chinese central committee had decided to re-publish its letter of June 14 together with the Soviet reply, and also to broadcast both documents in many languages. "There is only one reason", he said, "why we are broadcasting the open letter of the central committee of the CPSU—it is a remarkable piece of work. To quote a Chinese poem

> A remarkable work should be enjoyed together
> And doubts analysed in company."

He advised as many people as possible to study the Soviet letter, as it was "superlative material for learning by negative example".

The full text of the Soviet letter was published in the *People's Daily* on July 20, together with an editorial note which declared that "the methods used in the letter are the distortion of facts and the reversal of right and wrong—methods which Marxist-Leninists can in no circumstances tolerate". The *People's Daily* accused the Soviet leaders of "trying to pin the vicious charge of bellicosity on China, and in particular to attack Comrade Mao Zedong".

In reply to the Soviet charge that the Chinese leaders had reversed their attitude towards the decisions of the 20th congress of the CPSU, the *People's Daily* said that the Chinese party had never considered the 20th congress to be "wholly positive". It continued: "We have never agreed with its complete negation of Stalin, an action it took on the pretext of combating the personality cult, or with its one-sided emphasis on peaceful transition. . . . We repeatedly pointed out that Stalin's merits outweighed his faults. . . . Similarly, on the question of peaceful transition, the central committee of the CPC expressed differing opinions to the CPSU on many occasions. . . . At that time, however, we did not publicly criticize the leaders of the CPSU, for the sake of safeguarding the solidarity of the international Communist movement and out of consideration for the prestige of the CPSU and the Soviet Union".

In reply to the Soviet allegation that China had extended ideological differences to the sphere of state relations, the *People's Daily* said that the withdrawal of Soviet experts in 1960 had "inflicted incalculable difficulties and losses on China's economy, national defence, and scientific research, and was the main reason for the reduction in the economic and commercial links between China and the Soviet Union. China is the victim. Yet the central committee of the CPSU, in its open letter, blames China for reducing economic and commercial links with the Soviet Union and for extending ideological differences to the sphere of state relations! So complete a reversal of the truth is indeed astonishing".

Chinese Denunciation of Nuclear Test-ban Treaty (July 1963)

The Chinese Government issued a violently-worded statement on July 31, 1963, denouncing as a "dirty fraud" the partial nuclear test-ban treaty which had been initialled in Moscow on July 25 by the USSR, the USA and the United Kingdom. The statement said that the treaty "runs diametrically counter to the wishes of the peace-loving peoples", would not hinder America from pursuing her policy of "nuclear blackmail and proliferation of nuclear weapons", and represented an attempt on the part of America, Russia, and Britain to preserve their "nuclear monopoly". The exclusion of underground tests from the treaty's scope was regarded as particularly advantageous for "the further development of nuclear weapons by US imperialism". The Soviet Government was accused of having "willingly allowed US imperialism to get military superiority"; of having "betrayed the peoples of the socialist camp", including the peoples of the USSR and China; and of "allying with the forces of war and reaction against the forces of peace". Declaring that the peoples of the world wanted a real and not a "fake" peace, the Chinese statement said that the treaty reflected "the ugly face of US imperialism, which is aggressive by nature, as well as the servile features of those who are warmly embracing American imperialism".

Zhou Enlai sent identical letters on Aug. 2, 1963, to all heads of state calling for a world conference of heads of government to discuss "the question of complete, thorough, total and resolute prohibition of nuclear weapons". Apart from Albania, the only countries to accept this proposal were North Korea and North Vietnam (both at this time sympathetic to China's views in the ideological controversy) and Pakistan, which in recent years had adopted a policy of close friendship with China.

Liu Shaoqi described the atomic bomb as a "paper tiger" in a speech on Sept. 18, 1963. Saying that "the decisive factor in war is man, not new types of weapons", he declared that "in the eyes of the modern revisionists, to survive is everything. The philosophy of survival has replaced Marxism-Leninism".

The Soviet Government issued a lengthy statement on Aug. 3, 1963, in reply to the Chinese Government's statement of July 31. Describing the Chinese statement as "reeking of hopelessness and pessimism", the Soviet Government expressed amazement that any socialist country could have issued such a declaration; responding sharply to the "impudent" allegations made by the Chinese Government, the USSR described China's attitude as "tantamount to actual connivance with those who advocate thermo-nuclear world war and who are against the settlement round the conference table of international problems in dispute". The Chinese Government had thereby taken up a position which "runs counter to the Leninist policy of peaceful coexistence between states with different social systems", and the Chinese leaders had "placed themselves openly against the socialist commonwealth, the whole world Communist movement, and all the peace-loving peoples of Europe, Asia, Africa, and America".

A Soviet statement of Aug. 21, 1963, maintained that the real motive of the Chinese leaders' opposition to the treaty was their desire to acquire their own atomic bomb at any cost. In reply the Chinese Government accused the USSR on Sept. 1 of giving the USA details of the secret agreement of 1957 on nuclear weapons.

V: UNSUCCESSFUL ATTEMPTS TO REDUCE POLEMICS, 1963–64

The continuation of Sino-Soviet polemics in late 1963 and early 1964 was followed by attempts, notably by the Soviet side, to bring about a measure of reconciliation between the two sides, or at least a suspension of ideological hostilities. However, such moves produced little result, and by mid-1964 each side was castigating the other as strongly as ever.

Chinese Polemics against Soviet Party (September 1963–February 1964)

A series of seven articles replying to the Soviet party's open letter of July 14, 1963, appeared between Sept. 6, 1963, and Feb. 10, 1964, in the *People's Daily* and *Red Flag*.

After an introductory article reviewing the history of the controversy, the next two articles respectively defended Stalin and attacked the Yugoslav regime as "a brutal fascist dictatorship". The fourth described the Soviet leaders as "apologists for neo-colonialism" who adopted "a passive or scornful attitude" towards the struggles of the peoples of Asia, Africa, and Latin America, and accused them of inciting racial hatred by reviving the theory of the "yellow peril".

The fifth article, which dealt with the question of war and peace, said: "The leaders of the CPSU hold that with the appearance of nuclear weapons there is no longer any difference between just and unjust wars, that oppressed peoples and nations must abandon revolution and refrain from waging just popular revolutionary wars and wars of national liberation, and that the socialist countries must . . . yield to imperialist nuclear blackmail. . . . The CPC has always held that the socialist countries should actively support the peoples' revolutionary struggles. . . . At the same time we hold that the oppressed peoples and nations can achieve liberation only by their resolute revolutionary struggle and that no-one else can do it for them. . . . Socialist countries must not use nuclear weapons to support the peoples' wars of national liberation and revolutionary civil wars, and have no need to do so. . . . The socialist countries must achieve and maintain nuclear superiority. Only this can prevent the imperialists from launching a nuclear war and help to bring about the complete prohibition of nuclear weapons. . . . In the hands of a socialist country nuclear weapons must always be defensive weapons for resisting imperialist nuclear threats. A socialist country must not be the first to use nuclear weapons, nor should it in any circumstances play with them or engage in nuclear blackmail and nuclear gambling". In this latter respect the article maintained that Khrushchev had done so during the Cuban crisis.

The sixth article accused Khrushchev of having turned the Marxist-Leninist concept of peaceful coexistence into a policy of "class capitulation", whilst the seventh denounced the Soviet leaders as "the greatest splitters of our times".

Polemics against the Chinese party's policy continued in the Soviet press in the summer and autumn of 1963, but in general avoided personal vituperation of the type contained in the Chinese attacks on Khrushchev. The CPSU's theoretical organ *Kommunist* contended on Oct. 6, 1963, that although the CPC now claimed to support peaceful coexistence, which it had formerly attacked, it did not rule out the possibility of an international "revolutionary war" begun by a socialist state. "To strive to achieve revolution in other countries by means of world war", the article said, "is a path that is unacceptable to Communists in principle because it is based on the anti-Leninist idea of 'accelerating' revolution from outside. Moreover, it is a path which ignores the question of the real consequences of a world war fought by means of nuclear weapons. . . .".

On Oct. 23, 1963, *Kommunist* declared that Chinese propaganda was engaged in the "deification of Mao Zedong" and in "a campaign against the very fundamentals of Marxism-Leninism such as has not occurred since the days of Trotskyism". It was inspiring and supporting "anti-party and factional groups" in other countries, in an attempt to "knock together an international bloc out of such groups, mostly consisting of people who were expelled from Communist parties".

Soviet Proposals for World Communist Conference and Ending of Polemics (October 1963–February 1964)

During the autumn of 1963 the Soviet press published a large number of statements by foreign Communist parties calling for a world Communist conference in the near future. Khrushchev appealed on Oct. 25 for an end to public polemics, and suggested that if there were differences between the Chinese and Soviet parties "let us allow time to have its say as to which viewpoint is more correct". The New China News Agency, however, claimed on Nov. 15 that since this appeal Soviet papers had published more than 80 anti-Chinese articles, and described it as "nothing but a trick to cover up the Soviet leaders' frenzied anti-Chinese activities". On Nov. 29 the Soviet party, in a letter to the Chinese party, proposed a suspension of polemics in preparation for an international conference.

After emphasizing the harm done to the international Communist movement by public polemics, the letter observed that "besides the questions over which differences have arisen, there are also positions on which we are fully united or at least very close in our views". After appealing for "a calm and unprejudiced understanding of our present discussion and the elimination from it of everything that is non-essential", it proposed that negotiations should be opened on an increase of trade between the two countries and on increased Soviet technical aid to Chinese industry.

The letter suggested that public polemics should be replaced by an exchange of views through mutual consultations, negotiations, and exchanges of letters, which would create more favourable conditions for a world Communist conference. "It is the duty of all parties", it concluded, "to help to create a situation which will render such a meeting fruitful, so that it will lead not to a split in the world Communist movement but to the genuine unity and solidarity of all the fraternal parties. . . .".

The Soviet letter was ignored by the Chinese party, which did not reply until Feb. 29, 1964, and meanwhile continued to publish articles attacking the Soviet party and calling for the formation of pro-Chinese parties in countries where the local Communist leadership supported the USSR. The *People's Daily* on Feb. 4 openly advocated a split in the world Communist movement, maintaining that "like everything else, the international working-class movement tends to divide itself in two".

Mikhail Suslov's Report to CPSU Central Committee (February 1964)

After the publication of this article, the Soviet leadership abandoned its conciliatory attitude. In an unpublished letter of Feb. 12, 1964, which was sent to other Communist parties but not to the Chinese party, they stated that the central committee would discuss the Chinese party's activities at its forthcoming plenary session and thereafter would openly state its views, and again raised the question of a world Communist conference. On Feb. 14 Mikhail Suslov (a member of the CPSU secretariat) presented a long report on the controversy to the central committee, containing the most comprehensive Soviet indictment of the Chinese leadership to date; the report, however, was not published at the time, at the Romanian party's request [see below].

Suslov accused the Chinese leaders of "steering a course towards a split among the Communist parties and towards the setting-up of factions and groups hostile to Marxism-Leninism", and of seeking "to give orders in the socialist commonwealth as in their own estate, to impose their will on other countries, and to dictate the terms on which they would either admit parties and peoples into the socialist system or 'excommunicate' them from it at will". As an example, he cited the Chinese attitude towards Yugoslavia, which they had praised in 1955-56 but now denounced as a "fascist dictatorship".

Referring to the Albanian party, Suslov commented: "The Chinese-Albanian alliance . . . arose on the basis of opposition to the 20th congress of the CPSU on the basis of a hostile attitude to the elimination of the effects of the Stalin personality cult. Just as in the case of China, the defence by the Albanian leaders of the personality cult is due to the fact that for many years they have themselves been imposing the personality cult and using pernicious methods of leadership in the party and the country".

Suslov also accused the Chinese leaders of trying to sabotage the Soviet Union's efforts to avert the threat of a world war, as when in 1962 they had taken advantage of the Cuban crisis to extend the conflict on the Indian frontier. "The obviously adventurist position of the CPC leaders makes itself seen in their attitude to the question of nuclear weapons", he went on. The Chinese leaders had sought insistently to obtain the nuclear bomb from the Soviet Union, and had expressed deep mortification when the USSR did not give them samples of nuclear weapons. "We consider it inexpedient to help China to produce nuclear weapons", Suslov added. "The inevitable reaction to this would be the nuclear arming of powers of the imperialist camp, in particular West Germany and Japan. Having a higher level of economic, scientific and technical development, they could undoubtedly produce more bombs than China, and could build up a nuclear potential much faster."

Turning to the question of the transition from capitalism to socialism, Suslov maintained that the Chinese leaders had rejected "the Leninist teaching that the socialist revolution is the result of a mass struggle by the people" and were relying "solely on armed uprisings everywhere and in all cases, without taking into account the feelings of the masses of the people and their preparedness for revolution, or the internal and external situation". This approach rejected "painstaking and patient work with the masses and reliance on the maturing of the objective and subjective conditions for a socialist revolution, in favour of revolutionary phrase-mongering, or, what is still worse, in favour of adventurist actions by a handful of men who are cut off from the people. . .". Suslov commented: "If the Communist parties pin all their hopes solely on armed struggles, without taking into consideration the preparedness of the masses to support such a struggle, it will inevitably lead only to bitter failures."

After declaring that "the policy and activity of the Chinese leaders today are the main danger to the unity of the world Communist movement", Suslov continued: "Anti-party groups of renegades and splitters have been set up, with help and support from Beijing, in Belgium, Brazil, Australia, Ceylon, Britain, and some other countries. Some of these groups number less than 10 members; others comprise a few dozen people. . . . The CPC leadership is carrying things further, plainly intending to form in opposition to the world Communist movement a bloc of its fellow-thinkers which will have its own platform and group discipline, and will be centred on Beijing. . . . The CPC leadership is striving to spread the Mao Zedong personality cult to the whole world Communist movement, so that the leader of the CPC may, like Stalin in his day, sit aloft like God above all the Marxist-Leninist parties and arbitrarily settle all questions of their policy and work. . . ."

The report concluded: "It is now perfectly clear that the CPC leaders . . . intend to carry on with their factional activities in the world Communist movement. Our party favours convening another meeting of fraternal parties in order to discuss the basic problems of our time, and to hold the broadest possible exchange of opinions in the interest of surmounting the difficulties that have arisen in the Communist movement. These difficulties stem from the CPC leadership's differences with the world Communist movement. A collective effort by all the fraternal parties is therefore justified in order to determine the necessary ways and means for preserving and strengthening the Marxist-Leninist unity of the Communist ranks. . . ."

Exchange of Correspondence between Chinese and Soviet Parties (February–March 1964)

The Soviet party's letter of Feb. 12, 1964, provoked a lengthy and acrimonious correspondence between the Chinese and Soviet parties. In a letter dated Feb. 20, the central committee of the Chinese party demanded to be sent a copy of the Soviet letter, and accused the Soviet leaders not only of "vicious two-faced tactics" but also of "posing as the 'father party' " and intriguing for "a sham unity and a real split". The Soviet reply (Feb. 22) pointed out that the Chinese party had not yet replied to the Soviet letter of Nov. 29, 1963, and commented that "as you persistently failed to reply to our repeated letters and approaches and, what is more, presented them as expressions of our weakness, it was unnecessary and indeed useless to send you our letter of Feb. 12". A second Chinese letter (Feb. 27) peremptorily repeated the demand to be sent the letter of Feb. 12.

On Feb. 29, 1964, the central committee of the Chinese party replied at length to the Soviet letter of Nov. 29, 1963; it expressed its willingness to reach a negotiated settlement on the boundary question, but rejected the offer of economic aid and put forward its own terms for the holding of a world Communist conference. (The sub-headings below are taken from the original.)

Economic Aid. "So far from being gratis", the letter declared, "Soviet aid to China was rendered mainly in the form of trade and was certainly not a one-way affair. China has paid and is paying the Soviet Union in goods, gold or convertible foreign exchange for all Soviet-supplied sets of equipment and other goods, including those made available on credit plus interest. It is necessary to add that the prices of many of the goods we imported from the Soviet Union were much higher than those on the world market.

"While China has received aid from the Soviet Union, the Soviet Union has also received corresponding aid from China. . . . Up to the end of 1962 China furnished the Soviet Union with 2,100,000,000 new roubles' worth of grain, edible oils, and other foodstuffs. . . . Over the same period, China furnished the Soviet Union with more than 1,400,000,000 new roubles' worth of mineral products and metals. . . . Many of these mineral products are raw materials indispensable for the development of the most advanced branches of science and for the manufacture of rockets and nuclear weapons.

"As for the Soviet loans to China, it must be pointed out that China used them mostly for the purchase of war material from the Soviet Union, the greater part of which was used up in the war to resist US aggression and aid Korea. . . . For many years we have been paying the principal and interest on these Soviet loans, which account for a considerable part of our yearly exports to the Soviet Union. . . ."

Technical Aid. "When the leaders of the CPSU unilaterally decided to recall all the Soviet experts in China", the letter continued, "we solemnly affirmed our desire to have them continue their work. . . . But in spite of our objection you . . . withdrew the 1,390 Soviet experts working in China, tore up 343 contracts and supplementary contracts concerning experts, and scrapped 257 projects of scientific and technical co-operation, all within the short space of a month. . . . Many of our important designing and scientific research projects had to stop half way, some of the construction projects in progress had to be suspended, and some of the factories and mines which were conducting trial production could not go into production according to schedule. . . . Now you have again suggested sending experts to China. To be frank, the Chinese people cannot trust you. . . ." The letter added ironically: "We are very much concerned about the present economic situation in the Soviet Union. If you should feel the need for the help of Chinese experts in certain fields, we would be glad to send them."

Sino-Soviet Trade. The letter continued: "Nobody is in a better position than you to know the real cause for the curtailment of Sino-Soviet trade over the last few years. This curtailment was precisely the result of your extending the differences from the field of ideology to that of state relations. Your sudden withdrawal of all Soviet experts working in China upset the construction schedules and production arrangements of many of our factories, mines and other enterprises, and had a direct impact on our need for the import of complete sets of equipment. Such being the case, did you expect us to keep on buying them just for display? . . .

"Since 1960 you have deliberately placed obstacles in the way of economic and trade negotiations between our two countries, and held up or refused supplies of important goods which China needs. You have insisted on providing large amounts of goods which we do not really need, or which we do not need at all, while holding back or supplying very few of the goods which we need badly. . . . From 1959 to 1961 our country suffered extraordinary natural disasters for three years in succession and could not supply you with as large quantities of agricultural produce and processed products as before. This was the result of factors beyond human control. . . .

"You constantly accuse us of 'going it alone', and claim that you stand for extensive economic ties and division of labour among the socialist countries. But what is your actual record in this respect? . . . You bully those fraternal countries whose economies are less advanced, oppose their policy of industrialization, and try to force them to remain agricultural countries for ever and serve as your sources of raw materials and as outlets for your goods. You bully fraternal countries which are industrially more developed, and insist that they stop manufacturing their traditional products and become accessory factories serving your industries. . . .

"We hold that it is necessary to transform the Council for Mutual Economic Assistance (Comecon) of socialist countries to accord with the principle of proletarian internationalism, and to turn this organization—now solely controlled by the leaders of the CPSU—into one based on genuine equality and mutual benefit, which the fraternal countries of the socialist camp may join of their own free will. It is hoped that you will favourably respond to our suggestion."

Public Polemics. The Chinese letter accused the CPSU of beginning public polemics with its attack on Albania at its 22nd congress in 1961 and continued: "What you did was a bad thing. You created difficulties for fraternal parties and rendered a service to the imperialists and reactionaries. Now, with the extensive unfolding of the public debate, the truth is becoming clearer and clearer and Marxism-Leninism is making more and more progress. What was a bad thing is becoming a good thing."

Between July 15, 1963, and the end of October, the letter maintained, the Soviet press had published nearly 2,000 anti-Chinese articles and other items, and these had continued to appear even after the Soviet letter of Nov. 29. It added: "We have so far printed only seven articles in reply to your open letter [of July 14, 1963]. We have not yet completed our reply to the important questions you raised in the open letter, and have not even started to reply to the questions you raised in your other anti-Chinese articles." The letter concluded with the following proposals:

(1) "For the cessation of public polemics it is necessary for the Chinese and Soviet parties and other fraternal parties to hold various bilateral and multilateral talks in order to find, through consultation, a fair and reasonable formula acceptable to all, and to conclude a common agreement.

(2) "The Chinese Communist Party consistently advocates and actively supports the convening of a meeting of representatives of all Communist and workers' parties. . . . Together with the other fraternal parties, we will do everything possible to ensure that this meeting will be a meeting of unity on the basis of the revolutionary principles of Marxism-Leninsim.

(3) "The resumption of talks between the Chinese and Soviet parties is a necessary preparatory step for making the meeting of the fraternal parties a success. We propose that the talks between the Chinese and Soviet parties be resumed in Beijing from Oct. 10 to Oct. 25, 1964.

(4) "In order to make further preparations for the meeting of representatives of all fraternal parties, we propose that the Sino-Soviet talks be followed by a meeting of representatives of 17 fraternal parties—namely, the parties of Albania, Bulgaria, China, Cuba, Czechoslovakia, the German Democratic Republic, Hungary, Korea, Mongolia, Poland, Romania, the Soviet Union and Vietnam, and the parties of Indonesia, Japan, Italy and France."

In its reply to the Chinese letters of Feb. 27 and 29, 1964, the central committee of the Soviet party put forward on March 7, 1964, counter-proposals for a world Communist conference in the autumn. The Soviet letter declared that "while deliberately delaying an official answer to our appeal [of Nov. 29], you in fact replied to it by inflaming polemics, by intensifying schismatic activities in the Communist movement, and by directing even more slanderous accusations at the CPSU and other Marxist-Leninist parties. . . . In these circumstances we could no longer remain silent. . . . There was no sense at all in sending you our letter addressed to other fraternal parties . . . if only because we had already repeatedly approached you with the same questions and received no answer . . .".

Rejecting the Chinese charge that the CPSU was posing as the "father party", the Soviet letter commented: "We cannot avoid the impression that all this is done solely to enable you to fill the role of a 'father party' yourselves. But times are different now. Even in Stalin's lifetime this role had become obsolete, although he did take such a position. . . . Today the situation is not what it was, for instance, in

1919; today Lenin is no longer alive, and no-one living can take his place. It is only collectively that the Marxist-Leninist parties can work out a common line for the Communist movement. There are no 'father' or 'son' parties, nor can there be any, but there is and must be a family of fraternal parties with equal rights and collective wisdom. . . ."

The Soviet letter did not attempt to reply to the charges contained in the Chinese letter of Feb. 29, concentrating on the question of a world conference. "We note", it stated, "that after many months of stalling and delay the CPC has agreed with our view of continuing the bilateral meeting of representatives of the CPSU and the CPC, and of afterwards calling a meeting of all the Communist and workers' parties. . . . At the same time, we do not understand your motives for delaying these measures for a long period. . . . The delaying of the bilateral meeting between representatives of the CPSU and the CPC is all the more inexplicable. . . . Your proposal that the meeting . . . be held as late as October 1964 means in fact that the meeting of fraternal parties would be delayed by at least a year."

The letter rejected the Chinese proposal for a preparatory meeting of 17 parties, and suggested instead a meeting of representatives of the 26 parties which jointly prepared the 1960 Moscow statement—i.e., the 17 parties named in the Chinese letter, and in addition those of Western Germany, Britain, Finland, Argentina, Brazil, Syria, India, the United States, and Australia. It concluded with the following proposals: "(1) That the meeting of representatives of the CPSU and the CPC be continued in Beijing in May 1964. (2) That the preparatory meeting of representatives of 26 fraternal parties be called in June-July 1964. (3) That the international meeting be held, with the agreement of the fraternal parties, in the autumn of 1964."

In conclusion the Soviet letter declared: "The central committee of the CPSU emphasizes that for the successful implementation of all these measures it is necessary that there be a cessation of public polemics and an abandonment of all types of subversive and schismatic activity in the socialist community and the Communist movement. . . ."

Unsuccessful Romanian Attempt at Mediation (February–March 1964)

The Romanian Workers' Party which throughout the controversy had played an independent role, attempted in February and March 1964 to act as a mediator between the two sides. After receiving the Soviet letter of Feb. 12, 1964, the Romanian leadership appealed to the Soviet party not to publish Suslov's report, and to the Chinese party to put an immediate end to polemics, and suggested a meeting of the leadership of the two parties. The Soviet party agreed to delay publication of the report on condition that the Chinese ceased public polemics, whilst the Chinese party agreed to a temporary truce and invited a Romanian delegation to visit Beijing.

Talks took place in Beijing on March 2–11, 1964, between a Romanian delegation headed by the Prime Minister, Ion Gheorghe Maurer, and a Chinese delegation headed by Liu Shaoqi, but produced little result, as the Chinese leaders maintained that polemics could be stopped only after an agreement on the conditions of their cessation had been reached through bilateral or multilateral discussions.

In a new attempt to avoid an open split, President Gheorghiu-Dej of Romania on March 25, 1964, handed to the Soviet and Chinese ambassadors in Bucharest a draft appeal to all Communist parties for unity, and proposed that a joint commission of Soviet, Chinese and Romanian party officials should make preparations for an international conference comprising "all Communist parties of the world, not merely certain parties". The Soviet party agreed to examine the Romanian proposals, but no reply was received from the Chinese party.

Renewal of Polemics (March-April 1964)

Both sides had abstained from public polemics while the Sino-Soviet correspondence and the Romanian attempt at mediation were in progress, but at the end of March 1964 the truce was broken by the Chinese. Their new propaganda offensive was launched at the sixth meeting of the Afro-Asian Solidarity Council, held in Algiers on March 22–26, 1964.

Members of the Chinese delegation accused the Soviet Government of "racialism", "imperialism", "betraying the Algerian revolution", "refusing to help the Arabs to liberate Palestine", and being "morally responsible for the murder of Patrice Lumumba" (the former Premier of the Congo murdered in 1961). The leader of the Soviet delegation retorted by accusing the Chinese of "trying to set countries and whole continents against one another, on the principle of 'divide and rule.' " Most of the other delegations refused to align themselves with either side.

The eighth and longest of the series of articles replying to the Soviet open letter was published in Beijing on March 31, 1964. The article was largely devoted to refuting Khrushchev's "gross error" that in certain conditions there could be a peaceful transition from capitalism to socialism, and contended that "to realize the transition to socialism the proletariat must wage armed struggle, smash the old state machine, and establish a dictatorship of the proletariat". Admitting that the 1957 declaration and the 1960 statement, both of which the Chinese party had signed, envisaged the possibility of either a peaceful or a non-peaceful transition, it alleged that the Soviet draft had referred only to the peaceful variety, and that the non-peaceful one had been added only after a great deal of argument; the Chinese party, it added, was willing to accept criticism for agreeing to compromise on this issue. The rest of the article was largely devoted to personal invective against Khrushchev, who was described as having "assumed the mantle of Trotsky"—"the greatest capitulationist in history"— and as leading the Soviet Union back to capitalism. The article advised "leading comrades" of the Soviet party to throw Khrushchev "on the rubbish heap of history".

Khrushchev's Visit to Hungary (April 1964)

Nikita Khrushchev arrived in Budapest on March 31, 1964, for a visit to Hungary, during which he made a number of speeches defending the Soviet view on peaceful coexistence and the primary importance of the economic development of the Communist countries.

Khrushchev said on April 6: "Some people criticize us by saying, 'You are thinking all the time about a better life, but these are anti-Marxist, bourgeois slogans'. The working people of our countries reply to such critics, 'What then did we make the revolution for? We did not fight in order to live worse after the working class came to power' . . . There are people who say, 'And what about the world revolution? Are you ready to sacrifice the interests of the world revolution?' We resolutely reject this charge. . . . Our sympathies and our support are with our class brothers in the capitalist countries and with the peoples fighting for liberation, but we reject the theory according to which we should unleash a war against the capitalist states in the interests of world revolution. . . . We are against the export of revolution and against the export of counter-revolution. . . .

"There are people who criticize us for our stand on questions of peace and war. These people say 'You are afraid of war'. I have replied more than once to these brave men, 'Only a child or a fool does not fear war'. . . . The Chinese leaders say, 'Even if world war starts, what of it? Half of mankind will be destroyed, but the other half will survive'. . . . What can one say of such views? Let the people judge for themselves. . . .

"Some people are blabbering that the Soviet Union and the CPSU are begging for peace from the imperialists. This, of course, is slander. . . . We do not rely on entreaties, but on our own strength. . . . Even the leaders of the largest imperialist state, the United States of America, have to reckon with the new balance of forces in the world. . . .

"In our foreign policy we have always abided by the Leninist principle of peaceful coexistence between states with different social systems. . . . This is a good basis, and we would like to see the question of 'Who prevails over whom?' generally settled otherwise than by war. The system which gives the greater freedom to the peoples, which gives them more material and cultural benefits, will win in the final count. . . ."

Khrushchev made his strongest attack on the Chinese leaders in a speech in Budapest on April 9, 1964, in which he described them as "persons who, while using leftist, ultra-revolutionary phrases as a cover and while proclaiming their loyalty to Marxism-Leninism, are in fact sliding down on a number of questions into the mire of Trotskyism and Great-China chauvinism". He also accused them of "irresponsibly gambling with the destinies of millions of people" and of "trying to impose upon the fraternal parties their adventurist anti-Leninist course and to establish their hegemony over the international Communist movement".

Chinese Rejection of Soviet Proposals for Conference (May–July 1964)

In a letter of May 7, 1964, the central committee of the Chinese party rejected all the proposals contained in the Soviet letter of March 7, and in effect suggested that the proposed world conference should be postponed indefinitely. Rejecting any suggestion of a cessation of polemics, the letter stated: "Our press has not yet finished replying to your open letter of July 14, 1963. We have not yet started—to say nothing of completing—our reply to the more than 2,000 anti-Chinese articles and other items which you published after your open letter." After accusing the Soviet Union of "uniting with US imperialism, the common enemy of the people of the whole world", and of "opposing the national liberation movement, the proletarian revolution, and the dictatorship of the proletariat", it demanded: "How can you expect us and all other Marxist-Leninists to keep silent about these foul deeds of yours?"

In reply to the Soviet proposals for a conference, the letter said: "Judging by present circumstances, not only is it impossible to hold the two-party talks in May, but it will also be too early to hold them in October. We consider it more appropriate to postpone them till some time in the first half of next year, say May. And if either the Chinese or the Soviet party then considers that the time is still not ripe, they can be further postponed. . . . We maintain that a series of preparatory steps are necessary in order to make the international meeting of fraternal parties a success. . . . It may require perhaps four or five years, or even longer, to complete these preparations. . . ."

Reiterating the Chinese proposal that only 17 parties should take part in the preparatory meeting, the letter pointed out that in some of the countries mentioned in the Soviet letter (e.g. Australia and Brazil) the Communist party had split into a "Marxist-Leninist" and a "revisionist" party, whilst in India, it asserted, "the Dange clique have degenerated into pawns of the Indian big bourgeoisie and big landlords and into renegades from communism". In such cases the Soviet and Chinese parties differed as to which party should be invited but in the Chinese view "the first consideration should be given to those fraternal parties which uphold Marxism-Leninism".

The Soviet party repeated its proposals for an early conference in its reply, dated June 15, 1964. After claiming that "the overwhelming majority of the fraternal parties" favoured such a conference, the Soviet letter maintained that the Chinese party now opposed it "because you could not count on support for your ideological and political platform from a world Communist forum". The meeting of Communist party leaders in Moscow in 1957, it pointed out, had unanimously decided, with the support of Mao Zedong, to "entrust the Communist Party of the Soviet Union with the function of convening meetings of the Communist and workers' parties in consultation with the fraternal parties".

On the question of who should be entitled to attend, the letter maintained that "the anti-party groups in Australia, Brazil, Belgium, Ceylon, and certain other countries" were "made up of anti-party opposition elements expelled from Marxist-Leninist parties and fighting against lawfully elected central committees", and had been "joined by Trotskyists, anarchists, and renegades and apostates of all kinds". In reply to the Chinese attack on the leadership of the Australian, Brazilian, and Indian parties, it said: "We emphatically reject the unworthy methods by which the leaders of one party, the Communist Party of China, lay claim to a special position in the Communist movement, to the right to pass judgment on parties as a whole and on their leaders, and arbitrarily to decide issues that are only for the working class of the given country to decide."

The Soviet letter concluded: "We reiterate our proposal that a preparatory conference should be convened and attended by representatives of the 26 parties nominated by the world meeting of Communist parties as members of the drafting commission in 1960 and representing the interests of Communists in all the main regions of the world. We consider it necessary to reach agreement with the fraternal parties on the specific date of such a conference in the immediate future. As it has done in the past, the CPSU central committee expresses its readiness to hold a bilateral meeting of representatives of the CPSU and the CPC on any agreed date. . . ."

The Chinese reply (dated July 28, 1964) again rejected the Soviet proposals, declaring: "The Communist Party of China persists in its stand for an international meeting of the fraternal parties for unity on the basis of Marxism-Leninism, to be held after ample preparations, and we are firmly opposed to your schismatic meeting. The CPC solemnly declares: We will never take part in any international meeting or any preparatory meeting for it which you call for the purpose of splitting the international Communist movement. . . ."

The Chinese reply continued: "Since you have made up your minds, you will most probably call the meeting. Otherwise, if you break your word you will become a laughing-stock for centuries. . . . If you do not call the meeting, people will say that you have followed the advice of the Chinese and the Marxist-Leninist parties, and you will lose face. If you do, you will land yourselves in an impasse without any way out. . . . Dear comrades, we appeal to you once more to stop at the brink of the precipice, and not to attach too much importance to face. But if you refuse to listen and are determined to take the road to catastrophe, suit yourselves. . . ."

Soviet Proposal for Preparatory Conference—Invitation rejected by Chinese Party (July–August 1964)

The central committee of the Soviet party took a decisive step towards an open breach with the Chinese party on July 30, 1964, when it invited the 25 other parties which had formed the preparatory committee at the 1960 conference to send delegations to Moscow on Dec. 15 of that year to begin preparations for a world conference in 1965. The Soviet letter stated: "An absolute majority of the fraternal parties have spoken out in favour of the necessity for collective action to overcome the difficulties which have sprung up in our ranks. They advocate the holding of a new international meeting of representatives of the Communist and workers' parties, and, moreover, many parties insist that the convening of the meeting must not be postponed for a long period. . . ."

The letter continued: "At the 1957 meeting the fraternal parties unanimously adopted the following decision: 'Entrust the Communist Party of the Soviet Union with the function of convening meetings of the Communist and workers' parties in consultation with the fraternal parties.' Up to the present, necessary consultations have been held . . . and the positions of all the Communist parties have become manifest. . . . Taking into consideration the clearly expressed will of the absolute majority of the fraternal parties, the CPSU considers that the time is ripe to begin preparatory work for convening an international meeting. We hold that a drafting committee should be convened before the end of this year.

"As it has already become clear in the process of preliminary exchange of views that the question of the composition of the drafting committee could become a new obstacle to its convening, we regard as the only reasonable way out the convening of the drafting committee with the same composition with which it worked during the preparations for the 1960 meeting, that is, comprising the representatives of the Communist and workers' parties of the following 26 countries [which were then enumerated and which included the CPSU itself]. The CPSU invites the representatives of the fraternal parties listed above to come to Moscow by Dec. 15, 1964. . . .

"The meeting will not be called to condemn anyone, to 'excommunicate' anyone from the Communist movement and the socialist camp, to attach insulting labels, or to throw irresponsible charges at one another. . . . We consider that the meeting should concentrate its efforts on finding out the things in common which unite all the fraternal parties, and on seeking ways to overcome the existing differences. . . . It is possible that . . . unanimity may not be reached on all questions at once. . . . Nevertheless, we are deeply convinced that this would not mean the 'formalization' of the split or the creation of obstacles to the further seeking of ways to unity. . . .

"It is our deep conviction that there are no insurmountable obstacles to the international meeting starting its work as soon as drafts of documents are prepared by the drafting committee—about the middle of 1965. The representatives of all the 81 parties which participated in the 1960 meeting may take part in the international meeting. The refusal of this or that party to join in this collective work cannot serve as a ground for further delays. . . ."

The Chinese party rejected the invitation on Aug. 30, 1964, in a letter to the CPSU which began as follows: "You arbitrarily lay it down that a drafting committee shall be convened without the prior attainment of unanimous agreement through bilateral and multilateral talks by the Chinese and Soviet parties and all the other fraternal parties concerned. The members of the drafting committee must be the 26 parties you have designated, no more and no less. . . . You even decide before the convening of your appointed drafting committee that an international meeting shall be held in the middle of next year."

The Chinese letter continued: "Furthermore, you have the effrontery to declare in your letter that, whether or not the fraternal parties participate, the drafting committee you have designated shall open shop as scheduled, and that the international meeting unilaterally called by you shall begin on the day prescribed. Thus the day in December 1964 on which you convene your drafting committee will go down in history as the day of the great split in the international Communist movement. . . .

"What is there in common between yourselves and the world's Marxist-Leninists? Today the most urgent task before Communists and the revolutionary peoples of the world is to oppose US imperialism and its lackeys. But you are bent on collusion with the US imperialists and on seeking common ground with them. You have repeatedly indicated to US imperialism that you want to disengage from all fronts of struggle against it. When US imperialism recently launched its armed aggression against a fraternal socialist country, the Democratic Republic of Vietnam, not only did you fail to declare explicit support for Vietnam in its struggle against US aggression, but you even aided and abetted the aggressor by actively supporting the US attempt to intervene in Vietnam through the United Nations. While you pursue this anti-Communist, anti-popular, anti-revolutionary line, how can Marxist-Leninists reach any agreement or taken any common action with you? . . .

"Concerning the preparation and convening of an international meeting and its composition, we have repeatedly said that it is necessary to achieve unanimity of views through consultation among all the fraternal parties, including the old ones and those rebuilt or newly founded [i.e. pro-Chinese parties which had broken away from existing Communist parties, as in Australia, Belgium, Brazil, Ceylon, and India]. Otherwise, no matter what drafting committee or international meeting you convene, it will be illegal. . . ."

Intensification of Polemics (July–October 1964)

Polemics by both sides became increasingly virulent during the summer and autumn of 1964. On July 14 (the first anniversary of the Soviet party's open letter), the *People's Daily* and *Red Flag* published their ninth reply to it, which contained one of their most violent attacks to date on "Khrushchev's phoney communism".

The Chinese papers maintained that Khrushchev had carried out "a series of revisionist policies serving the interests of the bourgeoisie and rapidly swelling the forces of capitalism in the Soviet Union". They continued: "On the pretext of combating the personality cult, Khrushchev has defamed the dictatorship of the proletariat and the socialist system and thus paved the way for the restoration of capitalism in the Soviet Union. He has supported the degenerates in leading positions . . . [and] has accelerated the polarization of classes in Soviet society. Khrushchev sabotages the socialist planned economy, applies the capitalist principle of profit, develops capitalist free competition, and undermines socialist ownership by the whole people."

The Chinese press also made the following assertions: "Khrushchev is peddling bourgeois ideology and bourgeois liberty, equality, fraternity and humanity, inculcating bourgeois idealism and metaphysics and the reactionary ideas of bourgeois individualism, humanism, and pacifism among the Soviet people, and debasing socialist morality. The rotten bourgeois culture of the West is now fashionable in the Soviet Union, and socialist culture is ostracized and attacked. . . . The broad masses of the Soviet workers, collective farmers and intellectuals are seething with discontent against the oppression and exploitation practised by the privileged stratum. . . ."

Each side cited the US bombing attacks on North Vietnamese naval bases on Aug. 5, 1964, in support of its case against the other. The Chinese letter of Aug. 30 accused the USSR of supporting US "aggression" in North Vietnam, whilst Khrushchev said in Prague on Sept. 4 that "our opponents are trying to profit by the difficulties created by the actions of the Chinese diversionists". In the latter connexion he cited "the repeated aggressions of the US imperialists in South-East Asia, their armed attacks on the Democratic Republic of Vietnam, and their intervention in the internal affairs of Laos".

Both sides had previously intensified their radio propaganda from the summer of 1963 onwards, It was reported in August 1963 that powerful transmitters recently established in north-west China and Albania were broadcasting propaganda to the USSR and Eastern Europe, and a year later Moscow radio was broadcasting in Chinese for 70 hours a week and Beijing radio in Russian for 63 hours.

VI: THE POST-KHRUSHCHEV PERIOD, 1964–66

Nikita Khrushchev was removed from his party and governmental posts on Oct. 14, 1964, and was replaced by Leonid Brezhnev as first secretary of the party and by Alexei Kosygin as Prime Minister. According to Western correspondents, Khrushchev was accused of reducing the ideological conflict with China to the level of a personal feud between himself and Mao Zedong and underestimating the speed of Chinese scientific progress, which permitted China to explode her first atomic bomb on Oct. 16, 1964.

Temporary Improvement in Sino-Soviet Relations (October–December 1964)

Relations between the USSR and China temporarily improved after Khrushchev's dismissal. It was announced on Oct. 16, 1964, that Mao Zedong and other Chinese leaders had sent "warm greetings" to Brezhnev and Kosygin, coupled with the hope that "the unbreakable friendship between the Chinese and Soviet peoples may continue to develop." Zhou Enlai and six other leading Chinese Communists visited Moscow on Nov. 5–13, 1964, for the celebrations of the anniversary of the Bolshevik Revolution, and during their visit took part in talks with the Soviet leaders which were officially described as "frank and comradely". Addressing a public meeting on Nov. 6, at which Zhou Enlai was present, Brezhnev called for unity in the world Communist movement, while indicating that the USSR would continue Khrushchev's foreign policy.

Brezhnev said that the Soviet leaders considered it their duty to strengthen the unity of the Communist world, and that there was an "urgent necessity" for a new world conference of Communist parties; he made no reference, however, to Khrushchev's proposal for a preparatory meeting of 26 parties on Dec. 15, 1964. No Communist party or government, he said, had the right to impose its will on other parties or countries; there could be different forms of socialist society, and the choice between them might be determined by the political and economic conditions in the country concerned. Describing the Soviet Union's foreign policy as "consistent and immutable", Brezhnev gave as its main features unity of the socialist camp, support for national liberation movements, co-operation with the non-aligned countries, peaceful coexistence, and "delivering mankind from war". He gave a warning against "aggressive forces" and said that the Soviet Union would maintain its defence capability at the highest possible level so long as no agreement was reached on disarmament.

For several weeks after the fall of Khrushchev the Chinese and Soviet parties refrained from direct attacks on each other. Polemics nevertheless continued in indirect forms. The Chinese and Albanian Press attacked what was described as "Khrushchevism without Khrushchev", and the Soviet press defended policies which had been attacked by the Chinese in the past.

Red Flag published on Nov. 20, 1964, a violent denunciation of Khrushchev, which summed up its main accusations against him as follows: (i) He had attacked

Stalin on the pretext of combating the personality cult. (ii) He had sought all-round co-operation with "US imperialism". (iii) He had weakened the Soviet Union's defences and tried to prevent China from developing her nuclear strength by signing the test-ban treaty. (iv) He had obstructed revolutionary movements by advocating a peaceful transition to socialism. (v) He had opposed and sabotaged national liberation movements. (vi) He had supported the "renegade Tito clique". (vii) He had tried to injure and undermine Albania. (viii) He had spread calumnies against the Chinese party. (ix) He had opposed the development of other Communist countries in the name of "mutual economic assistance". (x) He had made use of "political degenerates, renegades and turncoats" to carry out disruptive activities against other Communist parties. (xi) He had violated the principle of unanimity by playing the "patriarchal father-party role" and had summoned an "illegal" meeting to split the Communist movement. (xii) He had pursued policies intended to lead the Soviet Union back to capitalism.

The *Red Flag* article also maintained that in his dealings with China Khrushchev had torn up several hundred agreements and contracts; recalled several hundred Soviet experts; organized frontier incidents; fomented subversive activities in Xinjiang and incited and aided the "Indian reactionaries" to make armed attacks on China. Any attempt to revive "Khrushchevism without Khrushchev", the article concluded, would "end in a blind alley".

Pravda replied in part to the Chinese criticisms in an editorial on Dec. 6, 1964, which declared that the condemnation of the personality cult was "irreversible", and defended the theory that during the transition to communism the dictatorship of the proletariat was replaced by "the state of the entire people". [This theory, put forward in the Soviet party's programme of 1961, had been attacked in the 19th of the Chinese party's "25 Points" of June 14, 1963—see page 35.]

Disagreements over Policy on Vietnam (January–April 1965)

The escalation of the war in Vietnam in the early months of 1965 contributed greatly to widen the gap between the USSR and China. Whereas the former made repeated efforts to bring about a negotiated settlement, the latter consistently opposed any suggestion of a compromise. Details of a number of secret Soviet peace moves were given in a letter from the Chinese Government and party which was published in *The Observer* (of London) on Nov. 14, 1965. According to this source, the US Government expressed the hope in January 1965 that the USSR would use its influence to persuade the North Vietnamese Government to stop supporting and arming the Viet Cong and to end attacks on South Vietnamese cities. These demands, which the Chinese letter described as "preposterous", were passed on to North Vietnam by the Soviet Government.

Kosygin paid a visit to Hanoi on Feb. 6–10, 1965, during which the USA began regular air raids on North Vietnam on Feb. 7. He flew on Feb. 10 to Beijing, where he had talks with Mao Zedong and Zhou Enlai; this was the first meeting between Mao and a Soviet leader since Khrushchev's visit to the Chinese capital in October 1959. According to the Chinese letter, "Comrade Kosygin stressed the need to help the USA 'find a way out of Vietnam'. We pointed out that since the US imperialists were intensifying their aggression against Vietnam this was no time to negotiate. . . . Comrade Kosygin expressed agreement with our views at the time, and stated that the new Soviet leadership 'would not bargain with others on this issue'." Kosygin left Beijing on Feb. 11, no communiqué on the talks being issued. On his return to the USSR he said in a broadcast on Feb. 26, 1965, that the talks had "helped to clarify the possibility of further developing our relations".

Earlier that month, on Feb. 16, 1965, the Soviet Government had proposed to China and North Vietnam that an international conference on Indo-China should be held, and without waiting for the Chinese reply submitted this proposal to the French Government on Feb. 23. The US government, however, announced on Feb. 25 that it was "not contemplating any negotiations".

On April 3, 1965, the USSR proposed a summit meeting of the Soviet, Chinese, and North Vietnamese leaders, contending that "the very fact of a demonstration of the unity of all the socialist countries, and particularly of the USSR and China . . . would constitute serious support for the Democratic Republic of [North] Vietnam and cool the ardour of the American militarists". The Chinese government rejected this proposal, according to the letter later published by *The Observer* because "you intended to lure us into your trap through such a meeting so that you could speak on behalf of Vietnam and China in your international manoeuvres, and strengthen your position for doing a political deal with US imperialism".

The Moscow Meeting of 19 Communist Parties (March 1965)

Pravda announced on Dec. 13, 1964, that "on the basis of joint consultations that have taken place among fraternal parties, and with a view to making better preparations for the meetings of the drafting commission and the international conference of Communist and workers' parties, the first meeting of the drafting commission has been fixed for March 1, 1965". This announcement was the first official intimation that the meeting of the 26 parties had been postponed. The invitation was accepted by all the parties invited except those of China, Albania, Romania, North Korea, North Vietnam, Indonesia, and Japan. The Chinese party revealed on March 20, 1965, that it had received the invitation in November 1964, but had not replied. Several of the parties which accepted the invitation, notably the British, Cuban, Italian, and Polish parties, did so with reservations; in consequence the Soviet party was obliged to abandon its original intention that the commission should prepare a draft programme for a world conference, and the March 1 conference was officially described only as a "consultative meeting".

At the meeting, which was held in Moscow on March 1–5, 1965, some delegations were reported to have pressed for the adoption of a resolution fixing the date for a world conference and condemning Chinese interference with other parties. This was opposed by the Italian and British representatives, who contended that it would widen the split in the international movement. The statement finally adopted suggested a preliminary consultative conference of the 81 parties taking part in the 1960 meeting to discuss the question of a new international conference, and called for the discontinuation of "open polemics, which are in character unfriendly and degrading to the fraternal parties". The meeting also adopted a resolution condemning the US air raids on North Vietnam.

Renewed Chinese Polemics (March 1965)

Direct attacks on the Soviet party began again in the Chinese press on March 1, 1965—the day on which the Moscow meeting opened. The *People's Daily* protested (on March 1) against the recent publication in Moscow of a book called *The International Revolutionary Movement of the Working Class,* edited by Boris Ponomaryov, which, it said, attacked the Chinese party "in an all-round, systematic and foul manner". The Chinese organ commented: "The fact that the editors of the book go to great pains to boost Khrushchev's revisionism is further proof that Khrushchev's downfall merely means a change of signboard, and that what is on sale in the shop remains the old wares of Khrushchevite revisionism. . . . The new anti-Chinese book once again reveals the hypocrisy of those who profess to reinforce the solidarity of the international Communist movement, but in reality . . . actually deepen the split.While talking about putting an end to the public debate, they intensify anti-Chinese agitation. . . ."

On March 4, 1965, the *People's Daily* published a number of recent extracts from the Soviet press supporting "the line of the 'three peacefuls' and 'two entires' " (i.e., peaceful coexistence, peaceful competition, peaceful transition to socialism, the state of the entire people, and the party of the entire people), which, it said, formed "the main content of Khrushchevite revisionism". It commented: "If the whole business of Khrushchevite revisionism is to be continued, then why oust Khrushchev? . . ."

The *People's Daily* published on March 23, 1965, its most violent attack on the new Soviet leadership to date, denouncing the Moscow meeting as "illegal" and "schismatic" and demanding that they should publicly renounce their "errors". "By replacing Khrushchev", it declared, "the new leaders have merely changed the signboard and employed more subtle methods in order better to apply Khrushchevism. . . . [They] continue Khrushchev's policy of US-Soviet co-operation for the domination of the world." Their policy could be described as "three shams and three realities"—"sham anti-imperialism but real capitulation, sham revolution but real betrayal, and sham unity but a real split". China, it stated, had no intention of accepting the "illegal and schismatic" Moscow meeting's appeal for a truce in polemics, and if the Soviet arguments could not be refuted in 9,000 years, "then we shall take 10,000 years".

Describing the Moscow meeting's protest against the bombing of North Vietnam as "a first class farce", the *People's Daily* declared: "The new Soviet leaders are now loudly proclaiming their support for the revolutionary struggle of the people of South Vietnam, but in reality they are trying to gain political capital for their dealings with the US imperialists and to carry out their plot for peace talks, in a futile attempt to extinguish the revolutionary struggle of the South Vietnamese people." In conclusion, it demanded that the Soviet leaders should publicly admit that the Moscow meeting was "illegal"; renounce "Khrushchevism", the revisionist" line of the 20th and 22nd congresses, and the 1961 party programme; admit their errors in their dealings with the Chinese, Albanian and other "Marxist-Leninist" parties; and undertake to return to Marxism-Leninism, proletarian internationalism, and the principles of the 1957 and 1960 declarations.

Chinese Student Demonstrations in USSR—Anti-Soviet Demonstration in Beijing (March-April 1965)

On March 4, 1965, about 2,000 Chinese and Vietnamese students again demonstrated outside the US embassy in Moscow. Although the embassy was protected by about 1,000 mounted and foot police, the students broke through them and stoned the building; order was not restored until about 500 soldiers were called in to clear the street. A soldier lost an eye in the fighting, and several policemen and students were injured. The Chinese Government protested against the "ruthless suppression" of the demonstration in a Note to the Soviet Union on March 6, demanding an apology and the punishment of those responsible; it alleged in particular that six injured students had been forcibly evicted from a Moscow hospital, although they needed treatment. In Beijing students staged a protest demonstration outside the Soviet Embassy on March 6—the first demonstration of the kind in the Chinese capital since the Communist revolution.

The Soviet reply (March 12, 1965) categorically denied the Chinese allegations, maintaining that the demonstrators had attacked unarmed policemen with sticks and stones and seriously injured over 30 policemen and soldiers. A group of Chinese citizens, it declared, had afterwards demanded hospital treatment, and when a medical examination had established that they did not need it they had insulted the staff. The Note concluded with a warning that foreigners guilty of disturbing public order would be brought to trial and punished. The Chinese Government's reply (March 16) rejected the Soviet Note, asserting that it "distorted the facts and reversed right and wrong".

The New China News Agency alleged on May 7, 1965, that the Soviet police had forcibly broken up a demonstration by Vietnamese students in Leningrad on April 3, injuring seven of the students and arresting 82.

Chinese Attacks on New Soviet Leaders (June-September 1965)

The Chinese Communist Party made its first direct attack on the Soviet leaders since the dismissal of Khrushchev in a long editorial published in the *People's Daily* on June 14, 1965, which declared that they "have not departed from the essence of Khrushchev's policies—revisionism, great-power chauvinism, and Soviet-American co-operation for the domination of the world". The Soviet party, which had refrained from open polemics against China since Khrushchev's removal from office, replied in an editorial in *Pravda* on June 19 deploring the Chinese attack, and appealing for international Communist unity against what it described as "US aggression in Vietnam".

In an article published on Sept. 2, 1965, Marshal Lin Biao envisaged the "encirclement" of the USA and Western Europe by a world-wide revolutionary movement characterized by "people's wars" in the countries of Asia, Africa and Latin America; he ridiculed "Khrushchev revisionists" for maintaining that "a single spark in any part of the globe may touch off a world nuclear conflagration and bring destruction to mankind". Describing the "Khrushchev line" of "peaceful coexistence, peaceful transition and peaceful competition" as "rubbish", Marshal Lin said: "The essence of the general line of the Khrushchev revisionists is nothing other than the demand that all the oppressed peoples and nations and all the countries that have won independence should lay down their arms and place themselves at the mercy of the US imperialists and their lackeys. . . ."

Soviet Reaction to New Sino-Indian Crisis (September 1965)

During the war between India and Pakistan, the Chinese Government sent an ultimatum to India on Sept. 16, 1965, declaring that unless India dismantled all her military installations on the Sikkim border within three days it must "bear full responsibility for all the grave consequences"; at the same time China moved up troops both on the Sikkim frontier and in Ladakh. China extended its ultimatum by another three days on Sept. 19, and in effect withdrew it on Sept. 21, when it claimed that the installations had been demolished, this allegation being denied by the Indian Government.

In the first Soviet comment on the Chinese ultimatum, *Pravda* stated on Sept. 23, 1965: "According to foreign news agencies, the handing over of the Chinese Notes has been accompanied by movements and concentrations of Chinese forces on India's borders. Reports of this kind cannot but evoke the concern of all those who are interested in the earliest liquidation of the Indo-Pakistani armed conflict, in consolidating the unity of all anti-imperialist forces, in restoring peace in South and South-East Asia, and in ending the machinations of imperialism in that region, especially US aggression in Vietnam". The Soviet article was denounced as "calumnious" by the New China News Agency on Sept. 24, 1965.

Further Polemics (October-November 1965)

In reply to further Chinese attacks, *Pravda* published on Oct. 27, 1965, a full statement of the Soviet position.

After emphasizing that "one cannot win over the masses to the side of socialism by words alone, even by the most revolutionary phrases", *Pravda* said that the Communist movement was made up of a number of detachments, each with its own special mission, and that the Soviet Union and other socialist countries made their most useful contribution by building up their own prosperity and strength. "The socialist countries", the article continued, "cannot replace other detachments of the liberation struggle in the solution of revolutionary tasks. They cannot replace the peoples of the young national states in the solution of tasks of the national liberation movement, or the working class and working people of the capitalist countries in the struggle for the overthrow of capitalism. This would be to force their will on other peoples. . . . Such actions might lead to the unleashing of world thermonuclear war, with all its severe consequences for all peoples. This would be for the socialist countries to fail in their international obligations to the working people of the world, and would do irreparable damage to the cause. . . ."

A violent attack on the Soviet party, entitled "Refutation of the New Leaders of the CPSU on 'United Action' ", appeared on Nov. 11, 1965, in the *People's Daily* and *Red Flag*. The article asserted that the new Soviet leaders were "still pursuing Khrushchev's line, but with double-faced tactics more cunning and hypocritical than his", and were "allied with US imperialism". They were "actively plotting new deals with the United States for the 'prevention of nuclear proliferation' and similar so-called 'disarmament' measures in an effort to maintain the monopoly of the two nuclear overlords, the Soviet Union and the United States, against China and all other independent countries"; in the previous September, claimed

the article, they had "openly sided with India against China on the Sino-
Indian border question".

"Some people ask", the Chinese article continued, "why is it that the Marxist-
Leninists and the revolutionary people cannot take united action with the new
leaders of the CPSU, yet can unite with personages from the upper strata in the
nationalist countries and strive for united action with them?" It answered this
question as follows: "In the contemporary world, opposition to or alliance with US
imperialism constitutes the hallmark for deciding whether or not a political force
can be included in the united front against the United States. . . . So far from
opposing US imperialism, the new leaders of the CPSU are allying themselves and
collaborating with it to dominate the world."
    Rejecting the Soviet proposal for united action on Vietnam, the Chinese article
repeated the details of Soviet attempts to bring about peace negotiations. Soviet aid
to North Vietnam, it continued, was "far from commensurate with the strength of
the Soviet Union. They have ulterior motives in giving a certain amount of aid—
they are trying to hoodwink the people at home and abroad, to keep the situation
in Vietnam under their control, to gain a say on the Vietnam question, and to
strike a bargain with US imperialism on it." After denying Soviet allegations that
China had obstructed the transit of Soviet military equipment for North Vietnam,
the article rejected Soviet proposals for an end to open polemics, declaring that
"we shall carry the debate to the finish".
    In reply to Soviet statements that all the Communist countries had "a socio-
economic system of the same type", the article asserted: "The report on the
problems of industry by Kosygin at the recent plenary session of the central
committee of the CPSU and the resolution which it adopted marked a big step
along the road of the restoration of capitalism in the Soviet economy. [This
resolution recommended greater freedom for individual enterprises, fuller use of
bonus schemes, and increased use of the profit motive as an incentive to greater
efficiency.] . . . In the countryside, too, the new leaders of the CPSU are
accelerating the growth of capitalism, developing the private economy, enlarging
the private plots, increasing the number of privately raised cattle, expanding the
free market and encouraging free trading. They are using a variety of economic and
administrative measures to encourage and foster the growth of a new kulak
economy. . . . Because they are the political representatives of the privileged
bourgeois stratum in the Soviet Union, just as Khrushchev was, the new leaders of
the CPSU pursue domestic and foreign policies which are not proletarian but
bourgeois, not socialist but capitalist. . . .
    "Comrade Mao Zedong has often said to comrades from fraternal parties that if
China's leadership is usurped by revisionists in the future, the Marxist-Leninists of
all countries should resolutely expose and fight them, and help the working class
and the masses of China to combat such revisionism. Taking the same stand we
consider it our bounden proletarian-internationalist duty firmly to expose the
revisionist leadership of the CPSU. . . ."

On Nov. 16, 1965, *Pravda* described the Chinese article as "saturated
with impermissible, utterly groundless, slanderous and provocative fabrications", and replied to it at length in an editorial on Nov. 28.

"Demonstrating its goodwill and striving for the cohesion of all revolutionary
forces, our party has refrained for over a year from open polemics", the *Pravda*
editorial said, and went on: "This is not because it had nothing to say. . . .
Unfortunately the Soviet Communist Party and other parties met with no positive
response from the Chinese Communist party leaders. . . . The policy of political

and organizational division, a policy of splitting the Communist movement, is now actually put forward in opposition to the stand of those parties favouring unity of action. . . . To oppose unity now and call for division is to act contrary to the interests of the revolution. . . . The Soviet Communist Party has always been implacably opposed to any opportunist who, donning various masks—including those of 'super-revolutionaries'—has tried to divert the Communist movement from the right road. . . ."

Soviet Letter to Other Communist Parties (February 1966)

The central committee of the Soviet Communist Party was reported on Feb. 14, 1966, to have recently sent a letter to the other Communist parties of Eastern Europe on its relations with the Chinese party. What was believed to be an authentic copy of the letter was published on March 22 in the Hamburg newspaper *Die Welt,* and is summarized below; this gave details of Soviet proposals for co-operation with China and of Soviet aid to North Vietnam, and accused the Chinese party of wishing to bring about war between the Soviet Union and the United States.

"Since the plenum of October 1964", the letter stated, "the CPSU central committee has done everything possible to normalize relations with the CPC [Communist Party of China]. . . . In endeavouring to create a favourable political atmosphere, the CPSU central committee has unilaterally discontinued open polemics. . . . In the negotiations with the Chinese party-government delegation headed by Zhou Enlai [in November 1964—see page 60] . . . we submitted an extensive programme for normalizing Chinese-Soviet relations at both the party and the state level. This programme included proposals on implementing bilateral meetings of delegations of the CPSU and the CPC on the highest level, on the mutual discontinuation of polemics, concrete proposals on extending Chinese-Soviet trade and scientific, technical and cultural co-operation, and on co-ordinating the foreign policy activities of the CPR [Chinese People's Republic] and the USSR . . . The CPC central committee completely ignored the proposal of a bilateral meeting on the highest level. The CPC leadership failed to accede to an expansion of economic, technical, and cultural co-operation, and even took additional steps to further curtail such co-operation. . . .

"The anti-Soviet course has now become an inseparable part of the entire ideological work of the CPC, both within and outside the country. . . . The Chinese leadership increasingly intensifies subversive activities against the Soviet state and social order. Beijing radio beams articles and material to the USSR in an attempt to pit various strata of the Soviet people against one another. . . . Direct appeals are being made to engage in political action against the CPSU central committee and the Soviet Union.

"The CPR leadership propagates ever more obstinately the thesis of potential military clashes between China and the Soviet Union. On Sept. 29, 1965, Chen Yi, Foreign Minister of the CPR, at a press conference in Beijing spoke utterly falsely of a possible 'co-ordination' of Soviet actions in the north of China with the aggressive war of the United States against the CPR . . . The idea is obstinately suggested to the Chinese people that it is necessary to prepare for a military conflict with the USSR. The CPSU central committee has already informed the fraternal parties that the Chinese side is provoking border conflicts. Such conflicts have again increased in recent months. . . . The Chinese Government refuses to resume the negotiations suspended in May 1964 on a precise delimitation of the border. It obviously prefers to leave this question unsettled. At the same time, allegations are being spread to the effect that the Soviet Union unlawfully holds Chinese territory in the Far East. . . .

"The attitude of the CPR leadership towards the struggle of the DRV [Democratic Republic of Vietnam] . . . against the US aggression is currently causing great damage to the joint cause of the countries of socialism", the letter continued. "The Soviet Union delivers large quantities of weapons to the DRV, including rocket installations, anti-aircraft artillery, aeroplanes, tanks, coastal guns, warships and other items. In 1965 alone weapons and other war material worth about 500,000,000 roubles were placed at the disposal of the DRV. The DRV is receiving support in the training of pilots, rocket personnel, tank drivers, artillerymen etc. Our military aid is being rendered to the extent the Vietnamese leadership itself thinks necessary. The Soviet Union grants extensive military and material support to the National Liberation Front of South Vietnam.

"The CPSU has proposed to the Chinese leaders more than once that joint action to support Vietnam be organized, but the Chinese leadership opposed such action. . . . Our party has proposed twice that the representatives of the three parties—the Vietnamese Party of Labour, the CPSU and the CPC—meet at the highest level to achieve agreement on co-ordinated action for aid to the DRV. These proposals, which were received by the politburo of the Vietnamese Party of Labour with approval, were not accepted by the Chinese leaders. At the same time, the CPC leadership hindered the implementation of the agreement of the Government of the USSR with the Government of the DRV on an immediate increase in military aid for the DRV. The CPC leaders did not permit Soviet transport planes with weapons to fly over CPR territory. Chinese personalities also placed obstacles in the way of the transportation of war material to Vietnam by rail. . . .

"From all this it becomes clear that the Chinese leaders need a lengthy Vietnamese war to maintain international tensions, to represent China as a 'besieged fortress'. There is every reason to assert that it is one of the goals of the policy of the Chinese leadership on the Vietnam question to originate a military conflict between the USSR and the United States . . . so that they may, as they say themselves, 'sit on the mountain and watch the fight of the tigers'. New facts constantly prove the readiness of the Chinese leaders to sacrifice the interests of the national liberation movement to their chauvinist big-power plans. . . . The nationalist big-power policy of the Chinese leaders has led to the fact that the CPR recently has suffered a number of serious setbacks on the international scene. The actions of the CPC leaders have led to a spreading of mistrust of the CPR, even in countries which until very recently were regarded as its friends. This became especially clear on the African continent and in a number of Asian countries. . . .

"The well-known disruptive agitation of the CPC leaders in the Communist movement has become very intensive. . . . The Chinese leaders have established factional groups in approximately 30 countries. . . . By supporting these groups and promoting their disruptive activity, the Chinese leaders openly interfere in the internal affairs of other Communist parties. . . .

"The role of the ideological-theoretical platform of the Chinese leadership is quite plain. Its exclusive purpose is to serve the nationalistic big-power policy of the Chinese leadership. . . . The course towards socialist revolution . . . has been replaced by a course towards a world war. These ideas were most completely explained in the recent article by Lin Biao. . . .

"The CPSU . . . has always recognized armed as well as peaceful forms of struggle of the working class for power. . . . The Chinese leaders, in contrast, derive from the whole arsenal of forms of struggle only one—armed revolt, war. . . . The efforts of the CPC leaders to force all parties of the non-socialist countries to accept the goal of an immediate revolution independent of actual conditions means in effect to try to force upon the Communist movement putschist, conspiratory tactics. These tactics, however, offer the imperialist bourgeoisie the opportunity to bleed the revolutionary Communist and workers' movement, and to expose the leadership and activists of a number of Communist parties to destruction. . . ." [This passage referred principally to the attempted coup on Oct. 1, 1965, by the pro-Chinese Communist Party of Indonesia, after the suppression of which at least 150,000 Communists, including most of the party's leaders, were massacred.]

"The Chinese leaders", the letter went on, "emphasize the idea that international tension is favourable for revolution by force, that it creates favourable prerequisites for their struggle. They come forth with statements that can hardly be assessed as anything but provocatory. Thus Chen Yi declared in one of his latest interviews: 'If the US imperialists have decided to force a war of aggression upon us, then we would welcome it. . . . We would welcome it if they came as early as tomorrow.' And what should one think, for example, of the statement of the same Chen Yi: 'With the help of the atom bomb one may destroy one or two generations of people. But the third generation will rise to offer resistance. And peace will be restored.' . . . Our people, who have taken up arms more than once to defend the achievements of the revolution, are not afraid of threats from imperialism. We are, however, definitely against adventures, against urging people towards nuclear world war. . . .

"We believe that the hegemonic activities of the Chinese leaders", the letter concluded, "are aimed at subordinating the policy of socialist countries, the international Communist and workers' movement, and the national liberation movement to their great-power interests. . . . It is not without intention that the Chinese leaders, while criticizing the other fraternal parties and socialist countries because of their alleged insufficient revolutionary spirit and indecisiveness in the fight against imperialism, show extraordinary caution in their own practical deeds. . . ."

The 23rd Soviet Party Congress (March-April 1966)

The Chinese party announced on March 23, 1966, that it had refused an invitation to send a delegation to the 23rd congress of the Soviet Communist Party, and published its letter rejecting the invitation. The Chinese letter alleged that the Soviet leadership had sent a letter to other Communist parties "instigating them to join you in opposing China", and had spread "rumours" that China was obstructing Soviet aid to North Vietnam and encroaching on Soviet territory. The Chinese Communist Party, it continued, had sent delegations to the last three congresses, but "at the 20th congress of the CPSU you suddenly lashed out at Stalin. Stalin was a great Marxist-Leninist. In attacking Stalin you were attacking Marxism-Leninism, the Soviet Union, Communist parties, China, the people, and all the Marxist-Leninists of the world. At the 22nd Congress you adopted an out-and-out revisionist programme, made a wild public attack on Albania, and reproached the Chinese Communist Party, so that the head of our delegation had to leave for home while the congress was only halfway through."

"Russia is the native land of Leninism", the letter declared, "and used to be the centre of the international working-class movement. After Stalin's death the leaders of the CPSU, headed by Khrushchev, gradually revealed their true features as betrayers of Lenin and Leninism. . . . The leadership of the CPSU has become the centre of modern revisionism. Over the last 10 years we have made a series of efforts in the hope that you would return to the path of Marxism-Leninism. Since Khrushchev's downfall we have advised the new leaders of the CPSU on a number of occasions to make a fresh start . . . but you have not shown the slightest repentance. Since coming to power the new leaders of the CPSU have gone farther and farther down the road of revisionism, splittism, and great-power chauvinism."

The letter went on to accuse the Soviet party of "pursuing US-Soviet collaboration for the domination of the world"; of "acting in co-ordination with the United States in its plot for peace talks, vainly attempting to sell out the struggle of the Vietnamese people against US aggression and . . . to drag the Vietnam question into the orbit of Soviet-US collaboration"; and of "actively trying to build a ring of encirclement around socialist China". The letter concluded: "Since you have gone so far, the Chinese Communist Party, as a serious Marxist-Leninist party, cannot send its delegation to attend this congress of yours."

In his report to the congress, which met in Moscow from March 29 to April 8, 1966, Brezhnev said that the party sincerely wanted friendship with China, and was "ready at any moment, jointly with the Communist Party of China, to re-examine the existing differences with the object of finding ways of overcoming them". He also expressed support for a new international Communist conference "when the conditions for it are ripe".

Increasing Isolation of Chinese Communist Party (1965–66)—Adoption of Neutral Position by North Korean and Japanese Parties (August 1966)

Of the five major Communist parties which, in varying degrees, had supported China in the past, only the Albanian party consistently maintained this attitude during 1965–66. Soviet influence in North Vietnam increased during this period at China's expense; the Indonesian party (previously the largest in any non-Communist country) was virtually wiped out after the attempted coup of Oct. 1, 1965; and the North Korean and Japanese parties adopted a neutral position in August 1966.

Suggested reasons for the Chinese party's increasing isolation included the greater tact and restraint shown by the Soviet leaders after Khrushchev's removal; China's failure to give effective aid to North Vietnam; her refusal of Soviet proposals for co-operation between the Communist countries for this purpose; her advocacy of "adventurist" policies, which was considered responsible for the massacre of Indonesian Communists; her interference in the affairs of other Communist parties and support for the formation of rival "Marxist-Leninist" parties; her alleged interference in the internal politics of the Afro-Asian countries, which had led to the severance of diplomatic relations by several African states and strained relations with Indonesia and Ghana; and her intervention in the Indo-Pakistani war of September 1965.

In a letter of Jan. 5, 1966, the Polish United Workers' Party proposed a conference of the Communist parties of the Warsaw Pact countries and the Communist countries of Asia to discuss the co-ordination of aid to North Vietnam. This proposal was rejected on Feb. 12 by the Albanian Party of Labour, which declared in its reply that it would not take part in any conference at which "the present perfidious revisionist leadership of the USSR" was represented.

An Albanian delegation led by the Prime Minister, Gen. Mehmet Shehu, visited China from April 26 to May 11, 1965. A joint communiqué issued at the conclusion of the visit asserted that "Marxist-Leninists of the whole world must . . . carry through to the end the struggle against modern revisionism, whose centre is the leading group of the CPSU, and never allow it any respite".

The communiqué continued: "It is necessary to wage uncompromising struggle against these renegades from Marxism-Leninism and never to show them any flexibility; to continue to expose and criticize them firmly and thoroughly and never to 'cease open polemics' with them; to continue to give full support to Marxist-Leninists of all countries in the struggle against modern revisionism and never to accept their call for 'cessation of factional activities'; to draw a clear line of . demarcation between ourselves and them politically, ideologically, and organizationally; and never to take any 'united action' with them. . . . Modern revisionism has long since been in league with US imperialism. . . . The fight against imperialism headed by the United States and its lackeys and the fight against modern revisionism are two inseparable tasks. . . ."

The general secretary of the Japanese Communist Party, Kenji Miyamoto, had previously stated on Jan. 1, 1966, that it was necessary to "organize concerted international action against imperialist aggression in Vietnam", even if ideological unity could not be re-established. In March 1966 a Japanese delegation led by Miyamoto visited Beijing in an unsuccessful attempt to persuade the Chinese party that Asian Communists should co-operate with the Soviet Union in support of North Vietnam, and afterwards visited Pyongyang, where it issued a joint statement with the North Korean party calling for united action. The Japanese party openly adopted a neutral position in August, and issued a statement early in September in which, while still critical of Soviet "revisionism", it strongly attacked the Chinese Government's attitude towards the Vietnamese war.

The Japanese statement rejected the Chinese contention that the purpose of Soviet aid was to make North Vietnam so dependent on it that she would have to yield to Soviet pressure in favour of unconditional negotiations with the United States, and denounced China's opposition to joint action as purely negative. It suggested that China feared that increased foreign aid to North Vietnam might lead to further escalation of the war and endanger China's own security, and commented that this resembled the arguments used by Khrushchev to justify Soviet passivity. Any agreement on joint action, however, must be conditional on Soviet assurances of "a maximum increase in weapons aid to the Vietnamese, positive aid to the Vietnamese to the very last, without deceiving them in their expectations, and a total ban on separate secret dealings with the United States". The statement suggested that the Soviet leadership was divided between "revisionists" who favoured a compromise settlement in Vietnam and "anti-revisionist elements", and advocated that foreign Communist parties should continue their struggle against "revisionism" while promoting the development of "anti-revisionist" policies within the Soviet party.

It was reported on Aug. 4, 1966, that the Japanese Communist Party had ordered its members to remove portraits of Mao from the party's local headquarters, to withdraw all Chinese books from party bookshops, not to visit China without permission, and not to listen to Beijing radio. Five party officials were expelled on Sept. 8 for disobeying these orders. The change in the Japanese party's policy was attributed in part to its growing strength, which rendered it more independent of Chinese support; since 1959 its membership had increased from 45,000 to 195,000 and that of its youth organization from 4,000 to 200,000, whilst the circulation of the party newspaper *Akahata* was over 1,000,000.

The North Korean party also issued a statement on Aug. 12, 1966, strongly advocating joint action on Vietnam and affirming its independence of both the Chinese and the Soviet parties. The statement accused the Chinese party by implication of attempting to impose its own theories and policies on the North Korean and Japanese parties, declaring that it was impermissible for a large party to put pressure on "a small party and the party of a capitalist country". All Communists could study Marx and Lenin for themselves, it added, and there was "no special master of Marxism-Leninism" (an obvious reference to Chinese claims of unique authority for "Mao Zedong's thought"). One party's guiding theory was "of importance only within the bounds of that country", and could not be applied to all parties, as their requirements were bound to differ. Hence each party must decide for itself whether it should follow another party's experience, without interference from outside, and must not "dance to music written by others" or be "ideologically chained to anyone".

An article in the North Korean party organ *Nodong Sinmun,* which was reprinted in *Pravda* on Sept. 18, 1966, attacked "Trotskyists" in terms which made it obvious that the attack was directed against the Chinese party. The "Trotskyists", it stated, tried to split the international Communist movement; maintained that the improvement of living conditions in Communist countries would lead to the restoration of capitalism; slandered the Soviet Union; and refused to combine peaceful with militant methods of struggle, insisting only on "insane revolts".

The Chinese party's isolation was further enhanced by Zhou Enlai's visits to Romania and Albania in June 1966, his failure to reach agreement with the Romanian leaders, and the subsequent Albanian attacks on Communist parties which pursued a neutral policy.

VII: THE PERIOD OF THE CULTURAL REVOLUTION, 1966–69

A new turning-point in the Sino-Soviet conflict was reached with the 11th plenary session of the Chinese party's central committee, held on Aug. 1–12, 1966, which officially endorsed the policy of the "Great Proletarian Cultural Revolution". A long communiqué issued on Aug. 13 reaffirmed the party's hostility to Soviet "revisionism", and its refusal to co-operate with the USSR on the Vietnamese question. Although the communiqué merely repeated views which had frequently been expressed in the past, its adoption by the central committee gave an official character to what was seen by Western observers as a definitive break with the Soviet party.

The CPC communiqué asserted that Soviet policy consisted in "safeguarding imperialist and colonialist domination in the capitalist world and restoring capitalism in the socialist world". Soviet policy in Vietnam "apparently supports the Vietnamese cause but in fact betrays it". The communiqué continued: "US imperialism is the most ferocious common enemy of the peoples of the world. In order to isolate US imperialism and deal it the heaviest blows, it is necessary to form the broadest possible international united front. The revisionist Soviet leading group, which pursues a policy of Soviet-American collaboration with a view to world domination and carries on splitting and subversive activities inside the international Communist movement and the national liberation movement, naturally cannot be included in such a front . . ."

The widening of the breach between the two parties in the past four years was illustrated by the contrast between the August 1966 Chinese communiqué and that issued after the central committee's previous plenary session, on Sept. 28, 1962 (see page 26). The 1962 communiqué had declared that "the modern revisionists are represented by the Tito clique" and that it was China's policy to "develop relations of friendship, mutual assistance and co-operation with the USSR", while expressing support for the 1957 Moscow declaration and the 1960 Moscow statement. The new communiqué referred to the Soviet leaders as heading the "modern revisionists"; adopted a violently hostile attitude towards the USSR; and made no mention of the 1957 declaration and the 1960 statement. Among those most violently denounced as "revisionists" during the next few months were Deng Xiaoping, who had headed the Chinese delegation at the 1960 Moscow conference and the 1963 Moscow talks, and Peng Zhen, who had been a member of the Chinese delegation on both occasions and had also represented China at the Bucharest conference.

Demonstrations outside Soviet Embassy in Beijing (August 1966)

Demonstrations by thousands of students and school-children, organized as "Red Guards of the Cultural Revolution", began in Beijing on Aug. 20, 1966. The Red Guards repeatedly demonstrated outside the Soviet embassy, carrying protraits of Mao Zedong and Stalin, and renamed the street leading to it "Struggle against Revisionism Street". On Aug. 20 a senior Soviet diplomat was prevented by mobs from leaving the embassy for an official appointment. The Soviet Government strongly protested to the Chinese embassy in Moscow on Aug. 26 against this "direct breach of generally recognized norms of international law", and demanded the immediate ending of the "hooliganism" outside the Soviet embassy in Beijing. The Chinese authorities retorted by organizing mass demonstrations outside the embassy on Aug. 29–30, during which thousands of Red Guards beat drums and shouted anti-Soviet slogans; the embassy gates were strongly guarded by troops and police, however, and no incidents occurred. A statement by the Soviet Communist Party on Aug. 31, 1966, described the "outrages" outside the embassy as "a new serious step damaging the cause of the unity of the international Communist movement". The East German embassy had previously made a strong protest on Aug. 28 after its military attaché and his family had been assaulted by Red Guards.

The anti-Soviet activities of the Red Guards in August 1966 were accompanied by widespread anti-religious demonstrations resulting in the closure of Catholic and Protestant churches in Beijing and other cities, the defacement of religious symbols and the expulsion of a number of foreign nuns.

During the first half of September 1966 the Soviet press concentrated on reporting criticisms of Chinese policy by other Communist parties, but on Sept. 20 *Izvestia* published an editorial describing recent developments in China as "not only a tragedy for the Chinese people but an unprecedented discreditation of the ideas of Marxism-Leninism". After stating that China had outlawed herself from the world Communist movement, the editorial expressed confidence that "in the end healthy forces of the Communist Party of China must lead the country back to the true path of Marxism-Leninism".

Soviet Criticisms of Chinese Foreign Policy (September–December 1966)

From September 1966 onwards the Soviet Government and Communist Party adopted an increasingly critical attitude towards the Chinese party's foreign policies. In reply to repeated Chinese allegations of "collusion" between the Soviet Union and the United States, Soviet spokesmen suggested that the Chinese Government, while itself developing contacts with the USA, was seeking to provoke a conflict between the United States and the Soviet Union.

This thesis was first put forward on Sept. 21, 1966, by *Izvestia* in an article composed entirely of quotations from Western newspapers. It quoted without comment the view attributed to "highly-placed Americans" that "if one set aside Beijing's verbal escalations, we have not yet seen any Chinese presence in the Vietnam conflict", and noted that a statement said to have been made by Marshal Chen Yi (as Chinese Foreign Minister) to a group of visiting Japanese politicians, that he did not exclude the possibility of talks with the United States about a negotiated settlement of the Vietnamese question, had never been officially denied in Beijing. The article also quoted reports that "clearly formulated conditions" had been drawn up at the Sino-American ambassadorial contacts in Warsaw on ways of avoiding a clash between China and the United States in Vietnam; US pilots, it alleged, had strict orders to keep clear of the Chinese frontier, and the Chinese Government had agreed to consider any "errors" which might take place as "regrettable incidents".

At the celebrations in Beijing on Oct. 1, 1966, of the 17th anniversary of the founding of the Chinese People's Republic the diplomatic representatives of the Soviet Union and the Eastern European countries, with the exception of Romania, left the rostrum when Marshal Lin Biao declared that "imperialism headed by the United States, and modern revisionism with leaders of the Soviet Communist Party at its centre, are actively plotting peace talk swindles for stamping out the rising flames of the Vietnamese people's national revolutionary war". On Nov. 7 the Chinese representatives walked out from the celebrations of the anniversary of the Russian revolution in Moscow when Marshal Malinovsky (then Soviet Defence Minister) said that China's divisive influence in the socialist camp "encouraged US imperialism to new crimes". A similar incident occurred at the May Day parade in Red Square on May 1, 1967, when Marshal Grechko (Marshal Malinovsky's successor) said that "the hour of failure for the aggressors' gamble in Vietnam would come much sooner if there existed unity of action of all the socialist countries, including China".

In the strongest Soviet attack on Chinese policies published since the fall of Khrushchev, *Pravda* openly accused the Chinese leaders, on Nov. 27, 1966, of attempting to promote war between the Soviet Union and the United States, and suggested that the Cultural Revolution was directed against those Chinese Communists who opposed this policy.

"The duplicity of the policy of the Chinese leaders is increasingly showing itself in the international arena", *Pravda* said. "On the one hand, they try to impose on the fraternal parties a course that would lead to a continuous aggravation of the international situation and ultimately to war, allegedly in the name of the world revolution. On the other, they pursue a policy which allows them to remain on the sidelines of the struggle against imperialism. While describing all Soviet-American contacts as 'collusion', the Chinese leaders do not miss any chance to develop their relations with capitalist countries, including the United States. Their 'escalation', which is purely verbal, is accompanied in the Chinese press by an intense exploitation of the theme of tension on the Sino-Soviet frontier. It is therefore not surprising that the bourgeois press publishes reports of a tacit agreement between China, the United States and other capitalist countries, which are very satisfied with Beijing's present policy. . . .

"Mao Zedong and his entourage could not disregard the fact that the party cadres who went through the school of revolution, despite the anti-Soviet campaign of the past years, came to realize increasingly all the harm caused to China by the split with the Soviet Union and other socialist countries. It is difficult to deceive them with fabrications about Soviet 'collusion' with the United States and the 'restoration of capitalism' in our country. That is why Mao Zedong and his group chose the road of defamation and destruction of the party cadres, or best representatives of the working class and the intellectuals, using for this purpose a section of the students and schoolchildren and the military and administrative apparatus. . . ."

Marshal Chen Yi, on the other hand, suggested in an interview published in a Brazilian paper on Dec. 11, 1966, that the Soviet Union was planning to attack China in alliance with the United States. "The Russians have 13 divisions on the Chinese frontier which have been moved from Eastern Europe", said Marshal Chen Yi, "but we are not afraid of a Soviet-American attack". He continued: "The Chinese people are ready for war and confident of final victory. We now have the atomic bomb and also rockets. We are not afraid of nuclear or conventional war, or any other kind of war that the Americans may invent". He went on to suggest that the aim of Soviet policy was the formation of "a new Holy Alliance" with the United States for a joint attack on China, the Russians attacking from the north and the Americans from the south, and added: "For this reason China is preparing for war, and all the nuclear bombs which fall on China will be returned with interest. . . ."

First Official Soviet Attack on Mao Zedong (December 1966)

The central committee of the Soviet Communist Party, at a plenary session on Dec. 12–13, 1966, adopted a resolution condemning the policy of "Mao Zedong and his group". This was the first time that Mao had been attacked by name in an official statement of the Soviet party.

"The anti-Soviet great-power policy of Mao Zedong and his group has entered a new and dangerous phase", the resolution said. "The policy of the present leaders of the Chinese Communist Party in the international arena has nothing in common with Marxism-Leninism, and their actions objectively assist imperialism. The central committee finds it necessary to expose resolutely the anti-Leninist views and the great-power nationalist course of the present Chinese leaders, and to intensify the struggle in defence of Marxism-Leninism and the general line laid down in Moscow by the conferences in 1957 and 1960. . . . The central committee expresses its agreement with the fraternal Marxist-Leninist parties on the appearance at the present time of favourable conditions for the convening of a new conference of representatives of the Communist and workers' parties, which must be well prepared in the course of mutual consultations between the parties. . . ."

Almost all the members of the Soviet party's politburo and secretariat addressed a series of meetings of party members in the leading cities of the Soviet Union during the first half of January 1967, at which they explained the significance of the central committee's resolution. Speaking at Gorky on Jan. 13, Brezhnev said that the Cultural Revolution was "a great tragedy for all true Chinese Communists, with whom we express our profound sympathy"; he emphasized that in denouncing the ideology and policy of "Mao Zedong and his group", the Soviet party was not attacking China or the Chinese party, which it hoped would return to the path of internationalism.

Expulsion of Foreign Students and Soviet Journalists from China— Expulsion of Chinese Students from USSR (September–December 1966)

Foreign embassies in Beijing were requested on Sept. 20, 1966, to repatriate all foreign students by Oct. 10, as their teachers were too busy with the Cultural Revolution to attend to them. The Soviet Government thereupon announced on Oct. 7 that, as the Sino-Soviet agreement on cultural co-operation provided for the exchange of students on a basis of reciprocity, all Chinese students must leave the Soviet Union by Oct. 31, but that it would consider resuming the exchange of students as soon as the Chinese Government was prepared to do so. After the Soviet embassy in Beijing had refused on Oct. 22 to accept a Chinese Note protesting against the expulsion of the Chinese students, demonstrations by Red Guards began outside the embassy on Oct. 23 and continued for several days.

A Soviet Note of Oct. 27, 1966, protested against the conduct of the Red Guards, who, it stated, had blocked the entrance to the embassy, threatened Soviet diplomats, and indulged in "unprintable abuse, obscene gestures and poses, and spitting". It commented that "it is impossible to avoid the impression that flagrant violations of universally recognized principles of relations between states, elementary standards of international law and the immunity of missions are becoming something of a standard practice in China".

The Chinese reply (Nov. 1) rejected the Soviet protest as "absurd and unreasonable" and asserted that the Soviet Government, "acting in collusion with US imperialism", had "intensified its efforts to aggravate Sino-Soviet relations and expelled all Chinese students from the Soviet Union without reason". The Note went on: "This act did not fail to arouse the unbounded indignation of large numbers of Chinese. It was a perfectly just and revolutionary act for the Chinese revolutionary youth to mass spontaneously in Struggle against Revisionism Street near the Soviet embassy and stick up large posters protesting against the unreasonable expulsion of Chinese students. Since the coming to power of the new leaders of the Soviet Communist Party, to say nothing of the previous period, you have collaborated with the United States, India and Japan to encircle China. You have perfidiously and arbitrarily torn up the agreements between China and the Soviet Union and taken a series of steps tending constantly to aggravate relations between the two countries. You have gone even farther than Khrushchev on the road of revisionism and splittism. . . ."

The Chinese Foreign Ministry demanded on Dec. 16, 1966, that three of the six Soviet correspondents resident in Beijing should leave the country within 10 days, as there were only three Chinese correspondents in Moscow; it also alleged that they had spread "rumours and slanders" about the Cultural Revolution "to meet the needs of the Soviet revisionist leading clique for attacking China". The Soviet Foreign Ministry commented on Dec. 23 that the question of limiting the number of correspondents had never before been raised by either side, and reserved the right to take appropriate measures if necessary against the Chinese correspondents, whose reports were full of "slanderous inventions".

The Red Square Incident (January–February 1967)

All Chinese studying abroad were recalled to China in January 1967 in order to take part in the Cultural Revolution. One party of students returning from France and Finland via Moscow became engaged in a brawl in Red Square on Jan. 25, of which widely differing accounts were given by the Soviet and Chinese Governments.

According to the Soviet version, the students, who were accompanied by Chinese embassy officials, lined up in front of the entrance to Lenin's mausoleum and chanted quotations from Mao Zedong. while 700 or 800 people waited in the freezing cold. When a policeman asked them to stop holding up the queue they began shouting "hysterically", and one of them struck a woman in the face. The others then began assaulting the bystanders, one woman being trampled on, until people in the queue linked arms, formed a line, and pushed the Chinese back to their buses. At a press conference on Jan. 28 a Soviet spokesman said that there were only two or three policemen near the mausoleum at the time, and not more than 10 in the whole of Red Square, whilst eye-witnesses of the incident denied that any of the Chinese had been injured.

A Chinese Foreign Ministry statement, on the other hand, asserted that "69 Chinese students returning from Europe via Moscow proceeded in an orderly and neat column to Lenin's mausoleum and Stalin's tomb to lay wreaths. . . . When they were reading out quotations from Chairman Mao Zedong, the Soviet Government called out the two or three hundred soldiers, policemen and plain-clothes men planted there in advance to encircle and savagely assault them, injuring over 30 of them with four seriously wounded, of whom one is in a critical state with broken ribs". After denouncing "this fascist atrocity", and comparing "the Soviet revisionist ruling clique" to the German, Italian and Japanese fascists, Chiang Kai-shek, Tsar Nicholas II, paper tigers, and "a few flies freezing to death in the whirling snow", the statement expressed confidence that the Soviet people would "rise in rebellion against the revisionist rulers, dismiss them from office, seize power from them, and smash the revisionist rule to smithereens".

In a Note of Jan. 26, 1967, the Soviet Foreign Ministry protested against the students' conduct, and demanded that the Chinese embassy should ensure that "Chinese citizens on Soviet territory conduct themselves in a seemly manner". A counterprotest delivered by the Chinese embassy on the same day demanded an apology and the severe punishment of those responsible for "this grave and premeditated crime".

Two of the students alleged to have been injured addressed foreign correspondents at a press conference at the Chinese embassy on Jan. 28, 1967, from which Soviet and US journalists were excluded. One of them, who according to the *Times* correspondent had "a suspicion of a black eye", asserted that the police had "kicked me in the lower part of the body so that I bled from my injury". The other appeared wearing a gauze mask over his face, apparently to give the impression that he had been gravely injured; in the course of an impassioned denunciation of "the fascist ordures Brezhnev and Kosygin", however, he removed the mask, revealing that his face was unharmed.

The Soviet Foreign Ministry asked the Chinese chargé d'affaires on Feb. 3, 1967, to remove the display cases outside the Chinese embassy, on which photographs of the incident in Red Square and texts denouncing Soviet leaders were on show. After this request had been refused the cases were removed by Soviet civilians later the same day.

A Chinese Government statement asserted that 160 to 170 plain-clothes policemen had entered the embassy grounds, forcibly removed the cases and assaulted 31 of the embassy staff, seriously injuring three of them. "Only Hitler's fascist Germany and US imperialism, the common enemy of the people of the world", the statement continued, "are capable of perpetrating this outrage committed by the Soviet revisionist ruling clique in brazenly violating the most elementary principles guiding international relations. It is entirely the making of the Soviet revisionist ruling clique that Sino-Soviet relations have been damaged to such a serious extent. . . ." Soviet spokesmen said that about 30 private individuals, "incensed by the materials displayed in the cases", had torn them down without entering the embassy grounds, and that members of the embassy staff had attacked them with their fists.

New Demonstrations outside Soviet Embassy in Beijing—Expulsion of Soviet and Chinese Diplomats (January–March 1967)

The Moscow incident of Jan. 25, 1967, was followed by the most violent outburst of anti-Soviet propaganda ever published in Communist China. A typical example was an editorial entitled "Hit back hard at the Rabid Provocations of the Filthy Soviet Revisionist Swine!" published in the *People's Daily* on Jan. 27 and including the following strictures:

"Listen, you handful of filthy Soviet revisionist swine! The Chinese people, who are armed with Mao Zedong thought, are not to be bullied! The debt of blood you owe must be paid! . . . How closely does your atrocious, bloody repression against the Chinese students resemble the atrocities committed by the Tsar, by Hitler and by the Ku Klux Klan! This clearly shows that what you are practising in the Soviet Union is in fact the most reactionary and most savage fascist dictatorship. . . ."

Demonstrations of unprecedented violence began outside the Soviet embassy in Beijing during the evening of Jan. 26, 1967. Huge crowds, which included armed soldiers, spat at and molested people entering or leaving the embassy, threw paint over their cars and assaulted them with sticks; they also hurled litter and burning torches over the fence, creating a danger of fire. The embassy gates and fence were plastered with anti-Soviet posters, and effigies of Brezhnev and Kosygin were hung from trees. Powerful loudspeakers blared out anti-Soviet slogans day and night, preventing the embassy staff from sleeping. Western correspondents, mistaken for Russians, had difficulty in escaping the violence of the Chinese demonstrators.

Although the Soviet Foreign Ministry presented a strong protest to the Chinese embassy in Moscow on Jan. 29, demanding that the embassy should be protected and compensation paid for damage done to the building, the demonstrations became increasingly violent. Soviet diplomats were besieged in their car by Red Guards for 16 hours on Feb. 2, and on the following day Soviet specialists returning from North Vietnam were mobbed. A second Soviet protest of Feb. 4 warned the Chinese Government that "the restraint and patience of Soviet men and women are not without limit", and that "the Soviet Union reserves the right to take steps, which will be guided by the situation, for the protection of the safety of its citizens and its lawful interests".

The wives and children of the Soviet embassy staff were evacuated from Beijing in three parties on Feb. 4–6, 1967. Those who left on Feb. 4 were jeered at by Red Guards at the airport, and on the following day the second party was prevented from boarding the aircraft for six hours by Red Guards, who broke into the bus taking them to the airport and on their arrival there struck them and spat at them. The most violent scenes took place on Feb. 6, when women (some of them carrying babies) and children were forced by Red Guards to crawl under portraits of Mao and Stalin. Soviet and other European diplomatists, including Donald Hopson (the British chargé d'affaires) and Lucien Paye (the French ambassador), were roughly handled when they tried to protect the women and children, and

Soviet officials returning to the embassy were attacked, one group being held prisoners in their bus for 12 hours. Demonstrators broke down the embassy gates, and paraded through the grounds waving signs threatening physical violence.

In the evening of Feb. 6, 1967, the Chinese Foreign Ministry notified the Soviet embassy that its officials were forbidden to leave the embassy compound, as otherwise their security could not be guaranteed, and for some days the embassy was under a virtual state of siege. Eastern European diplomats who delivered food to their Soviet colleagues on Feb. 7 were warned the following day that their safety could not be guaranteed if they went near the embassy. Ignoring this warning, the diplomats supervised the delivery at the embassy on Feb. 9 of food supplies which had been flown in from Moscow.

In a third protest Note, the Soviet Government stated on Feb. 9, 1967: "The steps taken by the Chinese authorities may signify either a deliberate intention to undermine relations between the People's Republic of China and the Soviet Union, or inability on the part of these authorities to ensure in their country elementary conditions for the life and work of the representatives of a state which maintains normal diplomatic relations with the People's Republic of China. The Soviet Government demands the immediate cessation of the arbitrary measures taken by the Chinese authorities and directed against the Soviet embassy in Beijing, and demands freedom of movement for the members of the embassy staff. Unless this is done within the shortest space of time, the Soviet side reserves the right to take necessary measures in reply".

The Soviet Government on the same day unilaterally cancelled the agreement allowing Chinese and Soviet citizens to visit each other's countries without a visa. Similar action was taken by the Chinese Government on Feb. 10, 1967.

The siege of the Soviet embassy, and particularly the harassment of women and children, aroused intense indignation in the Soviet Union, where protest meetings were held in many cities. Delegations visited the Chinese embassy in Moscow daily from Feb. 6–9 with protest resolutions, and when the embassy refused to accept them posted them up nearby. On Feb. 7 one Soviet delegation secured admittance, but subsequently the Chinese protested to the Soviet Foreign Ministry that they had forcibly broken into the embassy.

At a public meeting in Beijing on Feb. 11, 1967, Zhou Enlai violently denounced the Soviet "revisionists" but said that no reprisals should be taken against Soviet diplomats. His speech was broadcast but was not published in the press. On Feb. 12 the Soviet embassy staff were informed that they could now leave the building, "provided they did not provoke incidents", and the demonstrations outside the embassy came to an end.

In an analysis of the reasons for the demonstrations, published on Feb. 10, 1967, *Le Monde* (of Paris) said: "In the eyes of the small Cultural Revolution group around Mao Zedong, it is above all a question of consolidating internal unity against a 'foreign threat' from the Soviet Union, at a time when resistance to the excesses of the 'Revolutionary Rebels' threatens to assume increased proportions and even to develop into civil war in border regions such as Xinjiang, Tibet, Manchuria, and Yunnan. Some East European diplomats regard Gang Sheng (a former official of the Comintern in Moscow from 1933-35 and a specialist in relations with the former fraternal parties) as the most determined supporter of a complete break with the 'revisionist' socialist camp. . . . Zhou Enlai, on the other hand, seems to represent a slightly more moderate viewpoint, and to be seeking to avoid the worst. Apart from internal reasons, the campaign against the Soviet Union may be motivated by the following considerations:

"(1) The necessity to end the few remaining contacts between the Russians and their last Chinese informants. . . . Until recently the Soviet diplomats were better informed than any of their colleagues on certain events occurring even outside Beijing. The affair of Yang Shangkun, the former alternate member of the party secretariat accused by Red Guard papers of passing on party documents to the Russians, and even installing microphones in Mao Zedong's residence, may have played a determining role in the decision to provoke a break.

"(2) The prospect, now considered almost inevitable, of an international Communist conference in the near future makes it useless in Beijing's eyes to preserve even the appearance of organic unity, and it is now a question only of finding ways of making Moscow bear the responsibility for the final break. The support given to 'revisionism' last year by the Japanese Communist Party, one of the last to remain faithful to the Beijing line, is generally thought to have contributed to convince Mao that all consideration for foreign parties was useless.

(3) The desire to dissociate China in advance from any eventual settlement of the Vietnamese war. . . ."

The Chinese Foreign Ministry on March 11, 1967, declared two second secretaries of the Soviet embassy personae non gratae, on the ground that they had dismissed Chinese employees of the embassy who had gone on strike in protest against the Moscow incident of Jan. 25; this "political persecution" was described as "extreme contempt of Chinese law and a gross insult to the working class of China". The Soviet Government expelled a first secretary and a third secretary of the Chinese embassy on March 18, accusing them of having organized the embassy's anti-Soviet activities. *Le Monde* stated on March 25 that both the Chinese and the Soviet press had shown restraint in their reports of the expulsion of the two Chinese diplomats, and commented that "since Zhou Enlai's speech of Feb. 11 a sort of tacit agreement not to envenom relations further seems to have been reached".

Soviet Denunciation of Mao Zedong and Cultural Revolution (February–May 1967)

Following the siege of the Soviet embassy in Beijing, the Soviet press published a series of fierce attacks on Mao Zedong and his policies from February 1967 onwards, the most important of which was a long analysis of the Cultural Revolution published in *Pravda* on Feb. 16, 1967.

"There is no longer any doubt", *Pravda* stated, "that the desire to divert the Chinese people's attention from the privations and difficulties which they are enduring, and the many mistakes and failures in China's internal and foreign policies, is one of the immediate causes of the present Chinese leadership's anti-Soviet policy and propaganda. It is no accident that they fired the first shot in their political war against the Soviet state and party shortly after the failures of the 'Great Leap Forward' policy and the people's communes of unhappy memory. . . . Soon afterwards purely nationalist and even racialist elements had already become obvious in Chinese propaganda. . . . By making the Chinese people believe that they are surrounded by enemies on all sides, the leaders in Beijing are trying to organize them on a nationalist basis. They wish to divert the workers' attention from the real problems facing the country and justify the military and bureaucratic dictatorship of Mao Zedong and his group. . . .

"Following the economic adventures lauched by Mao Zedong, the Chinese leadership was forced practically to renounce economic planning and the construction of the material and technical basis of socialism, and openly to abandon a policy aimed at raising the workers' living standards. In these conditions the rulers in Beijing could only make a virtue of necessity by proclaiming that economic construction and the raising of living standards were 'anti-socialist' and 'bourgeois'. . . . As the practice of world socialism completely contradicts these ideas, the Chinese leaders have launched a campaign of calumnies against the Soviet Union and the other socialist countries, describing their struggle for economic progress and the raising of the people's material and cultural standards as 'revisionism', 'economism', and even 'restoration of capitalism'. . . .

"Faced with growing opposition to their policy, they have launched an unprecedented campaign of massive reprisals against those with different ideas. It is understandable that the whole practice of the Soviet party and the other Communist parties, which consistently develop the Leninist norms of party life, strengthen the principles of collective leadership, and strictly insist on democratic principles in the activities of all organizations from top to bottom, represents a danger to Mao Zedong and his power. For a long time Mao Zedong's group have been acting against their own party. The most elementary norms and principles—election of party organs, reports from the leaders to the party and its organizations, open discussion of the party line, etc.—are trampled upon in China. The personality cult of Mao Zedong is pushed to the point of absurdity and idolatry.

"The destruction of the party organizations and the persecution and extermination of party militants are now being carried on under the banner of the 'Cultural Revolution' by Mao Zedong's shock troops, with the support of the army and the security organs. To justify all this and silence the Chinese Communists, who cannot help comparing what is happening in their country with the practice of other Communist parties, Mao Zedong's group needs to blacken the Leninist line of the Soviet party with absurd accusations of 'revisionism'. The history of the working-class movement shows that renegades from Marxism have always felt a fierce hatred for the flag which they have betrayed. Mao Zedong's group is no exception. One of the principal aims of the anti-Soviet hysteria which they are stirring up is to cut off the Chinese people from authentic Marxism-Leninism and the experience of world socialism. Today this experience is not only foreign to the Chinese leaders but dangerous to them, for a knowledge of it could only show the Chinese Communist Party and people how far their leaders have departed from the interests of the revolution and of socialism. . . .

"The actions of Mao Zedong's group are dictated not by strength but by weakness, by fear of the party and the people. Recent events have shown that the leaders in Beijing have good reason to fear. The 'Cultural Revolution' has revealed the extent of the discontent which has spread among the workers, peasants and intellectuals and even infiltrated into the army and the young people, on whom Mao Zedong's group have relied. The events which have taken place under the banner of the 'Cultural Revolution' in reality have developed into a bitter struggle for power by Mao Zedong and his collaborators. Their policy shows that to keep power they are ready to sacrifice everything—the interests of socialism, the interests of their people, and the interests of the revolution. . . ."

Other articles published in the Soviet press during the next two months described Mao Zedong as a "megalomaniac"; *Izvestia* accused him of practising "cultural genocide" against the national minorities in China, while the *Literaturnaya Gazeta* said that Mao "thinks of creating something like a racialist *Reich* in Asia and even outside it".

Moscow radio increased its Chinese broadcasts to 84 hours a week, and a second station, "Radio Peace and Progress", which had previously broadcast only in European languages, began broadcasting in Chinese on March 1, 1967. Both stations made violent attacks on Mao and his closest supporters, such as Marshal Lin Biao and Gang Sheng, whose hands were said to be "dripping with the blood of thousands of Communists whom he has tortured and shot". The Chinese radio retaliated by sending out propaganda broadcasts in Russian almost continuously for 22 hours every day.

Pravda's correspondent in Beijing was ordered on May 6, 1967, to leave China within seven days, on the ground that he had "slandered the Cultural Revolution, the Chinese people and Mao Zedong".

The "Svirsk" Incident—Attack on Soviet Embassy in Beijing (June–August 1967)

The Tass agency reported on June 13, 1967, that the Soviet Foreign Ministry had recently protested to the Chinese embassy in Moscow against hostile actions by Red Guards against Soviet diplomats, demanding that measures should be taken to ensure the necessary conditions for their normal work and safety. Despite this protest, while visiting Shenyang [Mukden] on business two members of the Soviet trade mission were attacked on June 17 by Red Guards, who accused them of collecting information about the Cultural Revolution and staged a "trial" of them. To a Soviet protest of June 21 the Chinese Foreign Ministry replied on July 3 with a counterprotest against the "stealing of intelligence" by Soviet diplomats.

Another serious incident occurred on Aug. 10, 1967, when the port authorities at Tailien [Dairen] alleged that the second officer of a Soviet merchant ship, the *Svirsk,* had not only refused to accept a badge bearing a portrait of Mao Zedong but had thrown it into the sea. The ship was prevented from sailing, and when the captain went ashore for clearance papers on the following day he was arrested, while Red Guards overran the ship and painted anti-Soviet slogans. Although a Soviet Note demanded the captain's immediate release and the ship's unhindered departure, the captain was paraded through the streets in a lorry on Aug. 12, and a mob again invaded the ship, blocking the funnel, tearing down the aerial and breaking other equipment. After Kosygin had sent a telegram to Zhou Enlai, warning him that these "arbitrary and lawless acts" were "placing in doubt the fulfilment of existing trade relations between the Soviet Union and China", the *Svirsk* was allowed to sail on Aug. 13; a Chinese Note of the same date asserted that its crew had been instructed to insult Mao Zedong while in port, and that it had therefore been decided to "deport" the captain and conduct the ship out of Chinese waters.

A Soviet Note of Aug. 20, 1967, recalled that in addition to the *Svirsk* incident another Soviet ship had been detained at Tailien for 20 days under a pretext in December 1966, and stated that two others had been forced to sail from the port on Aug. 15 without taking on cargo. These incidents, the

Note declared, "place in question the implementation of the trade and navigation agreements . . . as in these abnormal conditions Soviet ships are unable to enter the port".

Protest demonstrations against the *Svirsk* incident began outside the Soviet embassy in Beijing on Aug. 14, 1967, and culminated in an attack on the building on Aug. 17, when Red Guards smashed windows, destroyed furniture and documents, beat up a Soviet diplomat and set fire to an embassy car. A Soviet Note of Aug. 18 denounced the attack as "a great provocation, premeditated, organized and carried out by the Mao Zedong group", and as a criminal act "incompatible with normal relations between states".

Celebrations of 50th Anniversary of Bolshevik Revolution (November 1967)

The celebrations of the 50th anniversary of the Bolshevik Revolution, held in Moscow in November 1967, were attended by delegations from all the Communist countries except China, which had ignored an invitation, and Albania. At a joint session of the Supreme Soviets of the USSR and the Russian Federation and the Communist Party central committee held on Nov. 3–4 Brezhnev criticized "the ideological and political degradation of some of the leaders of the Communist Party of China"; praised "the stubborn struggle waged by the finest sons of the Communist Party in China and by the progressive forces of the Chinese people to preserve the gains of socialism"; and declared that "the attitude of Mao Zedong's group hampers co-ordinated assistance to Vietnam from all socialist countries". At this point Chinese diplomats walked out of the meeting.

At a mass meeting in Beijing on Nov. 6, 1967, Marshal Lin Biao denounced the Soviet leaders as "accomplices of US imperialism" who had betrayed the revolution and restored capitalism. An editorial published on the same day in the *People's Daily, Liberation Army Daily* and *Red Flag* described them as "renegades to the October Revolution", and claimed that the Cultural Revolution represented "the third great milestone in the history of the development of Marxism."

Chinese Reaction to Soviet-led Invasion of Czechoslovakia (August 1968)

Soviet forces, together with Polish, Hungarian, East German and Bulgarian units, invaded Czechoslovakia during the night of Aug. 20–21, 1968, with the object of suppressing Alexander Dubcek's liberal Communist regime. Zhou Enlai described the invasion on Aug. 23 as "the most barefaced and typical specimen of fascist power politics played by the Soviet revisionist clique against its so-called allies", and declared: "The Chinese Government and people strongly condemn the Soviet revisionist clique and its followers for their crime of aggression, and firmly support the Czechoslovak people in their heroic resistance struggle against the Soviet occupation. . . ." The Soviet revisionist clique of renegades has long since degenerated into a gang of social-imperialists and social-fascists." At the same time, Chinese statements strongly denounced Dubcek's regime both for its "revisionism" and for its failure to organize armed resistance to the invasion.

The Soviet Theory of "Limited Sovereignty"—Marshal Lin Biao's Reply
(November 1968—April 1969)

Addressing the Polish United Workers' Party congress on Nov. 12, 1968, Leonid Brezhnev attempted to justify the invasion of Czechoslovakia by putting forward the so-called theory of "limited sovereignty", i.e. that when internal developments in a Communist country endangered "the socialist community as a whole" other Communist countries were justified in intervening.

After insisting that Communist countries stood for strict respect for sovereignty, Brezhnev continued: "But when internal and external forces that are hostile to socialism try to turn the development of some socialist country towards the restoration of a capitalist regime, when socialism in that country and the socialist community as a whole is threatened, it becomes not only a problem of the country concerned, but a common problem and concern of all socialist countries. Naturally, an action such as military assistance to a fraternal country designed to avert the threat to the social system is an extraordinary step, dictated by necessity." Such a step, he added, "may be taken only in case of direct actions of the enemies of socialism within a country and outside it, actions threatening the common interests of the socialist camp".

Although the so-called "Brezhnev doctrine" was one which the Soviet Government had already applied in Hungary in 1956 at Chinese instigation, it was strongly denounced in China, presumably because it could be used to justify Soviet intervention in that country. Marshal Lin Biao commented on the theory on April 1, 1969, in his report to the ninth congress of the Chinese Communist Party, and prophesied that the Soviet Government would be overthrown by its own people.

"Since Brezhnev came to power", he said, "with its baton becoming less and less effective and its difficulties at home and abroad growing more and more serious, the Soviet revisionist renegade clique has been practising social-imperialism and social-fascism more frantically than ever. Internally, it has intensified its suppression of the Soviet people and speeded up the all-round restoration of capitalism. Externally, it has stepped up its collusion with US imperialism and its suppression of the revolutionary struggles of the people of various countries, intensified its control over and its exploitation of various East European countries and the People's Republic of Mongolia, intensified its contention with US imperialism over the Middle East and other regions, and intensified its threat of aggression against China . . .

"In order to justify its aggression and plunder, the Soviet revisionist renegade clique trumpets the so-called theory of 'limited sovereignty', the theory of 'international dictatorship', and the theory of 'socialist community'. What does all this stuff mean? It means that your sovereignty is 'limited', while his is unlimited. You won't obey him? He will exercise 'international dictatorship' over you— dictatorship over the people of other countries, in order to form the 'Socialist community' ruled by the new tsars . . . We firmly believe that the proletariat and the broad masses of the people in the Soviet Union, with their glorious revolutionary tradition, will surely rise and overthrow this clique consisting of a handful of renegades."

In another passage of his report, in which he reaffirmed the party's views on the inevitability of war, Marshal Lin Biao opposed the "social-imperialist" countries (i.e. the USSR) to the socialist countries (i.e. China and Albania), and suggested that a conflict existed in the former between the proletariat and the "bourgeoisie," implying that the USSR had ceased to be a socialist country.

"Lenin pointed out, imperialism means war," he said. "'Imperialist wars are absolutely inevitable under such an economic system, as long as private property in the means of production exists.' Lenin further pointed out: 'Imperialist war is the eve of socialist revolution.' These scientific theses of Lenin's are by no means out of date.

"Chairman Mao has recently pointed out: 'With regard to the question of world war, there are but two possibilities; one is that the war will give rise to revolution, and the other is that revolution will prevent the war.' This is because there are four major contradictions in the world today: the contradiction between the oppressed nations on the one hand and imperialism and social-imperialism on the other; the contradiction between the proletariat and the bourgeoisie in the capitalist and revisionist countries; the contradiction between imperialist and social-imperialist countries and among the imperialist countries; and the contradiction between socialist countries on the one hand and imperialism and social-imperialism on the other. The existence and development of these contradictions are bound to give rise to revolution. According to the historical experience of World War I and World War II, it can be said with certainty that if the imperialists, revisionists, and reactionaries should impose a third world war on the people of the world, it would only greatly accelerate the development of these contradictions and help arouse the people of the world to rise in revolution and send the whole pack of imperialists, revisionists, and reactionaries to their graves."

VIII: FRONTIER DISPUTES AND ARMED CLASHES, 1960–69

The Sino-Soviet frontier falls into two sections, divided by the buffer state of the Mongolian People's Republic: (i) the Central Asian sector, which divides the Chinese province of Xinjiang from the Soviet republics of Tajikistan, Kirghizia and Kazakhstan, and (ii) the Far Eastern sector, which divides Manchuria from north-eastern Siberia. From the 18th century onwards the Russian frontier in Central Asia was pushed steadily eastwards from Lake Balkhash, and large areas formerly under Chinese suzerainty were annexed in 1864 and 1881. Under the Kuomintang regime and for some years after the Communist revolution in China, Chinese maps of the region laid claim to large areas of Soviet territory, and more recent maps showed as "undefined" sections of the frontier which the USSR regarded as final. Before the Chinese Communist revolution the Soviet Government actively encouraged anti-Chinese movements in Xinjiang, where the majority of the population are non-Chinese; after a revolt against the local Chinese administration, which was driven out, an "East Turkestan Republic" was established under Soviet protection in 1944 in the Ili region, which has a population of over 1,000,000, and was reintegrated into Xinjiang only after 1949. Although at least 2,000,000 Chinese have been settled in Xinjiang since 1949, the majority of the population still consists of Kazakhs, Tajiks, Kirghiz, Uighurs and Uzbeks—the same peoples which form the majority of the population in the adjacent Soviet republics.

In the Far East the sparsely populated wastelands north of the Amur (Heilong) and east of the Ussuri (Wusuli) river became part of the Chinese empire in the 17th century as a result of the Manchu conquest of China, but were never effectively settled by the Chinese. The Treaty of Aigun (1858), which was imposed on China by the Tsarist Government at a time when that country had been weakened by a war with Britain and France in 1856–58, gave Russia sovereignty over 230,000 square miles north of the River Amur and placed 150,000 square miles east of the Ussuri (the Amur's principal tributary) under joint Sino-Russian control. The Treaty of Beijing (1860) incorporated the territory east of the Ussuri into the Russian empire, which later founded the port and city of Vladivostok on the newly acquired territory.

The so-called "unequal treaties", as well as others recognizing Russian spheres of influence and extra-territorial rights in China, were intensely resented by the Chinese. After the Russian revolution the Soviet Government proclaimed on Sept. 27, 1920, that it "declares null and void all the treaties concluded with China by the former governments of Russia, renounces all seizure of Chinese territory and all Russian concessions in China, and restores to China, without any compensation and for ever, all that had been predatorily seized from her by the Tsar's Government and the Russian bourgeoisie". An agreement with China signed in 1924

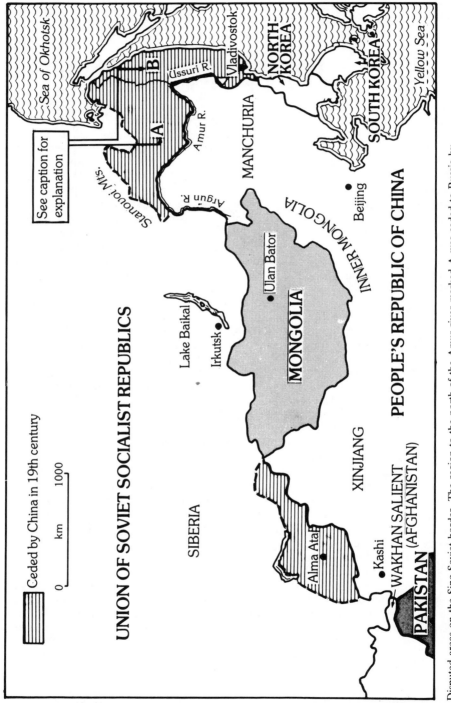

Disputed areas on the Sino-Soviet border. The region to the north of the Amur river marked A was ceded to Russia by China under the 1858 Treaty of Aigun, while the area further to the east marked B was ceded under the 1860 Treaty of Beijing.

repudiated all unequal and secret treaties with China, and renounced all Russian spheres of influence, extra-territorial rights, and consular jurisdiction in China; however, it did not deal with frontier questions.

The boundary question, which had been in abeyance since the Communist revolution in China, again came to the fore as relations between the two countries deteriorated. Later statements from both Soviet and Chinese sources revealed that border incidents began on July 1, 1960, after the recall of Soviet technicians from China, although no publicity was given to them at the time. In his speech of April 1, 1969, Marshal Lin Biao stated that China had proposed to the Soviet Government on Aug. 22 and Sept. 21, 1960, that negotiations should be held to settle the boundary question.

Boundary Question Raised by China (1963)

The possibility of a revision of the frontiers was first mentioned publicly by China in March 1963, in response to a passage in Khrushchev's speech of Dec. 12, 1962, in which when defending his policy during the Cuban crisis he referred to China's attitude towards former Chinese territory annexed by Western powers.

"One must be very cautious", Khrushchev declared, "and not rush in with irresponsible charges such as that some pursue an orthodox and others a mistaken policy, some are attacking imperialism while others tolerate it." After ironically contrasting the expulsion of the Portuguese from Goa by India with the Chinese Government's omission to take similar action against Macao and Hong Kong, he continued: "The odour coming from these places is by no means sweeter than that which was released by colonialism in Goa. But no one will denounce China for leaving these fragments of colonialism intact. It would be wrong to prod China into actions which she considers untimely. If the Chinese Government tolerates Macao and Hong Kong, it clearly has good reasons for doing so. It would therefore be ridiculous to levy against it the accusation that these are concessions to the British and Portuguese colonialists, that this is appeasement. . . ."

In reply to this remark, the *People's Daily* mentioned on March 8, 1963, nine treaties which former Chinese Governments had been forced to sign, including the treaties of Aigun and Beijing, and inquired: "In raising questions of this kind do you intend to raise all the questions of unequal treaties and invite a general settlement?" This comment was interpreted as a suggestion that China reserved the right to demand the return of these territories at some future date.

A Soviet Government statement issued on Sept. 21, 1963, alleged that the Chinese had "systematically violated" the Soviet border, and that Chinese propaganda was demanding the revision of the frontier.

"Since 1960", the statement said, "Chinese servicemen and civilians have been systematically violating the Soviet border. In the single year 1960 over 5,000 violations of the Soviet border from the Chinese side were recorded. Attempts are also being made to 'develop' some parts of Soviet territory without permission." The statement went on to quote a document, allegedly issued by the Chinese administration in Manchuria, instructing fishermen to ignore orders by Soviet border guards to keep off disputed islands in the Amur and the Ussuri.

"The Soviet Government", the statement continued, "has invited the Chinese Government a number of times to hold consultations on the question of ascertaining separate sections of the border line, to exclude any possibility of misunderstanding. The Chinese side, however, evades such consultations while continuing to violate the border. This cannot but make us wary, especially in view of the fact that Chinese propaganda is making definite hints at the 'unjust demarcation' of some sections of the Soviet-Chinese border allegedly made in the past. However, the artificial creation of any territorial problems in our times, especially between socialist countries, would be tantamount to embarking on a very dangerous path. . . ."

Tension on Central Asian Border (1963)

Chinese and Soviet statements issued in September 1963 indicated that a tense situation existed on the Xinjiang border. The *People's Daily* alleged on Sept. 6 that Soviet agencies and personnel had carried out "large-scale subversive activities in the Ili region of Xinjiang and incited and coerced several tens of thousands of Chinese citizens into going to the Soviet Union". In an interview with the Soviet newspaper *Komsomolskaya Pravda,* published on Sept. 20, 1963, four refugees from Xinjiang stated that the Chinese attitude to such peoples as the Kazakhs and Kirghiz had greatly deteriorated, especially if they claimed Soviet citizenship, and that about 400 officials who sympathized with the Soviet Union had been sent to a labour camp.

According to reports from Moscow, riots had occurred in Xinjiang in recent years among the Moslem Kazakhs, Uighurs and other nationalities, who resented Chinese attempts to suppress their religion and languages, and between the middle of 1962 and September 1963 about 50,000 Kazakhs and other tribesmen had fled into the USSR.

Boundary Negotiations—Further Controversy over Frontiers (1964–66)

Boundary negotiations began in Beijing on Feb. 25, 1964, but were suspended in the following May without any progress having been achieved. According to Soviet sources, the Soviet delegation put forward proposals for the "clarification" of certain sections of the border, but the Chinese delegation laid claim to over 1,500,000 square kilometres (580,000 square miles) of Soviet territory, whilst stating that China would not press her claims for the present. According to the Chinese version, the Chinese delegation, while regarding the treaties of Aigun and Beijing as "unequal treaties", offered to take them as a basis for determining the entire alignment of the boundary, subject to "necessary readjustments at individual places on the boundary by both sides", but the Soviet delegation refused to accept these proposals. Although it was agreed in principle to resume the talks in Moscow at a later date, no further negotiations took place.

The controversy was revived by an interview given by Mao Zedong on July 10, 1964, to a group of Japanese Socialists, at which he was reported to have said: "There are too many places occupied by the Soviet Union. . . . Some people have said that Xinjiang province and the territory north of the Amur River must be included in the Soviet Union. The USSR is concentrating troops on its border. . . . China has not yet asked the Soviet Union for an account about Vladivostok, Khabarovsk, Kamchatka, and other towns and regions east of Lake Baikal, which became Russian territory about 100 years ago."

Pravda printed the Mao interview on Sept. 2, 1964, together with a long editorial which gave warning that any attempt to enforce the Chinese territorial claims could have "the most dangerous consequences".

The *Pravda* editorial said: "We are faced with an openly expansionist programme with far-reaching pretensions. This programme did not appear today or yesterday. In 1954 a text-book on modern history was published in China with a map showing China as it was, in the authors' opinion, before the First Opium War. This map included Burma, Vietnam, Korea, Thailand, Malaya, Nepal, Bhutan and Sikkim in China. In the north the border ran along the Stanovik mountain range, cutting off the Maritime Territory from the USSR. In the west a part of Kirghizia, Tajikistan and Kazakhstan up to Lake Balkhash were included in China. Sakhalin was also shown as Chinese. If one is to believe the text-book, all these lands and countries were 'state territory of China' and had been taken away from it . . .
"By what right do the Chinese leaders lay claim to territories which have never belonged to China? They refer to the fact that centuries ago Chinese troops passed through these territories and Chinese emperors sometimes collected tribute from the population. If the problem were not so serious, so-called historical arguments of the type used by Mao Zedong could only be described as childish. . . . Do those who question the Soviet Union's possession of a territory of more than 1,500,000 square kilometres think how these claims will be taken by Soviet people who have been living and working on this land for several generations and regard it as their homeland? . . ." In conclusion, *Pravda* declared that "any attempt to re-carve the map of the world" could lead to "the most dangerous consequences".

In an interview with a Japanese delegation on Sept. 15, 1964, Khrushchev replied to Mao's statements by advocating self-determination for the non-Chinese peoples of Xinjiang and Inner Mongolia.
"Mao Zedong" said Khrushchev, "has declared that the Soviet Union is too large and that Tsarist Russia conquered too much Chinese territory. I have no wish to defend Tsarism; the Tsars and the Chinese emperors were much the same. But the Chinese emperors conquered Inner Mongolia, Manchuria, Tibet and Xinjiang. Xinjiang is not China; Kazakhs and Uighurs live there. The bulk of the Kazakhs and Kirghiz live in Soviet Kazakhstan and Kirghizia, but there are also Kazakhs, Kirghiz and even Uzbeks in Xinjiang. So, too, the independent state of Mongolia contains only half the Mongol people. The other half lives in China. Mao Zedong wishes to settle political questions not on a political but on an ethnographical basis. If questions are to be discussed on that basis, we do not lack arguments. Kazakhstan must decide its own destiny. We support self-determination. The Chinese must do the same. . . ."
In its letter sent early in 1966 to other Communist parties [see Chapter V] the Soviet party accused China of "provoking border conflicts". In reply to this allegation Marshal Chen Yi (then Chinese Foreign Minister) accused the USSR on May 20 of provoking over 5,000 incidents between July 1960 and the end of 1965, of concentrating troops on the Chinese frontiers and of conducting military manoeuvres which presupposed that China was the enemy.

Incidents during the Cultural Revolution (1966–68)

The tension on the borders greatly increased during the earlier stages of the Cultural Revolution. It was reported from Moscow on Oct. 2, 1966, that 2,000,000 Chinese were estimated to have taken part in mass demonstrations on the Soviet frontier in support of China's territorial claims, especially on the border between Manchuria and the Soviet Far East, and that Chinese troops had opened fire several times on Soviet ships plying on the River Amur. In view of the strained situation, military training schools were reported on Dec. 7 to have been established for the civilian population in the Soviet republics of Kazakhstan, Tajikistan and Kirghizia.

The situation became particularly tense during the siege of the Soviet embassy in February 1967. Beijing radio alleged on Feb. 2 that a plot by the "Soviet revisionists and US and Japanese imperialists" to attack China through Heilongjiang province (Manchuria) had been smashed, and on Feb. 11 all Chinese frontier troops were placed on the alert. On the following day wall newspapers in Beijing alleged that a company of the Chinese army had recently repulsed an attack by a Soviet battalion near Vladivostok, taking a number of prisoners; this report was not confirmed by any other source.

Western sources estimated the number of troops on the Sino-Soviet border at this time at nearly 40 Soviet divisions, many of which had recently been transferred from Eastern Europe, and between 50 and 60 Chinese divisions, or more than 600,000 men. It was reported from Moscow on Feb. 21, 1967, however, that except for frontier guards all Chinese troops had been withdrawn about 100 miles from the Soviet and Mongolian borders, creating a "no man's land" from which all civilians had been evacuated.

The Soviet press reported in January 1967 that several hundred thousand Uighurs and Kazakhs had crossed the border from Xinjiang in recent months and taken refuge in the Soviet Union; this exodus was attributed to fear of the Cultural Revolution and the hunt for Soviet sympathizers which accompanied it, the mass settlement of Chinese in Xinjiang, and the alleged persecution of national minorities. The evacuation of civilians from the frontier areas was reported on Feb. 21 to have been particularly thorough in Xinjiang, with the result that the flight of refugees into the Soviet Union had been almost brought to an end.

According to diplomatic sources in Moscow, many minor incidents took place in 1968, but neither side gave them any publicity; a Chinese protest Note of Sept. 16, 1968, however, alleged that Soviet military aircraft had flown over Heilongjiang province 29 times between Aug. 9 and 29.

The Damansky Island Fighting (March 1969)

Armed clashes between Soviet and Chinese frontier guards, causing considerable loss of life, occurred on March 2 and March 15, 1969, on the River Ussuri. The scene of the fighting was a small uninhabited island 1½ miles long by half a mile wide, known to the Russians as Damansky Island and to the Chinese as Chenpao Island, which lies about 110 miles south of Khabarovsk and 250 miles north of Vladivostok. The status of the island under the treaties of Aigun and Beijing is disputed.

A Chinese Foreign Ministry statement of March 10, 1969, contended that under international law the central line of the main channel of the Ussuri formed the boundary line, that the island was situated on the Chinese side of this line, and that it had always been under Chinese jurisdiction and had been admitted to be Chinese by the Soviet delegation at the boundary negotiations in 1964. A Soviet Note of March 29 [see below], on the other hand, maintained that a map approved by both Governments in 1861 showed the Chinese bank of the Ussuri as the boundary line in this area. The problem was complicated by the fact that after the breaking up of the ice in spring the Ussuri regularly flooded its banks and frequently shifted its channel.

The Chinese statement of March 10, 1969, asserted that Soviet frontier troops had intruded into "the Chenpao Island area of China" 16 times between Jan 23, 1967, and March 2, 1969, wounding Chinese frontier guards on several occasions, whilst Maj.-Gen. Vasily Lobanov (Soviet commander in the Pacific frontier district) claimed on March 16 that Chinese troops had repeatedly attempted to capture the island during the past 18 months.

Diametrically opposite accounts of the clash on March 2, 1969, were given by the two sides. According to the Soviet version, about 300 Chinese soldiers, camouflaged in white cloaks, crossed the frozen river during the night of March 1–2 to Damansky Island, where they lay in ambush. In the morning about 30 more Chinese approached the island and, when Soviet frontier guards came up to them to protest, opened fire without warning. At the same time both the troops on the island and others on the Chinese bank of the river opened fire with rifles and artillery on another group of Soviet frontier guards. With the help of reinforcements from a neighbouring post, it was stated, the Soviet troops had expelled the intruders after a two-hour battle, in which they had lost 31 killed, including an officer, and 14 wounded. Chinese official statements, on the other hand, stated that a large Soviet force, accompanied by four armoured vehicles, had opened fire on Chinese frontier guards who were on normal patrol duty, killing and wounding many of them.

Both Governments sent strongly worded protest Notes to the other on March 2, 1969. The Soviet Note demanded an immediate investigation, the punishment of those responsible for the incident and immediate steps to preclude any further violation of the frontier; it also declared that "reckless and provocative actions by the Chinese authorities" would be "met on our side by a rebuff". The Chinese Note similarly demanded the punishment of the culprits, reserved the right to demand compensation, and declared that if the Soviet Government continued to "provoke armed conflicts" it would receive "resolute counter-blows".

Mass protest demonstrations began on March 3, 1969, outside the Soviet embassy in Beijing which for four days was virtually besieged by thousands of Chinese servicemen and civilians shouting such slogans as "Hang Kosygin" and "Fry Brezhnev". Similar demonstrations, in which according to the New China News Agency 260,000,000 people took part, were held in the next few days throughout China. On the Russian side, although demonstrations took place in Khabarovsk and Vladivostok on March 3–4, there were no demonstrations in Moscow until March 7, when over 50,000 people marched past the Chinese embassy in the largest organized protest seen in the city for many years; some of the crowd threw stones, lumps of ice, ink bottles and paint bombs at the building, and many windows were broken.

At a press conference on March 7, 1969, Leonid Zamyatin (head of the Soviet Foreign Ministry press department), after giving the first detailed account of the incident, alleged that the Chinese had shot and bayoneted wounded men, and that the faces of some of those killed had been "so mutilated as to be unrecognizable". An even larger demonstration than that of the previous day occurred outside the Chinese embassy in Moscow on March 8, over 100,000 people taking part, although on this occasion there were no disorders; protest meetings were also held on March 8–9 in many other Russian cities. In Beijing protest demonstrations against the stoning of the Chinese embassy in Moscow began outside the Soviet embassy on March 11, and continued for three days. *Red Flag* (the Chinese Communist Party's theoretical organ) declared on March 14 that if the Soviet leadership wanted to fight, "let us thoroughly annihilate them". The article added: "The Soviet revisionists have created such theories as 'limited sovereignty' to help Soviet troops march into other countries [i.e. Czechoslovakia]. This makes us understand that their recent armed provocation is no mere coincidence."

A Chinese Note of March 13, 1969, which the Soviet embassy refused to accept, alleged that between March 4 and March 12 Soviet armoured vehicles had "intruded into China's territory, Chenpao Island", on six occasions, and that Soviet helicopters had twice flown over it during this period. Soviet official statements claimed that a group of Chinese soldiers had attempted to "invade" the island on March 14 but had been driven off.

Further fighting occurred on March 15, 1969, and was apparently on a much larger scale than that on March 2. Gen. Lobanov told the press on March 16 that Chinese infantry in regimental strength—or up to 2,000 men—had launched repeated attacks on the island under cover of artillery and mortar fire from the Chinese bank, and had been driven back, with the aid of frontier guards from neighbouring posts and the reserve, only after seven hours' fighting. According to the version given by Beijing radio, large numbers of Soviet troops supported by tanks repeatedly attacked the Chinese frontier guards on duty on the island, and were driven back after an 11-hour battle during which Soviet heavy artillery and tanks shelled the island and the Chinese bank of the river. Although neither side gave details of the casualties, these were evidently heavy; Soviet press reports mentioned by name 12 officers and NCOs who had been killed, including a colonel, suggesting—according to the Moscow correspondent of *The Times*—that a full regiment of frontier guards and reserves, or nearly 3,000 men, had been engaged on the Soviet side.

Only minor incidents were subsequently reported from the area. The Soviet press reported on several occasions between March 18 and April 8, 1969, that the Chinese had directed mortar and machine-gun fire against the island and were digging fortifications on their side of the river, whilst Beijing radio alleged on April 13 that the Russians had committed "new acts of aggression" on the Ussuri frontier, without giving any further details.

A Chinese Note of March 15, 1969, accused the Soviet Government of "incessantly " sending troops to intrude into Chinese territory, and demanded that it should immediately stop its "armed provocations". A Soviet Note of the same date maintained that "Damansky Island is an inalienable part of Soviet territory", and declared that "if further attempts are made to violate the inviolability of Soviet territory, the USSR and all its peoples will resolutely defend it and will deliver a crushing rebuff to such violations".

For some days after the fighting on March 15, 1969, both the Chinese and the Soviet press published virulent and bellicose attacks on the other country's leaders. The Beijing *People's Daily* described "Khrushchev, Kosygin, Brezhnev and company" on March 20 as "a herd of swine", asserting that the Soviet people hated "the new tsars", whilst the Soviet armed forces newspaper *Red Star* denounced Mao Zedong on March 23 as "a traitor to the sacred cause of communism . . . painted with human blood" and compared him to Hitler. The fact that protest demonstrations were not resumed in either country, however, despite the seriousness of the latest fighting, suggested that both Governments were anxious not to push matters to extremes.

Soviet Proposals for Boundary Negotiations (March–April 1969)

Kosygin asked on March 21, 1969, to communicate with the Chinese leaders by telephone. The Chinese Government replied on the following day with a memorandum stating that "in view of the present relations between China and the Soviet Union, it is unsuitable to communicate by telephone. If the Soviet Government has anything to say, it is asked to put it forward officially to the Chinese Government through diplomatic channels."

In a long and moderately worded Note of March 29, 1969, the Soviet Government reaffirmed in detail its claim to sovereignty over Damansky Island, and proposed that the boundary negotiations broken off in 1964 should be resumed as soon as possible.

After giving the Soviet version of the incidents on March 2 and 15, 1969, the Note contended that the Chinese Government had signified its acceptance of the existing frontiers by concluding an agreement on shipping on the Amur and the Ussuri in 1951, and by asking the competent Soviet authorities for permission to use certain islands in those rivers for cutting hay and timber—an indication that they did not question the Soviet claim to those islands, including Damansky Island.

The Note went on to recall the friendly relations between the two countries in the 1950s, and commented: "If it were not for the position adopted by the Chinese side, trade, economic and scientific technical co-operation between our countries would undoubtedly have developed successfully further. This also holds true for today. . . . Whenever a danger arose to the security of the People's Republic of China, the Soviet Union, loyal to its commitments under the Treaty of Friendship, Alliance, and Mutual Assistance, always came out in support of People's China." [These statements were interpreted by Western observers as a suggestion that in the event of a change in Chinese policy the Soviet Union would be prepared to resume its economic aid and diplomatic support to China.]

After deploring the breaking off of boundary negotiations, and recalling that the then Chinese Premier, Zhou Enlai, had said in 1960 that the unestablished sections of the Soviet-Chinese frontier were "insignificant discrepancies in the maps, easy to solve peacefully", the Soviet Note urged the Chinese Government to "refrain from any actions on the frontier that may cause complications and to solve any differences that may arise in a calm atmosphere and through negotiations". It proposed that the consultations started in Beijing in 1964 should be resumed as soon as possible, and concluded: "The Soviet Government is firmly convinced that in the final count the vital interests of the Soviet and Chinese peoples will make it possible to remove and overcome difficulties in Soviet-Chinese relations. The Soviet Government has stated, and considers it necessary to repeat, that it resolutely rejects any encroachments by anyone on Soviet territory, and that any attempts to talk to the Soviet Union and the Soviet people in the language of weapons will be firmly repulsed."

Marshal Lin Biao stated on April 1, 1969, that the Chinese Government was considering its reply to the Soviet Note. A second Soviet Note of April 11 proposed that the boundary negotiations should be resumed in Moscow on April 15, 1969, or at any other early date convenient for the Chinese.

IX: POLEMICS AND BILATERAL DEVELOPMENTS, 1970–76

Talks on the Sino-Soviet border question opened in Beijing on Oct. 20, 1969, but made little progress in the following months [see Chapter XII]. Accordingly, anti-Soviet polemics, which for a time had largely disappeared from the Chinese press, resumed in the second half of November 1969, while the Soviet press in turn resumed its anti-Chinese campaign. *Pravda* denounced on Jan. 6, 1970, "the war preparations being carried on in China, which are accompanied by increasingly malicious attacks by the Chinese press against the Soviet Union". Articles appearing in the Soviet press during the next few weeks repeatedly accused the Chinese leaders of stirring up war hysteria.

In the period following the death of Mao Zedong in 1976, events were influenced by the increasing predominance of a moderate faction within the Chinese Government led by Zhou Enlai. The Soviet Union was still regarded as China's major security threat and relations continued to be characterized more by confrontation and competition than co-operation. However, the militant hostility of the Chinese radicals towards Moscow, unleashed during the Cultural Revolution, was replaced by Zhou's more pragmatic foreign policy which sought to avoid unnecessary provocation of the Soviet Union. Moreover, from the early 1970s China developed a closer relationship with the United States [see Chapter X] as a strategic counterweight to the perceived Soviet threat.

Brezhnev's Speech at Lenin Centenary Celebrations—Chinese Responses (April–July 1970)

Celebrations in Moscow in April 1970 marking the centenary of the birth of Lenin were attended by representatives from all Communist countries except China and Albania, neither of which had been invited. Brezhnev, in an address to a joint meeting of the CPSU central committee and the Supreme Soviets of the USSR and the Russian Federation held in the Kremlin on April 21–22, repeated that the Soviet intervention in Czechoslovakia had been necessary to defend the international socialist movement, and contrasted Soviet action with China's policy of self-aggrandizement in Asia which abetted the "enemies of socialism".

In passages referring to the Soviet intervention in Czechoslovakia, Brezhnev said: "The anti-socialist conspiracy in Czechoslovakia . . . was a long-premeditated attempt, prepared behind a screen of demagogy, on the part of the remnants of the former exploiting classes, in alliance with right-wing opportunists and with the support of world imperialism, to destroy the foundations of the socialist system in Czechoslovakia, to isolate her from the fraternal countries, and thereby to strike a heavy blow against the positions of socialism in Europe. But the staunchness of the Marxist-Leninist core of the Czechoslovak Communist Party and the determined action by Czechs and Slovaks devoted to the cause of socialism and by allied countries loyal to the principles of socialist internationalism frustrated the dangerous enemy plans directed against the common interests of socialism and, in the long run, against peace on the continent of Europe. . . ."

China, Brezhnev continued, was "regrettably" an example of "cases of co-operation between socialist countries being disrupted in a most serious manner". He continued: "This situation is obviously the result of the nationalistic policy of the Chinese leadership and its break with the principles laid down by Lenin. . . . The enemies of socialism are the only ones to benefit from the virulent anti-Soviet campaign that has been conducted in China during the past few years. Lately it has been carried on under the screen of an alleged threat from the Soviet Union. By their actions against the country of Lenin and against the world Communist movement the initiators of this campaign expose themselves before the masses as apostates from the revolutionary cause of Lenin.

"As for the Soviet Union, we take a resolute stand in favour of socialist internationalism and the restoration of good relations between socialist countries wherever they have been broken. We shall not be found wanting. The central committee of the CPSU and the Soviet Government will continue to work actively and consistently in this direction. . . ."

A long editorial on the Lenin centenary was published on April 22, 1970, in three leading Chinese papers (*People's Daily, Red Flag* and *Liberation Army Daily*), in what was seen as the most violent attack on the Soviet leadership since the opening of bilateral negotiations. It reiterated the Chinese assertion that the Soviet Union had ceased to be a socialist country, declaring that Khrushchev's "secret report" of 1956 (in which he announced the de-Stalinization policy—see Chapter II above) was "a counter-revolutionary coup d'état which turned the dictatorship of the proletariat into the dictatorship of the bourgeoisie, and which overthrew socialism and restored capitalism". The editorial quoted Mao Zedong as having said in May 1964 that "the Soviet Union today is under the dictatorship of the bourgeoisie, a dictatorship of the Hitler type". It also violently attacked the so-called Brezhnev doctrine used to justify the invasion of Czechoslovakia, calling it an "assortment of fascist theories" which it defined as follows:

"(1) *The theory of 'limited sovereignty'*. Brezhnev and co. . . . declare that Soviet revisionism has the right to determine the destiny of another country, including the destiny of its sovereignty. . . . In other words, you have the right to order other countries about, whereas they have no right to oppose you. . . .

"(2) *The theory of 'international dictatorship'*. Brezhnev and co. assert that they have the right to 'render military aid to a fraternal country to do away with the threat to the socialist system'. . . . The 'international dictatorship' you refer to simply means the subjection of other countries to the rule of the new tsars. . . .

"(3) *The theory of 'socialist community'*. Brezhnev and co. shout that 'the community of socialist States is an inseparable whole' and that the 'united action' of 'the socialist community' must be strengthened. . . . By 'united action' you mean unifying under your control the politics, economies and military affairs of other countries. By 'inseparable' you mean forbidding other countries to free themselves from your control. . . .

"(4) *The theory of 'international division of labour'*. Brezhnev and co. . . . have not only applied 'international division of labour' to a number of East European countries and the Mongolian People's Republic, but have extended it to other countries in Asia, Africa and Latin America. . . . The Soviet revisionist clique has taken over this colonial policy from imperialism. Its theory of 'international division of labour' boils down to 'industrial Soviet Union, agricultural Asia, Africa and Latin America' or 'industrial Soviet Union, subsidiary processing workshop Asia, Africa and Latin America'. . . .

"(5) *The theory that 'our interests are involved'*. Brezhnev and co. clamour that 'the Soviet Union, which as a major world power has extensive international contacts, cannot passively regard events that, though they might be territorially remote, nevertheless have a bearing on our security and the security of our friends'. . . . This theory that 'our interests are involved' is a typical argument used by the imperialists for their global policy of aggression. . . . How strikingly similar are the utterances of the Soviet revisionists to those of the old tsars and the US imperialists!"

These polemics were followed by a series of exchanges when each country accused the other of having expansionist intentions. *Pravda* on May 18, 1970, published a vigorous 5,000-word editorial headed "Pseudo-Revolutionaries with their Masks Off" which stated that:

"For a number of years the Chinese leadership has been promoting in Asia a line of undermining progressive regimes, provoking conflicts between states and isolating the national liberation struggle of the peoples from their genuine allies, the countries of the socialist community and the international Communist and workers' movement. By acting thus Beijing shows the imperialists that it does not intend to take concerted action with the USSR and other socialist countries against imperialist aggression. This stand enables imperialist quarters to carry out their anti-popular designs and plans, the latest events in Indo-China [i.e. the US intervention in Kampuchea] being added proof of this. By their actions the Beijing leaders leave no doubt that they strive to use the heroic freedom struggle of the peoples in their global intrigues, which stem from the Great Han dreams of becoming new emperors of 'the Great China' which would rule at least Asia, if not the whole world. . . ."

On July 31, 1970, the *People's Daily, Red Flag* and the *Liberation Army Daily* accused the Soviet Union of preparing to attack China, in a joint editorial which called on the Chinese people to be "ready at any moment to repulse an aggression or a surprise attack by imperialism or social imperialism".

Exchange of Ambassadors (September–October 1970)

Relations between China and the Soviet Union showed a marked improvement in the autumn of 1970 when an important step was taken towards their normalization with the exchange of ambassadors. The appointment of Vasily Tolstikov (Communist Party secretary for the Leningrad region) as ambassador to China was announced in Moscow on Sept. 16. Tolstikov arrived in Beijing on Oct. 10, and the new Chinese ambassador, Liu Xinzhuan (previously a Deputy Foreign Minister) arrived in Moscow on Nov. 22. Both countries had recalled their ambassadors in 1967 during the period of extreme tension caused by the Cultural Revolution, diplomatic relations having since been conducted at chargé d'affaires level.

The more conciliatory mood was further reflected in the Soviet Government's message on the occasion of China's National Day on Oct. 1, 1970, and the Chinese Government's message on the occasion of the anniversary of the Russian revolution on Nov. 7, both of which were unusually warm in tone. The Soviet message expressed the hope of "normalization of state relations" and "restoration of good neighbourliness and friendship between the Soviet and Chinese peoples", whilst the Chinese message said that "China had held all along that the differences of principle between China and the Soviet Union should not hinder the two countries from maintaining and developing normal state relations on the basis of the five principles of peaceful co-existence".

Brezhnev's Report to 24th Congress of Soviet Communist Party (March 1971)

The 24th CPSU Congress opened in Moscow on March 30, 1971, when Brezhnev delivered the central committee's report. Reviewing relations with China, he noted that there had been a recent improvement and urged China to co-operate in normalizing relations further.

Brezhnev said: "The Chinese leaders have put forward an ideological-political platform of their own which is incompatible with Leninism on key questions of international life and the world Communist movement, and have demanded that we should abandon the line of the 20th congress [at which Khrushchev denounced Stalin's repression and the "personality cult"] and the programme of the CPSU. They have developed an intensive and hostile propaganda campaign against our party and country, made territorial claims on the Soviet Union, and in the spring and summer of 1969 brought matters to the point of armed incidents along the frontier. . . .

"In the past 18 months, as a result of the initiative displayed by us, there have been signs of some normalization in the relations between the USSR and the People's Republic of China. A meeting of the heads of government of the two countries took place in September 1969, and this was followed by negotiations in Beijing between government delegations on a settlement of the border issues. These negotiations are going forward slowly, and it goes without saying that their favourable completion calls for a constructive attitude, and not only on the part of one side.

"An exchange of ambassadors took place between the USSR and the People's Republic of China at the end of last year. After a considerable interval, trade agreements have been signed and trade has somewhat increased. These are useful steps. We are prepared to continue to act in this direction. But, on the other hand, we cannot fail to see that the anti-Soviet line in China's propaganda and policy is being continued, and that the ninth congress of the Communist Party of China laid down this line, which is hostile to the Soviet Union, in its decisions. . . . Our party and the Soviet Government are profoundly convinced that an improvement in the relations between the Soviet Union and the People's Republic of China would be in keeping with the fundamental long-term interests of both countries, and with the interests of socialism, the freedom of the peoples and the strengthening of peace. That is why we are prepared to help in every way not only to normalize relations but also to restore neighbourliness and friendship between the Soviet Union and the People's Republic of China. . . ."

However, in a later passage, Brezhnev again criticized China for undermining the unity of the socialist movement, saying:

"Success in the struggle against imperialism largely depends on the cohesion of the anti-imperialist forces and above all of the world Communist movement. . . . It has been precisely in the period under review that the attempts on various sides to attack Marxism-Leninism as the ideological-theoretical basis for the activity of the Communist movement have been most acute. The Chinese leadership went over in a number of countries to setting up splinter groupings labelled as 'Marxist-Leninist parties'. . . . The Trotskyites have now and again formed blocs with these groupings. Here and there tendencies towards nationalistic self-isolation have been intensified. . . . It is precisely the nationalistic tendencies, and especially those which assume the form of anti-Sovietism, that bourgeois ideologists and bourgeois propaganda have most willingly relied upon in their fight against socialism. . . ."

Renewal of Polemics (December 1970–July 1971)

Anti-Soviet polemics in the Chinese press had revived in December 1970 following widespread food riots in Poland which posed a serious challenge to the Soviet-backed Polish regime. The first major theoretical attack on the Soviet Union since April 1970, however, appeared in an article entitled "Long Live the Victory of the Dictatorship of the Proletariat", which was published in the *People's Daily, Red Flag* and the *Liberation Army Daily* on March 18, 1971, to commemorate the centenary of the Paris Commune. Notwithstanding, Leonid Ilyichev, the Soviet Deputy Foreign Minister, met with Zhou Enlai on March 21 for talks on border issues (see Chapter XII).

The article declared: "With its leadership usurped by the Soviet revisionist renegade clique, the Soviet state is no longer an instrument with which the proletariat suppresses the bourgeoisie, but has become a tool with which the restored bourgeoisie suppresses the proletariat. The Soviet revisionist renegades have turned the Soviet Union into a paradise for a handful of bureaucrat monopoly capitalists of a new type, a prison for the millions of working people." It also accused "the Soviet revisionist renegades" of using "the most savage and brutal means . . . to suppress the people of different nationalities in their country", to "impose a tight control" over some East European countries and Mongolia, to occupy Czechoslovakia, and to "engage in military expansion everywhere and insidiously conduct all manner of subversive activities against other countries".

Chinese attacks on alleged Soviet expansionism were renewed in the April 1971 issue of *Red Flag* which declared that the Soviet Union had "intensified its transformation into a fascist dictatorship, and practises a policy of aggression and collusion with American imperialism, its rival in the struggle for world hegemony". A further *Red Flag* article published on July 1, 1971 (the 50th anniversary of the founding of the Chinese Communist Party), denounced the Soviet leaders as "renegades" and "world storm-troopers opposing China, opposing communism and opposing the people".

The Soviet press was for its part particularly critical during this period of the improvement in relations between China and the United States. Articles published in April 1971 accused the Chinese Government of "collusion" with the United States, charges which were stepped up after the announcement in July 1971 of President Nixon's forthcoming visit to China.

The Lin Biao Connexion (September 1971–August 1973)

Soviet propaganda against China relaxed in September 1971 after reports that Marshal Lin Biao, the former Chinese Defence Minister, vice-chairman of the Communist Party and designated successor of Chairman Mao Zedong, had been killed on Sept. 12, 1971, when an aircraft in which he was fleeing to the Soviet Union crashed in Mongolia, it being alleged in China that he had attempted a coup d'état and tried to assassinate Mao. *The Times* commented on Sept. 30, 1971: "The drying up of the anti-Chinese propaganda suggests that the Russians are hoping for a political change in Beijing which would be in their favour, and are not going to make themselves seem more than usually anti-Chinese while they wait to see what happens. . . ."

Western commentators suggested that the Lin Biao crisis arose from disagreements inside the Chinese party leadership primarily over foreign but also over internal political and economic policies, reflecting a split between the left wing of the party on which Marshal Lin largely relied for support, and the moderate faction led by Zhou Enlai, the Prime Minister. The division had become apparent following a session of the central committee held from Aug. 23 to Sept. 6, 1970, after which two prominent left wingers, Chen Boda and Li Xuefeng, disappeared from public life. The main issues were thought to have been as follows:

(1) Marshal Lin was believed to have opposed the moderate faction's policy of détente with the United States and other Western countries which was actively pursued in the early months of 1971, culminating in the announcement on July 15 of President Nixon's visit to China. According to some sources he had advocated that such a policy, if adopted, should be accompanied by an attempt to improve relations with the Soviet Union. Previously, he had put forward a strategy for world revolution; in an essay published in 1965 entitled "Long Live the Victory of the People's War", he prophesied that revolutionary wars in the under-developed countries would end the "encirclement of the United States and Western Europe".

(2) Lin, together with a section of the army, opposed steps to reduce the political ascendancy of the army; the Cultural Revolution, while severely disrupting the Communist Party organs, had greatly strengthened the political role of the army which largely controlled the provincial revolutionary committees as well as many ministries and economic enterprises. In December 1970 the re-establishment of provincial party committees was begun and was accompanied by an intensification of the campaign against the extreme left which had been in progress since 1969 and which strengthened the position of the moderate faction. Attacks on the radical "May 16 Detachment" (which had organized a number of assaults on foreign diplomatic missions in Beijing) formed an integral part of the Government's policy of détente.

(3) Proposals for the fourth five-year plan put forward in September 1970 envisaged a massive programme for the mechanization of agriculture. Marshal Lin and other military leaders were believed to have been opposed to financing such a programme by reducing military expenditure, arguing that the policy of détente with the United States would exacerbate China's relations with the Soviet Union and would thus necessitate strong armed forces.

No details of Marshal Lin's alleged plot (which was apparently discovered on Sept. 11 or 12, 1971) were officially published but a number of unofficial accounts, said to be derived from Chinese sources, appeared nearly a year later in July and August 1972, and included allegations of Soviet involvement in the affair.

The Chinese Nationalist Government Information Service (in Taiwan) published on July 23, 1972, what it claimed to be the official report sent to provincial party leaders. According to this document, Marshal Lin had quarrelled with Chairman

Mao after the 1970 session of the central committee and formed the "571" plot with his wife (Ye Qhun), his son, Gen. Huang Yongsheng, Gen. Wu Faxian, Admiral Li Zuopeng and Gen. Qiu Huizuo (head of the army's logistics department and a member of the politburo). The conspirators were said to have planned an uprising, for which they expected Soviet support, and to have proposed either to capture Chairman Mao and force him to accept their demands or to assassinate him. The code name "571" in Chinese characters was said to resemble those for "armed uprising".

The accusation of Soviet collusion was repeated in subsequent Chinese polemics against the Soviet Union. Zhou Enlai's report to the 10th CPC congress, presented on Aug. 24, 1973, was mainly devoted to a denunciation of the late Marshal Lin and to polemics against the Soviet Union which, Zhou suggested, had supported Marshal Lin's attempted coup.

Recounting the details of Marshal Lin's conspiracy, Zhou Enlai said: "The course of the struggle to smash the Lin Biao anti-party clique and the crimes of the clique are already known to the whole party, the army and the people. . . . [The struggle] was an acute expression of the intense domestic and international class struggles". "The Lin Biao anti-party clique", Zhou continued, "sprang out to continue the trial of strength with the proletariat" following the downfall of Liu Shaoqi and his supporters. (Liu, a former Chairman of the Republic, had been removed from his post at the height of the Cultural Revolution for being an alleged "capitalist roader".) The Soviet Union, which had denounced such purges at the time [see Chapter VII], was associated by Zhou with the alleged new rightist threat:

"As early as Jan. 13, 1967, . . . Brezhnev, the chief of the Soviet revisionist renegade clique, . . . openly declared that they stood on the side of the Liu Shaoqi renegade clique, saying that the downfall of this clique was 'a great tragedy for all true Chinese Communists, with whom we express our profound sympathy'. At the same time Brezhnev publicly announced the continuation of the policy of subverting the leadership of the Chinese Communist Party, and ranted about 'struggling to bring it back to the path of internationalism'. . . . The Brezhnev renegade clique has impetuously voiced the common wish of the reactionaries, and blurted out the ultra-rightist nature of the Lin Biao anti-party clique. . . .

Returning to Marshal Lin and his supporters, Zhou Enlai continued: "The essence of the counter-revolutionary revisionist line they pursued and the criminal aim of the counter-revolutionary armed coup d'état they launched was to usurp the supreme power in the party and the state, thoroughly betray the line of the ninth congress, radically change the party's basic line and policies for the entire historical period of socialism, turn the Marxist-Leninist Chinese Communist Party into a revisionist fascist party, subvert the dictatorship of the proletariat, and restore capitalism. Inside China they wanted to reinstate the landlord and bourgeois classes . . . and to institute a feudal-comprador-fascist dictatorship. Internationally, they wanted to capitulate to Soviet revisionist social-imperialism and ally themselves with imperialism, revisionism and reaction to oppose China, communism and revolution.

"Lin Biao . . . engaged in machinations within our party not just for one decade but for several decades. . . . Lin Biao joined the Communist Party in the early days of China's new democratic revolution. Even at that time he was pessimistic about the future of the Chinese revolution. . . . At important junctures of the revolution he invariably committed right opportunist errors. . . . As the Chinese revolution developed further and especially when it turned socialist in nature . . . Lin Biao and his like . . . sprang out for a trial of strength with the proletariat. When under the baton of Soviet revisionism he attempted to have his decisive say in order to serve the needs of domestic and foreign class enemies, his exposure and bankruptcy became complete. . . .

"In the last 50 years our party has gone through 10 major struggles between the two lines. The collapse of the Lin Biao anti-party clique does not mean the end of the two-line struggle within the party. . . . For a long time to come there will still be two-line struggles within the party . . . and such struggles will occur 10, 20 or 30 times. . . ."

At the end of the 10th CPC congress, a resolution was passed posthumously expelling the "bourgeois, careerist conspirator, counter-revolutionary double-dealer, renegade and traitor", Marshal Lin Biao, from the Chinese Communist Party.

Further Polemics (late 1971–early 1974)

After an interval occasioned by the Lin Biao crisis, Soviet anti-Chinese propaganda revived as a result of the December 1971 war between India and Pakistan, during which the Soviet Union supported India while China and the United States supported Pakistan [see Chapter XIII]. *Pravda* accused China (on Dec. 22) of attempting to "do a deal with the United States" and described Zhou Enlai, who had not previously been attacked in the Soviet press, as "one of the leaders of the anti-Indian and anti-Soviet campaign". Soviet attacks on China died down in March 1972, when border negotiations were resumed after a three months' break, but polemics by both sides were intensified in the autumn of that year.

The Times commented on March 7, 1973: "Recently China has accused the Russians of spying over Japanese airspace; plundering Pakistan's fish resources; disrupting the Venezuelan (and by implication the Chinese) economy through massive buying on the world grain market; arming themselves to threaten Western Europe; making a mess of their own agriculture; and harming the Arab countries by permitting mass emigration of Jews to Israel. Russia in its turn has accused China of being involved in the world narcotics business. . . ."

Another lull of several months ended on Aug. 15, 1973, when Brezhnev declared that Soviet attempts to normalize relations had failed because of China's "openly anti-Soviet" policy. Soviet propaganda in August and September 1973, before and during the Algiers conference of non-aligned countries, alleged that China was no longer socialist and was ruled by a military-bureaucratic dictatorship which aimed at becoming a nuclear super-power and dominating Asia. Zhou Enlai made similar attacks on Soviet expansionist intentions in his speech to the Chinese Communist Party congress on Aug. 24, 1973, when he called for vigilance against a possible surprise attack by the Soviet Union. Apparently in reply to criticism inside the party of the Government's policy of détente with the United States, Zhou emphasized throughout the speech his belief that the Soviet Union posed a far greater threat to the security of China than US imperialism; the United States, he claimed, had "started to go downhill" and had "openly admitted that it is increasingly on the decline", with the result that "it could not but pull out of Vietnam . . .".

Zhou said: "Today it is mainly the two nuclear super-powers, the USA and the USSR, that are contending for hegemony. . . . The West always wants to urge the Soviet revisionists eastward to divert the peril towards China. . . . At present the Soviet revisionists are making a feint to the east while attacking in the west, and stepping up their contention in Europe and their expansion in the Mediterranean, the Indian Ocean and every place their hands can reach. . . .

"Over the last two decades the Soviet revisionist ruling clique, from Khrushchev to Brezhnev, has made a socialist country degenerate into a social-imperialist country. Internally it has restored capitalism, enforced a fascist dictatorship, and enslaved the people of all nationalities. . . . Externally it has invaded and occupied Czechoslovakia, massed its troops along the Chinese border, sent troops into the People's Republic of Mongolia, supported the traitorous Lon Nol clique, intervened in Egypt, causing the expulsion of the Soviet experts, dismembered Pakistan, and carried out subversive activities in many Asian and African countries. . . . The Brezhnev renegade clique . . . alleges that China is against relaxation of world tension and unwilling to improve Sino-Soviet relations. . . . If you are so anxious to relax world tension, why don't you show your good faith by doing a thing or two— for instance, withdraw your armed forces from Czechoslovakia or the People's Republic of Mongolia and return the four northern islands to Japan? . . ." (This last reference was to Etorofu, Kunashiri, Shikotan and the Habomai group—islands off northern Japan held by the Soviet Union since the end of World War II and claimed by Japan to be part of its national territory.)

Zhou emphasized that "necessary compromises between revolutionary countries and imperialist countries must be distinguished from collusion and compromise between Soviet revisionism and US imperialism", and continued: "We must maintain high vigilance and be fully prepared against any war of aggression that imperialism may launch, and particularly against a surprise attack on our country by Soviet revisionist social-imperialism. Our heroic People's Liberation Army and our vast militia must be prepared at all times to wipe out any enemy that may invade. . . ."

In late 1973 and early 1974, both sides made biting attacks on the alleged repressive nature of the other's domestic policies, each claiming that the other country was a seething mass of discontent and that the opposing regime lacked any substantial degree of popular support.

The journal of the Soviet Writers' Union, *Literaturnaya Gazeta,* accused the Chinese Government on Nov. 7, 1973, of practising a policy "close to genocide" against national minorities, some of which were alleged to have been completely wiped out. Between 1967 and 1972, it asserted, uprisings by minorities had been brutally suppressed in Xinjiang, Inner Mongolia, Tibet, Sichuan, Hainan and Yunnan, and over 12,000 people had been killed when a new revolt in Tibet was suppressed in 1972. (The allegation concerning a major revolt in Tibet in 1972 was not confirmed by Tibetan exiles.)

The Beijing *People's Daily* replied to this attack on Jan. 8, 1974, alleging that the Soviet Union was in a state of turmoil caused by popular resistance to "the Soviet revisionist renegade clique", and that "the new tsars are sitting on a volcano". It asserted inter alia that more than a million people were confined in over 1,000 labour camps, in addition to mental hospitals where dissidents were given mind-destroying drugs; that tanks, armoured cars and parachute troops had been used to suppress popular unrest, which since 1960 had taken the form of strikes, sabotage, demonstrations, and the formation of underground revolutionary organizations; and that thousands of students in the Baltic republics and the Ukraine had demonstrated against the regime.

Reciprocal Expulsion of Diplomats (January 1974)

Relations between the Soviet Union and China sank to their lowest level since the border fighting of 1969 in January 1974, when five Soviet nationals, including three diplomats, were expelled from China for alleged espionage and a Chinese diplomat was expelled from the Soviet Union on similar charges. A Chinese Note of Jan. 19 alleged that V. I. Marchenko (first secretary at the Soviet embassy), U. A. Semyonov (the third secretary), their wives and A. A. Kolosov (an interpreter) had been arrested at a secret meeting with two Soviet agents, and declared them personae non gratae.

A long statement issued by the New China News Agency on Jan. 22, 1974, alleged that on the evening of Jan. 15 the five diplomats had driven to a bridge on the outskirts of Beijing, under which Semyonov and Kolosov had met a Chinese named Li Hongshu and an unnamed accomplice. Li had handed over intelligence in secret writing to Semyonov, who gave him a bag containing a miniature radio transmitter and receiver, directions written in invisible ink, "a copy of the programme for establishing a secret counter-revolutionary organization in China", a forged border pass, a large sum of money, and other espionage materials. At this point a signal flare had been fired, and the police had arrested the four men and filmed the scene. When the other three Soviet citizens returned to pick up Semyonov and Kolosov they had also been arrested.

An alleged confession by Li Hongshu, which was also published, asserted that he had fled to the Soviet Union in 1967, and after receiving training in Moscow had secretly returned in June 1972, since when he had been engaged in espionage in north-east China under the orders of the military intelligence agency in Moscow and the Soviet embassy in Beijing. He had received a radio message from Moscow on Dec. 27, 1973, ordering him to go to Beijing with his "friend" to meet embassy personnel under the bridge on Jan. 15. After arriving in Beijing he had sent coded radio signals to the embassy on the morning of Jan. 15, and had received reply signals confirming the appointment.

A Soviet protest Note of Jan. 21, 1974, alleged that Marchenko, his wife and Mrs Semyonov had been stopped in the street, dragged from their car, and driven to another street where a crowd had been assembled and film cameras installed. After a film had been made they were taken to a building where attempts were made to secure a confession that they were engaged in espionage. Semyonov and Kolosov, the Note claimed, had been arrested while walking in the street and similarly treated. Despite protests by the Soviet embassy, the Chinese authorities had denied all knowledge of their whereabouts, and had not released them until Jan. 19.

Kuan Hengguang, an attaché at the Chinese embassy in Moscow, was arrested at Irkutsk (Siberia) on Jan. 19, 1974, on a charge of attempting to obtain military information from a Soviet woman and was expelled from the country. In reply to a Soviet protest, a Chinese Note of Jan. 25 described his arrest as "an anti-China farce" and "a mean act of retaliation".

The Chinese Note alleged that the international train in which Kuan was returning to Beijing on completing his tour of duty was stopped at Irkutsk station on the pretext that a passenger had been found to be suffering from smallpox. He had been taken from the train and forcibly detained in the quarantine station, where a woman had tried to put a "picture folder" into his hand. Police had then entered the room, arrested him and flown him to Moscow, where he had been questioned until he was released on the following day.

Zhou Enlai referred to the incident in his report on the work of the Government presented to the National People's Congress (NPC) which met in Beijing on Jan. 13–17, 1975. He stated that the "Soviet leading clique have betrayed Marxism-Leninism, and our debate with them on matters of principle will go on for a long time. However, [although] we have always held that this debate should not obstruct the maintenance of normal state relations between China and the Soviet Union . . . , [the Soviet leadership] have taken a series of steps to worsen the relations between the two countries, conducted subversive activities against our country and even armed conflicts on the border."

At the same NPC session a new constitution was adopted which altered the reference in the preamble to the previous constitution drawn up in 1954, which referred to China's "indestructible friendship with the great Union of Soviet Socialist Republics and the people's democracies" and replaced it with the statement that "we should strengthen our unity with the socialist countries".

Chinese Internal Developments (1973–76)

These and subsequent developments in Sino-Soviet relations occurred against a background of continuing competition within the Chinese Government, after the fall of Lin Biao, between the moderate and radical factions. The moderates, led by Zhou Enlai, whose prestige was second only to Chairman Mao's, were believed to command strong support inside the party, the administration and the armed forces. They were further strengthened by the return to public life of many officials and officers who had been removed from their posts during the Cultural Revolution, the most conspicuous example being Deng Xiaoping, who had been rehabilitated in April 1973. The radicals were represented in the Government by Zhang Chunqiao, Yao Wenyuan, Wang Hongwen and Jiang Qing (Chairman Mao's wife), who later became known as the "gang of four". Although weakened by Marshal Lin's fall, they continued to control the press and radio, and drew their support from the trade unions, the militia and the Communist Youth League; they were also believed to have access to Chairman Mao, who was living in retirement, through Jiang Qing. The differences between the two factions in domestic policies largely turned upon the question of priorities.

In his report to the National People's Congress on Jan. 13, 1975, Zhou Enlai laid down an ambitious programme for building "an independent and relatively comprehensive industrial and economic system" before 1980 and for "the comprehensive modernization of agriculture, industry, national defence, and science and technology" (usually referred to as "the four modernizations") "before the end of the century, so that our national economy will be advancing in the front ranks of the world". While both sides fully supported this programme, the radicals maintained that survivals of capitalism in the economy such as market relations, differentials in pay and distribution on the principle of "To each according to his work" formed the basis for a possible restoration of capitalism under "revisionist" leadership such as, they alleged, had already occurred in the Soviet Union. They therefore emphasized Chairman Mao's slogans "Class struggle is the key link" and "Put politics in command", and called for the elimination of "bourgeois rights" and a speedy advance towards an egalitarian society based on the principle "To each according to his needs".

The moderates, on the other hand, held that political advance was dependent on economic progress; hence they advocated political stability in the interests of the economy, were prepared to reinstate officials accused of "revisionism" during the Cultural Revolution who possessed useful technical qualifications, and opposed experiments in university education which might lower the standard of scientific and technological research. Their pragmatic viewpoint was summed up in a widely quoted saying of Deng Xiaoping's: "What does it matter if the cat's black or white, so long as it catches mice?"

In foreign policy matters, while both factions were suspicious of the Soviet Union, the pragmatic attitude of Zhou and Deng favoured tempering the policy of confrontation pursued by the radicals and their unrestrained antipathy towards the "Soviet revisionist clique".

The struggle between the two groups was apparent in internal developments during 1973–76. The radicals were believed to be responsible for a series of campaigns intended to continue the work of the Cultural Revolution, beginning with the "Criticize Lin Biao, criticize Confucius" campaign of 1973–74, which led to a wave of industrial unrest beginning in the summer of 1974, and continuing at least until July 1975. In reaction to the indiscipline which the campaign provoked, Mao issued in autumn 1974 an appeal for stability and unity. This was viewed as a setback for the radicals, as was Zhou Enlai's report to the National People's Congress in Beijing in January 1975, in which he put great emphasis on the need for economic development.

The radicals resumed the offensive in February 1975, however, with the "proletarian dictatorship" campaign which emphasized that at China's present stage of development many vestiges of capitalism still survived and that unless these "bourgeois rights" were restricted, the danger of the restoration of capitalism would remain. In the autumn of 1975 a new campaign was launched against "capitulationists" which was partly directed against Communists who advocated a conciliatory attitude to the Soviet Union.

Moderate influence nevertheless remained strong. A large number of political and military leaders who had been denounced as "revisionists" during the Cultural Revolution were rehabilitated in the summer and autumn of 1975, and a campaign for the mechanization of agriculture launched in September tended to divert attention from political and economic policy issues.

Zhou Enlai died on Jan. 8, 1976, resulting in a direct clash between the two factions over the choice of his successor as Prime Minister. The final selection of Hua Guofeng to succeed Zhou as acting Prime Minister, instead of Deng Xiaoping (who as First Deputy Premier had increasingly discharged many of Zhou's duties during the latter's last illness) was interpreted by foreign commentators as a compromise move as Hua was not associated with any faction inside the party leadership. His appointment as premier was confirmed on April 7, 1976.

The struggle between the two factions intensified in February 1976, however, when the radicals began a violent campaign against "unrepentant capitalist roaders". Deng Xiaoping in particular appeared to be in disgrace, making no public appearances after January 1976, while in April 1976 he was reportedly removed from office.

Brezhnev's Report to 25th CPSU Congress (February 1976)

Leonid Brezhnev, presenting the central committee's report at the 25th congress of the CPSU held in Moscow from Feb. 24 to March 5, 1976, denounced Maoism as "directly hostile" to Marxism-Leninism, although at the same time he offered to normalize relations with China. This more conciliatory approach appeared to stem from Soviet hopes that the recent changes in the Chinese political leadership would produce a more favourable policy towards the Soviet Union.

Brezhnev said with regard to China: "The policy of China's present leaders is openly directed against the majority of the socialist states. . . . It is far too little now to say that the Maoist ideology and policy are incompatible with Marxist-Leninist teaching. They are directly hostile to it. . . . We shall continue the struggle against Maoism, a principled and irreconcilable struggle. At the same time, we should like to repeat once again that in our relations with China, as with other countries, we adhere firmly to the principles of equality, respect for sovereignty and territorial integrity, non-interference in each other's internal affairs and non-use of force. In short, we are prepared to normalize relations with China in line with the principles of peaceful co-existence. What is more, we can say with assurance that if Beijing reverts to a policy which is genuinely based on Marxism-Leninism, if it abandons its hostile policy towards the socialist countries and takes the road of co-operation and solidarity with the socialist world, there will be an appropriate response from our side. . . . The matter rests with the Chinese side."

The Soviet willingness to improve relations was reiterated following the confirmation of Hua Guofeng's appointment as Prime Minister on April 7, 1976, when Alexei Kosygin (the Soviet Prime Minister) sent him a telegram of congratulations in which he said that the Soviet Union was "prepared to normalize relations with China on the basis of the principles of peaceful co-existence".

A long article, signed "I. Alexandrov" (a pseudonym often used for important Soviet policy pronouncements), was published in *Pravda* on April 28, 1976, which appeared to align the Soviet Government with the moderate faction in the Chinese Government in the hope of producing an initiative to improve relations. It attributed the Chinese Government's anti-Soviet policy to "the Mao Zedong group" and commented: "The Chinese people are not going along with Maoism, as was shown by the recent large-scale unrest in Beijing and other Chinese cities". It also called for the resumption of border negotiations [see Chapter XII].

This approach produced no response from the Chinese Government, while at a banquet on April 29, 1976, in honour of Robert Muldoon, then New Zealand Prime Minister, Hua denounced the Soviet Union as "wildly ambitious" and "the most dangerous source of war". Also on April 29, 1976, an explosion occurred at the gates of the Soviet embassy in Beijing, two Chinese guards and a civilian being killed. A Chinese official spokesman said on May 13 that the explosion was "an act of sabotage by a counter-revolutionary who was killed on the spot".

Sino-Soviet Economic Relations (1970–76)

Since the split between China and the Soviet Union in 1959 (when the Soviet Union was China's main trading partner and the two countries' mutual exchanges totalled the equivalent of over US$2,000 million, or 47 per cent of China's foreign trade), Sino-Soviet trade had steadily declined. This process was accelerated by the Cultural Revolution and in 1970 the volume of trade had fallen to $45,000,000. After that date, however, trade expanded: China's import needs—of capital goods in particular—had grown with the rapid expansion of the country's economy, and although much of China's imports of industrial equipment came from the West and from Japan, commercial relations with the Soviet Union were especially attractive to China because of the barter basis for such trade and the ease of direct deliveries by rail.

A new trade and payments agreement was concluded on Nov. 22, 1970, by the Chinese Government and a Soviet delegation headed by Ivan Grishin, a Deputy Minister for Foreign Trade. Despite the deterioration in relations between the two countries in summer 1971 [see above], two further trade and payments agreements were signed on Aug. 5, 1971, and June 13, 1972. Under these agreements the value of trade between the two countries was planned to increase from $167,000,000 in 1971 to $288,000,000 in 1972.

A non-stop air service between Beijing and Moscow was introduced on Jan. 30, 1974, under an agreement signed the previous month. Hitherto the Soviet Aeroflot airline had handled the route alone, with a stopover at Irkutsk, while the Civil Aviation Administration of China had served only the Beijing-Irkutsk line. It was agreed that the Soviet and Chinese companies would each handle one weekly direct flight, both using Ilyushin 62s.

Annual trade and payments agreements were signed on July 4, 1974, July 24, 1975, and May 21, 1976, the agreed volume of trade being $200,000,000 in 1974, $158,700,000 in 1975 and $210,500,000 in 1976. The pattern of trade remained constant, the Soviet Union supplying machinery and equipment and China raw materials and consumer goods. *The Financial Times* commented on June 16, 1976: "The size of the trade now puts the Soviet Union in roughly the same bracket as the UK in the list of Beijing's partners, though it is far outclassed by Japan, West Germany, France and increasingly the US".

X: THE US CONNEXION, 1969–82

As China emerged from the Cultural Revolution, its isolation from the non-socialist world slowly decreased, notably after the admission of the People's Republic to the United Nations in October 1971. The continued tension in relations with the Soviet Union encouraged the Chinese to seek outside contacts, and made them responsive to overtures by the USA. The process of rapprochement between the two countries accelerated after the fall of the "gang of four" in 1976.

The development of closer relations was helped by the decision to stimulate the Chinese economy by importing foreign technology, and by the USA's desire to maintain its influence in Eastern Asia after the Vietnam war. Both sides saw each other as a counterweight to Soviet power. Later, as relations between China and the Soviet Union improved, and problems arose over US aid to Taiwan, Chinese interests were safeguarded by an apparent policy of balancing the two super-powers against one another.

The 1970s were also a period of détente between the Soviet Union and the USA. As their relations grew warmer, mutual contacts developed and several important agreements on nuclear arms limitation were signed. However, after 1976 the anti-Soviet overtones of China–US relations, and American suspicions of Soviet expansionism, led to increasing strain between the two super-powers. The Soviet invasion of Afghanistan in December 1979 and the election of Ronald Reagan as US President in 1980 effectively halted the process of US–Soviet détente, which in turn had important ramifications for Sino–Soviet relations.

Relaxation of US Restrictions on China (July 1969–March 1971)

Certain relaxations of the US travel restrictions with China which had been in force since 1950 were announced on July 21, 1969. These were: (i) American citizens travelling abroad would be permitted to bring back to the United States up to $100 worth of goods produced in mainland China, whereas hitherto the importation of anything that had originated in China— except for printed matter—had been forbidden. (ii) The ban on travel to China was lifted for certain categories of US citizens. The then State Department spokesman, Robert McCloskey, explained that these measures had been taken unilaterally, without consultation with the Chinese authorities and with little expectation of any reciprocation by Beijing. He added that the measures were intended to help the development of contacts between the two countries.

It was announced on Dec. 19, 1969, that President Nixon had decided to relax some of the controls on US trade with China. Under this relaxation the embargo would be lifted in the following respects: (i) Foreign subsidiaries of US companies would be allowed to trade with China in non-strategic goods. (ii) US companies would be able to buy Chinese goods and to resell them in third countries, although the ban on direct trade between the United States and China remained in force. (iii) American citizens would be allowed to buy, when overseas, an unlimited amount of Chinese goods for their own private use at home.

The lifting of the last remaining restrictions on travel by US nationals to China was announced on March 15, 1971. The decision was a further unilateral step taken by the US Government in seeking to ease tensions between Washington and Beijing, although the Chinese had made no visible response to the US initiatives.

Table Tennis Diplomacy (April 1971)

On April 6, 1971, at the end of the world table tennis championships in Nagoya, Japan (in which both Chinese and US teams had taken part), the US team received a surprise invitation to visit China. This was immediately accepted. The visit was the first by American sportsmen and sportswomen to China since the establishment of Communist rule in 1949. In Washington, the State Department welcomed the invitation, noting that it would never have been issued without official approval by Beijing.

The US team's visit lasted from April 10–17, 1971, and involved extensive trips around China, sight-seeing and exhibition matches. Premier Zhou Enlai received the players on April 14 in Beijing. Welcoming the American party, he said; "With your acceptance of our invitation, you have opened a new page in the relations of the Chinese and American peoples. I am confident that this new beginning of our friendship will certainly meet with the major support of our two peoples."

Warm tributes to the courtesy and friendliness of the Chinese were paid by the Americans after their return to the United States. Graham B. Steenhoven, president of the US Table Tennis Association, announced that a Chinese table tennis team would visit the USA soon at his invitation—a statement officially welcomed by the White House.

On April 14, 1971, President Nixon announced further relaxations on trade and travel in respect of China: (i) The United States was prepared to expedite visas for visitors from China to the United States. (ii) US currency controls would be relaxed to permit the use of dollars by China. (iii) Restrictions would be ended on American companies providing fuel to ships or aircraft proceeding to or from China, except on Chinese carriers bound to or from North Vietnam, North Korea or Cuba. (iv) US vessels or aircraft could carry Chinese cargoes between non-Chinese ports, and US-owned foreign-flag carriers could call at Chinese ports. The currency controls were duly lifted on May 7, 1971, thereby enabling the resumption of direct trade between the United States and China for the first time since December 1950.

Nixon further relaxed restrictions on trade with China on June 10, 1971, when the 21-year embargo on the export of non-strategic goods to China was ended. The effect of the announcement was greatly to liberalize the conditions of trade with China, including the importation of Chinese goods into the USA. Direct telephone links between the two countries were resumed on Sept. 16, 1971 (having been deactivated in 1968). The Chinese authorities on Dec. 13, 1971, released two US detainees, one of them a pilot shot down over north-east China in 1952.

Admission of People's Republic of China to United Nations—Expulsion of Taiwan (October 1971)

During its 26th session, the UN General Assembly on Oct. 25, 1971, adopted, by 76 votes to 35 with 17 abstentions, a resolution to admit the

People's Republic of China to membership of the United Nations, including a permanent seat on the Security Council; at the same time it voted to expel "forthwith" the Chinese Nationalist regime on Taiwan—the first time in the history of the Organization that a member had been expelled. The resolution to this effect was presented by Albania with the co-sponsorship of 22 other countries, and was adopted at the end of a six-day debate on the Chinese representation question. The Soviet Union voted in favour of the admission of Communist China.

Before adopting this resolution, the Assembly had rejected a US resolution, co-sponsored by 18 other countries, asking the Assembly to rule that any proposal to deprive the Republic of China (i.e. Taiwan) of representation in the United Nations was an "important question" requiring, under the UN Charter, a two-thirds majority for adoption. The voting on this resolution was 55 in favour and 59 against (including the Soviet Union), with 15 abstentions.

The US Secretary of State, William Rogers, had made it clear on Aug. 2, 1971, that at the forthcoming General Assembly session the United States would support the entry of the People's Republic of China into the UN, while opposing any action to deprive Taiwan of representation. This standpoint was reiterated in a memorandum which the US representative at the United Nations, George Bush, sent on Aug. 17 to U Thant (Secretary-General) asking that the General Assembly, in debating the Chinese representation question, should "take cognizance of the existence of both the People's Republic of China and the Republic of China and reflect that incontestable reality in the manner in which it makes provision for China's representation". The US memorandum continued:

"In so doing, the United Nations should not be required to take a position on the respective conflicting claims of the People's Republic of China or the Republic of China pending a peaceful resolution of the matter as called for by the Charter. Thus the People's Republic of China should be represented and at the same time provision should be made that the Republic of China is not deprived of its representation. If it is to succeed in its peace-keeping role and in advancing the well-being of mankind, the United Nations should deal with the question of the representation of China in a just and realistic manner."

At an impromptu press conference on Sept. 16, 1971, President Nixon said that the US decision to vote for the admission of the People's Republic of China to the UN, with a seat on the Security Council, "reflects the realities of the situation". At the same time he emphasized that the United States would "vote against the expulsion of the Republic of China" and "work as effectively as we can to accomplish this goal". The Foreign Ministry in Beijing, however, had previously emphasized on Aug. 20 that the People's Republic of China would not enter the United Nations unless the "Chiang Kai-shek clique" was expelled from the Organization, the statement saying:

"The Chinese Government solemnly declares that the Chinese people and Government firmly oppose 'two Chinas', 'one China, one Taiwan', or any similar absurdities; firmly opposes the fallacy that 'the status of Taiwan remains to be determined'; and firmly opposes the scheme of creating an 'independent Taiwan'.

Should a similar situation occur in the United Nations, the Government of the People's Republic of China will have absolutely nothing to do with the United Nations. This just stand of the Chinese Government is unshakable. No schemes of 'two Chinas,' 'one China, one Taiwan', or the like pushed by anyone at any time or in any form will ever succeed. The Taiwan President Chiang Kai-shek's clique must be expelled from the United Nations and all its organs, and all the legitimate rights of the People's Republic of China in the United Nations must be completely restored."

This statement was the first official Chinese reaction to the US Government's "two Chinas" policy in the UN, although the New China News Agency had previously made a strongly-worded attack on Mr Rogers's statement of Aug. 2, 1971. [For later developments involving the "Taiwan factor", see pp. 117–19 below.]

President Nixon's Visit to China (February 1972)—The Shanghai Communiqué

President Nixon visited China on Feb. 21–28, 1972, accompanied by William Rogers, the Secretary of State, and Dr Henry Kissinger, Assistant to the President for National Security Affairs. On his arrival in Beijing, Nixon met Zhou Enlai and later, accompanied by Kissinger, was received by Chairman Mao for an hour-long talk. No details were given beyond a statement that the discussions had been "serious and frank".

Nixon and Zhou met for lengthy talks several times during the remainder of the visit, and the presidential party made a number of trips to notable sites in various parts of China. Rogers had several meetings with the Chinese Foreign Minister, Ji Pengfei. Whereas little publicity had at first been given to Nixon's arrival, the leading Chinese newspapers on Feb. 22, 1972, and on subsequent days prominently featured the meeting between the US President and Chairman Mao. The visit ended on Feb. 27, 1972, in Shanghai, where Nixon and Zhou concluded their talks.

At the banquet given for him on that day in Shanghai, Nixon described his visit to China as a "week that changed the world". A lengthy communiqué was issued on Feb. 27, 1972, which stated that "the Taiwan question is the crucial question obstructing the normalization of relations between China and the United States" and that the US would "progressively withdraw its forces and military installations on Taiwan as the tension in the area diminishes", with complete withdrawal as the "ultimate objective". The communiqué set out in detail the positions of China and the United States on important international questions in addition to detailing those aspects on which there was bilateral agreement. Apart from undertakings to develop "contacts and exchanges" in the fields of science, technology, culture, journalism and sport, it was also agreed that China and the United States would "stay in contact through various channels, including the sending of a senior US representative to Beijing from time to time for concrete consultations to further the normalization of relations between the two countries and continue to exchange views on issues of common interest". Finally, the communiqué expressed the hope of both sides that President Nixon's visit would "open new prospects for the relations between the two countries".

The White House announced on March 10, 1972, that the United States and China had designated their ambassadors in Paris to serve as the diplomatic channel agreed upon by President Nixon and Zhou Enlai for continuing contacts between the two countries. The two ambassadors then immediately proceeded to hold their first meetings at the Chinese and US embassies.

The 22-year-old restrictions on travel to China by US ships and aircraft were lifted by Nixon on Nov. 22, 1972. It was stated that this action reflected the US Administration's intention to "facilitate the development of trade and contacts between the American and Chinese people" in the spirit of the Shanghai communiqué. Chinese permission was still required before each American ship or aircraft could travel to China.

Dr Kissinger's Missions to Beijing (February and November 1973)

Dr Kissinger arrived in Beijing on Feb. 15, 1973, and during his five-day visit had talks with Zhou Enlai, Ji Pengfei (Foreign Minister) and Jiao Guanhua (Deputy Foreign Minister). On Feb. 17 Kissinger had a two-hour meeting with Chairman Mao.

A brief communiqué issued at the end of the visit said that the talks had been "conducted in an unconstrained atmosphere and were earnest, frank and constructive". In addition to agreeing to broaden contacts in all fields, including trade, the two countries had agreed to establish a liaison office in each other's capitals. Both sides reaffirmed the principles of the Shanghai communiqué, and "agreed that the time was appropriate for accelerating the normalization of relations".

In a statement in Washington on Feb. 22, 1973, after his return, Kissinger said that contacts between the United States and China "have moved from hostility to normalization", adding that the liaison offices to be set up in Beijing and Washington would constitute the closest formal contact the two countries could have short of full diplomatic relations. (Three US pilots, detained by the Chinese authorities since 1952 and the Vietnam war, were released on March 12 and 15.)

Kissinger (now Secretary of State) again visited China from Nov. 10–14, 1973, when he had further discussions with Zhou Enlai and Ji Bengfei, as well as a two-hour meeting with Chairman Mao. Speaking on Nov. 14 at a banquet given in his honour, Kissinger expressed the view that "no matter what happens in the United States in the future, friendship with the People's Republic of China is one of the constant factors of American foreign policy".

At the end of Kissinger's visit to Beijing both sides again repeated their commitment to the principles established in the Shanghai communiqué. The US side reaffirmed its acknowledgment "that there is but one China and that Taiwan is a part of China", while the Chinese side "reiterated that the normalization of relations between China and the United States can only be realized on the basis of confirming the principle of 'one China'".

The final communiqué added: "Both sides noted with satisfaction that the liaison offices in Beijing and Washington are functioning smoothly. Both sides agreed that the scope of the functions of the liaison offices should continue to be expanded." The rapid development of trade between the two countries during the past year was noted, and both sides stated they would continue their efforts to promote the normalization of relations.

President Ford's Visit to China (December 1975)

President Gerald Ford, accompanied by Dr Henry Kissinger, visited Beijing from Dec. 1 to 5, 1975, for talks with Deng Xiaoping, the Chinese Deputy Premier. He also had a meeting with Chairman Mao. Details of the visit had been arranged by Dr Kissinger during discussions in Beijing on Oct. 19–23, 1975. In the course of the visit references to differences between China and the United States over détente with the Soviet Union were made by Deng and Ford at a banquet held on Dec. 1.

Deng, dealing with the international situation, said: "The basic contradictions in the world are sharpening daily. The factors for both revolution and war are clearly increasing . . ., the contention for world hegemony is intensifying, and strategically Europe is the focus of this contention. Such continued contention is bound to lead to a new world war. . . . Today it is the country which most zealously preaches peace that is the most dangerous source of war. Rhetoric about 'détente' cannot cover up the stark reality of the growing danger of war. . . . We consider that it is in the interest of the people of the world to point out the source and danger of the war, dispel illusions of peace, fully arouse the people, make all preparations, unite with all the forces that can be united with and wage a tit-for-tat struggle."

President Ford, pointing out that in the international field China and the United States had a "mutual interest in seeing that the world is not dominated by military force or pressure", continued: "In pursuing our objectives each of us will, of course, determine our policies and methods according to our differing positions in the world and our perceptions of our respective national interests. . . . The United States will strive both to reduce the dangers and to explore new opportunities for peace without illusions. The current situation requires strength, vigilance and firmness. But we will also continue our efforts to achieve a more peaceful world even as we remain determined to resist any actions that threaten the independence and well-being of others."

Although no communiqué was issued at the conclusion of the talks, Dr Kissinger told a press conference on Dec. 5, 1975, that they had been beneficial because they enabled the "leaders of both sides to understand the perceptions of the other and to see where parallel policies can be pursued". Although Europe and Angola were areas of "parallel policies", it was clear that it would take time to resolve the basic issue of continuing US recognition of the Nationalist Chinese Government on Taiwan, that the two Governments had not yet bridged their differences over the American military presence in South Korea, and that attempts to broaden trade, cultural and scientific exchanges would proceed through normal channels.

Commenting on his talks in Beijing, Ford said: "We reaffirmed that we share very important areas of concern and agreement. . . . We share opposition to any form of hegemony in Asia or in any other part of the world. I reaffirmed the determination of the United States to complete the normalization of relations with the People's Republic of China on the basis of the Shanghai communiqué. . . . Our relationship is becoming a permanent feature of the international political landscape".

The State Department announced on Dec. 5, 1975, that the Chinese authorities, as a gesture of friendship, were returning the ashes of two US Navy airmen shot down during the Vietnam war.

Normalization of US–Chinese Relations (December 1978)—Soviet Reactions

After the December 1975 visit to China of Ford and Kissinger, no member of the US Administration went to China until August 1977, when Cyrus Vance, the new Secretary of State, held talks in Beijing with Huang Hua (now Foreign Minister), Deng Xiaoping (who had recently been reinstated as a Deputy Premier) and Chairman Hua Guofeng. The interruption in contacts between the two Governments had been largely due to the major political changes in China which had followed the death of Zhou Enlai and Chairman Mao in 1976, and to the election of Jimmy Carter as President of the USA at the end of that year.

Vance again met Huang Hua on Sept. 28, 1977, in New York. It was later revealed that they had formally agreed at this meeting to enter into discussions leading to the establishment of diplomatic relations. The following year, Zbigniew Brzezinski (Carter's Assistant for National Security Affairs) visited Beijing on May 20–23, 1978, for talks with the Chinese leadership. He announced that "the United States has made up its mind on the issue" of normalization of relations.

While in Beijing Brzezinski made a number of statements which were regarded as strongly anti-Soviet in tone. At a banquet on May 20, 1978, he said: "We recognize and share China's resolve to resist the efforts of any nation which seeks to establish global or regional hegemony. . . . Only those aspiring to dominate others have any reason to fear further development of US–Chinese relations." In informal remarks made publicly and reported in the press he referred to the Soviet Union as "the barbarians" and "the polar bear". *Izvestia* commented on Aug. 4: "None of his anti-Soviet statements made there has been contradicted by the US Government. . . . We have unequivocally pointed out that forming a bloc with China on the basis of anti-Sovietism will close the possibilities for co-operation with the United States in reducing the danger of a nuclear war and limiting arms. Washington should give serious thought to this instead of thinking in terms of petty anti-Soviet scheming. . . ."

During the following months a number of senior US officials visited China for discussions leading to agreements on educational and scientific exchanges, energy projects and agricultural development. Moreover, Brzezinski's visit to Beijing gave added impetus towards normalization of relations, and serious negotiations began in mid-July 1978. This was helped by suggestions from the Chinese Government that it was prepared to adopt a more flexible attitude towards the Taiwan question.

Deng Xiaoping said on Nov. 29, 1978, that the Chinese Government recognized that Taiwan's political system differed from that of the mainland, and would seek a solution which took account of that reality. China wished to discuss with the Taiwan authorities conditions for their return, but it could not give a pledge to abstain from the use of force, as such a pledge would make the Taiwan authorities refuse to negotiate. He indicated that China would not drop its three conditions for normal relations with the United States—severance of diplomatic relations with Taiwan, cancellation of all existing treaties with Taiwan and withdrawal of all US forces from the island—but the United States could continue less formal links with Taiwan.

US Government officials stated on Dec. 16, 1978, that the United States had acceded to the three basic Chinese conditions on US relations with Taiwan, but had also insisted on three conditions of its own: (i) that the mutual defence treaty with Taiwan of 1954 would not be terminated immediately, but after a year's notice had been given, as provided in the treaty itself; (ii) that the United States would say that it expected the Taiwan issue to be settled peacefully, and that China would not make any statement to the contrary; and (iii) that the United States would continue the sale of arms to Taiwan even after normalization of relations with China and termination of the mutual defence treaty.

The proposed continuation of US arms supplies to Taiwan constituted the main obstacle to an agreement on normalization of US–Chinese relations. However, on Dec. 13, 1978, Deng reportedly stated that, although the Chinese Government still insisted that arms supplies to Taiwan should be ended, it no longer made this a prerequisite to normal relations.

The US Government had announced on Nov. 6, 1978, that it had decided to offer the Taiwan authorities fighter jets for strictly defensive use, and would not (as requested by Taiwan) supply fighters which could strike the Chinese mainland. Cyrus Vance on Nov. 3 indicated a change in US policy towards arms sales by other NATO members to China; stating that each nation "must decide for itself" on the matter, he implied that the United States would not now discourage such sales.

Boris Ponomaryov, then a candidate member of the Soviet Communist Party politburo and a member of its secretariat, said during talks with a visiting US senatorial delegation on Nov. 15, 1978, that the normalization of relations between the United States and China was "a legitimate process", but added: "What we do not understand is how one can speak of aspirations to peace and the necessity of international understanding and at the same time arm China, creating a dangerous military centre from which the fires of war can not only spread in Asia but attain world dimensions."

The establishment of diplomatic relations between the United States and China was announced in a joint communiqué issued on Dec. 15–16, 1978. It stated: "The People's Republic of China [PRC] and the USA have agreed to recognize each other and to establish diplomatic relations as of Jan. 1, 1979. The USA recognizes the Government of the PRC as the sole legal government of China. Within this context, the people of the USA will maintain cultural, commercial and other unofficial relations with the people of Taiwan."

The communiqué reaffirmed the principles agreed in the Shanghai communiqué, and also included the following clauses:

(1) "Neither should seek hegemony in the Asia-Pacific region or in any other region of the world and each is opposed to efforts by any other country or group of countries to establish such hegemony.

(2) "Neither is prepared to negotiate on behalf of any third party or to enter into agreements or understandings with the other directed at other states.

(3) "The Government of the USA acknowledges the Chinese position that there is but one China and Taiwan is part of China.

(4) "The PRC and the USA will exchange ambassadors and establish embassies on March 1, 1979."

The two Governments at the same time issued statements defining their respective positions on the Taiwan question.

US Statement. "As of Jan. 1, 1979, the USA recognizes the PRC as the sole legal government of China. . . . On that same date . . . the USA will notify Taiwan that it is terminating diplomatic relations and that the mutual defence treaty between the USA and the Republic of China is being terminated in accordance with the provisions of the treaty. The USA also states that it will be withdrawing its remaining military personnel from Taiwan within four months. In the future, the American people and the people of Taiwan will maintain commercial, cultural and other relations without official government representation and without diplomatic relations. The Administration will seek adjustments to our laws and regulations to permit the maintenance of commercial, cultural and other non-governmental relationships in the new circumstances. . . . The USA continues to have an interest in the peaceful resolution of the Taiwan issue, and expects that the Taiwan issue will be settled peacefully by the Chinese themselves. . . ."

Chinese Statement. "As of Jan. 1, 1979, the PRC and the USA recognize each other and establish diplomatic relations. . . . As is known to all, the Government of the PRC is the sole legal government of China, and Taiwan is a part of China. The question of Taiwan was the crucial issue obstructing the normalization of relations between China and the USA. It has now been resolved between the two countries in the spirit of the Shanghai communiqué and through their joint efforts. . . . As for the way of bringing Taiwan back to the embrace of the motherland and reunifying the country, it is entirely China's internal affair. . . ."

Hua Guofeng announced the decision at a press conference in Beijing on Dec. 16, 1978. In reply to a question on the effect of the agreement on relations with the Soviet Union he said: "It is neither an alliance nor an axis. . . . It is out of the question that the normalization of relations is directed at any country. . . . Undoubtedly, of course, it is also favourable to the struggle of all peoples against hegemonism. We have mentioned our opposition to hegemonism in our joint communiqué. We oppose both big hegemony and small hegemony, both global hegemony and regional hegemony." (Chinese propaganda frequently accused the Soviet Union of seeking "global hegemony" and Vietnam of seeking "regional hegemony".)

In a message to President Brezhnev, President Carter gave an assurance that this step had no aims other than those of protecting world peace. A Tass report of Dec. 21, 1978, stated that Brezhnev had said in his reply that the establishment of normal relations between two sovereign states was a natural thing, but it was another question on what basis normalization took place and what aims were pursued by the parties. He drew attention to the fact that "the joint US–Chinese communiqué contains expressions whose direction is beyond doubt, if one bears in mind the usual vocabulary of the Chinese leaders" (i.e. the reference to "hegemony"). The Soviet Union, the letter concluded, would follow most closely what the development of US–Chinese relations was in practice, and from this would draw appropriate conclusions for Soviet policy.

The Soviet press in general adopted a sceptical attitude towards the agreement. *Pravda* on Dec. 19, 1978, welcomed an assurance given by

Carter on Dec. 15 that "we have no desire whatsoever to use our new relationship with China to the disadvantage of the Soviets or anyone else", but commented that "time will show if these words accord with practical deeds and political actions". The army newspaper *Red Star* suggested on Dec. 17 that "the American imperialists, the Japanese *revanchards* and the Chinese great-power chauvinists" were preparing to form a military bloc, and accused China of seeking to provoke a war in which the United States and the Soviet Union would destroy each other, leaving the way clear for Chinese "world hegemony".

US Government spokesmen stated on Jan. 25, 1979, that President Carter had repeated in his reply to President Brezhnev that US recognition of China was not directed against the Soviet Union, and that it was not US policy to supply arms to Beijing. It was, however, the sovereign right of other countries to sell defensive weapons and of China to purchase them, and the United States would not prevent the export of defensive weapons to China by other countries.

During an official visit to the United States, Deng Xiaoping had talks with President Carter in Washington from Jan. 29 to Feb. 1, 1979, accompanied by Huang Hua. In addition, four agreements covering scientific, technological, educational and diplomatic exchanges were signed.

A joint communiqué issued at the end of the talks stated that the two sides had "agreed that in many areas they have common interests and share similar points of view", and had "also discussed those areas in which they have differing perspectives". The communiqué added: "They reaffirm that they are opposed to efforts by any country or group of countries to establish hegemony or domination over others. . . ."

During his visit Deng caused considerable embarrassment to the US Administration by certain public statements, in which he repeatedly attacked the Soviet Union. In an interview with the magazine *Time*, published on Jan. 29, 1979, he referred to the Soviet Union as "a hotbed of war", maintained that the United States was in "strategic retreat", and declared: "If we really want to be able to place curbs on the polar bear, the only thing is for us to unite."

In other remarks Deng said on Jan. 31 that the nuclear test ban treaty of 1963 and the strategic arms limitation agreements of 1972 and 1974 had had "no effect whatsoever on curtailing unbridled Soviet military build-up", and whilst denying that China was opposed to such agreements declared that "what is needed are more realistic steps, tactical steps—for instance, unity between the United States, China, Japan, Western Europe and other countries of the Third World, unity among these to deal with Soviet hegemonism".

On the Taiwan question he told a meeting of senators on Jan. 30: "So long as Taiwan is returned to the motherland and there is only one China, then we will fully respect the present realities of Taiwan. . . ." Early in the month the Chinese leadership had given further indications of a conciliatory attitude towards Taiwan.

A Tass despatch on Feb. 1, 1979, commenting on Deng's remarks, demanded clarification of the US Administration's attitude towards his "incendiary statements". *Pravda* said on Feb. 4: "The Soviet public cannot close its eyes to the fact that a broad forum was provided for the Chinese visitor, for slander against the USSR. It seems that anti-Sovietism is what is meant by the 'common interests' and 'identical views' mentioned in the American–Chinese communiqué. It would be interesting to know in what concrete aspects the views of Washington coincide with the policies of the leaders of Beijing. . . ."

At a press conference on Feb. 12, 1978, President Carter effectively dissociated himself from Deng's statements on the Soviet Union, and stressed his wish for good relations with the Soviet Union.

US–China Economic and Military Agreements (1979–June 1981)

Before 1979 trade between China and the United States had grown to a considerable level, although it had fluctuated substantially. The normalization of relations was expected to lead to a steady rise in trade between the two countries. Li Qiang, the Foreign Trade Minister, said on Dec. 18, 1978, that American companies would be able to open permanent offices in Beijing and enter into joint ventures with Chinese trade corporations. He added that China was prepared to accept foreign loans "as long as the conditions are appropriate". Among other things, this represented a fundamental departure from China's previous policy of "self-reliance".

The US Steel Corporation on Jan. 5, 1979, signed an agreement to build a $1,000 million ore processing complex at Ji-da Shan, in northern China, by 1983. On March 2, 1979, the US and Chinese Governments signed an agreement on the settlement of outstanding claims.

Four agreements on scientific and technological exchanges between the United States and China were signed in Beijing on May 8, 1979, while an agreement signed on June 12 provided for US aid to China in the construction of a 50,000 million electron-volt high-energy accelerator. A five-year agreement on co-operation in medicine and public health was signed on June 22, 1979.

A trade agreement under which the United States granted China most-favoured-nation status was signed on July 7, 1979, and entered into force on Feb. 1, 1980. As a result, US tariffs on Chinese goods were reduced from 20 per cent to around 10.5 per cent (i.e. in line with tariff rates for US trade with the non-Communist world).

Following the Soviet military intervention in Afghanistan in December 1979, Harold Brown, then US Defence Secretary, visited Beijing on Jan. 5–9, 1980. He had talks with his Chinese counterpart, Marshal Xu Xiangqian, with Deputy Premiers Deng Xiaoping and Geng Biao and with Foreign Minister Huang Hua. During the visit Brown implied that China and the United States could co-operate in the area of defence as well as of diplomacy, although no joint steps were planned to strengthen "other nations in the region" to deal with the Soviet presence in Afghanistan (about which the two countries held similar views).

Brown stated on Jan. 10, 1980, that the United States would provide China with new technology but not weapons, although some of the technology could be adapted for military purposes. On Jan. 24 the Defence Department announced that the United States was now prepared to sell military equipment (excluding offensive weapons) to China. It was disclosed that Brown had given an undertaking about such sales during his visit to Beijing. Agreements on certain deliveries were announced during visits to Washington in mid-March by Zhang Wenjin, the Chinese Deputy Foreign

Minister, and in late May by Geng Biao. By September 1980 the US Administration had approved over 400 export licences for advanced electronic and military support equipment, and it was also reported that China was prepared to sell the United States scarce metals with a strategic importance.

On Jan. 24, 1980, the USA and China also signed a memorandum of understanding to build a ground-receiving station for data transmitted by the US Landsat-D satellite system, as announced during Brown's visit to China. The Defence Department admitted that, although the system was designed for civilian purposes, the technology involved could have military applications.

An agreement was signed in March 1980 opening the way for large-scale US assistance in the development of the Chinese hydroelectric industry, resulting from a visit to China by Vice-President Walter Mondale in August 1979.

President Carter authorized the US Export-Import Bank on April 4, 1980, to finance loans to China to help the sale of American goods there. An agreement between the Bank of China and the Export-Import Bank was signed in May 1981. Agreements on consular services, shipping and civil aviation were signed in Washington on Sept. 17, 1980. Annual quotas for six categories of Chinese textile imports into the United States for 1980–82 were agreed on the same date.

An agreement in Beijing on Oct. 22, 1980, provided that China would purchase 6,000,000 to 8,000,000 tonnes of US grain in each of the years 1981 to 1984. The total value of trade between the United States and China increased from $1,100 million in 1978 to $2,300 million in 1979, $4,800 million in 1980 and $5,500 million in 1981. The balance of trade was heavily in favour of the United States, the bulk of US exports to China consisting of agricultural products.

Alexander Haig, the new Secretary of State, paid an official visit to Beijing on June 14–17, 1981, during which he had talks with Huang Hua, Geng Biao (recently appointed Defence Minister) and Bo Yibo, then the Deputy Premier responsible for economic questions. He also met Zhao Ziyang (the Prime Minister), who accepted an invitation to visit the United States, and Deng Xiaoping. On June 16, 1981, Haig announced that the United States had agreed in principle to consider Chinese requests to buy arms, it being emphasized by the State Department the following day that any sales would be for defensive purposes only (although it was admitted that "some equipment obviously can be used for both defensive and offensive purposes").

The US Secretary of State said the talks had been productive, and emphasized President Reagan's wish to develop relations with China, to introduce legislation amending laws which "lump the People's Republic of China with the Soviet bloc", and to make changes in export control procedures to facilitate expanded trade with China. It had been agreed that a joint US–Chinese commission on commerce and trade would be established. Although he had not come to China "on an arms-selling mission", Haig added, "we did agree that exchanges between our respective defence establishments would continue to expand", and he said that a delegation of the People's Liberation Army would visit the United States in August, when arms sales would be discussed. There would, however, be "a substantial loosening-up of dual-use technology", i.e. items with both a commercial and a military potential, and munitions list restrictions would be removed.

Pravda described Haig's announcement on June 19, 1981, as "one more step towards widening the military-strategic aspects of Chinese–US rapprochement in an effort to use its anti-Soviet direction for a risky gamble aimed at the erosion of détente and the incitement of local conflicts threatening world peace". A fuller analysis appeared in *Pravda* on June 27 in an article signed "I. Alexandrov", the pseudonym often used for semi-official Soviet statements.

"The danger of China's militarization . . . lies in the fact that American weapons in the hands of the Chinese will be used in the first place against relatively small neighbouring countries, among which, incidentally, there are America's allies as well", the article declared, continuing: "It seems that China is being pushed towards the realization of its territorial claims in South-East and Southern Asia. . . . If Washington counts on using the rabid anti-Sovietism of the current Chinese leadership for the advance of the United States in its global anti-Soviet strategy, Beijing has its own interests to pursue, viz., to set the United States and the Soviet Union against each other so as to be able to dominate the world after a nuclear conflict which, according to Beijing's plans, will annihilate America and Europe but, possibly, spare some dozens or a few hundreds of millions of Chinese. . . . The teaming up of the USA and China on an anti-Soviet basis will be taken into account in an appropriate way in the USSR in the general context of Soviet–US and Soviet–Chinese relations."

The US National Broadcasting Corporation reported on June 16, 1981, that two electronic intelligence-gathering stations in north-western China, operating with American equipment and Chinese personnel, were monitoring Soviet missile tests in Central Asia. The report was supported on the following day by *The New York Times*, which stated, however, that there was only one station. Both US and Chinese official spokesmen refused to confirm or deny the story. Tass cited the reports on June 18 as evidence that the Chinese had assumed the "disgraceful role" of "voluntary agents of the imperialist intelligence services". (Deng Xiaoping had told a visiting delegation from the Senate foreign relations committee in April 1979 that China was prepared to accept US equipment for monitoring stations and to share the information with the United States, on condition that they were staffed solely by Chinese.)

The Taiwan Factor (1979–August 1982)

The Taiwan Relations Act, which enabled the United States to maintain unofficial relations with Taiwan through the American Institute in Taiwan, was passed by Congress on March 28–29, 1979, and was signed by President Carter on April 10 of that year. The Act stated that any attempt to resolve the Taiwan question by other than peaceful means would be considered "of grave concern to the United States", and required the United States "to assist the people on Taiwan to maintain a sufficient self-defence capability through the provision of arms of a defensive character". It also specified that in principle Taiwan might be regarded as an independent state for immigration purposes. The Act led to Communist Chinese protests, Deng Xiaoping stating on April 19 that it had come close to nullifying the normalization of US–Chinese relations.

The American Institute in Taiwan, which opened on April 16, 1979, was staffed by Foreign Service officers temporarily on leave from the State Department. According to an agreement signed with the Co-ordination Council for North

American Affairs (the Taiwanese non-governmental body in the United States), its members and those of the Co-ordination Council enjoyed diplomatic privileges.

Following the notice of termination of the mutual defence treaty with Taiwan, given on Jan. 1, 1979, the last members of the US Military Assistance Advisory Group in Taiwan left the island on April 30 of that year. The mutual defence agreement automatically expired on Jan. 1, 1980.

Harold Brown, the Defence Secretary, stated on Feb. 5, 1979, that the US would make no new commitments to supply arms to Taiwan during 1979, although weapons which the US had agreed already to sell would be delivered. However, the State Department announced on Jan. 3, 1980, that the US would sell certain defensive weapons to Taiwan. The New China News Agency (NCNA) on June 20, 1979, strongly condemned US arms sales to Taiwan as "a breach of the principles embodied in the agreement on the establishment of diplomatic relations".

Ronald Reagan, the Republican candidate in the 1980 presidential election, suggested during his campaign that the US should restore official relations with Taiwan. This drew sharp criticism from the Chinese media. A Chinese official statement on Reagan's election as President issued on Nov. 5, 1980, said: "We hope and expect that the new Administration will adhere to the principles set forth in the Shanghai communiqué and the communiqué on the establishment of diplomatic relations between China and the United States, so that Sino-US relations may continue to make good progress and grow stronger."

Relations between China and the United States were extremely strained during the early months of Reagan's Administration, due to his statements during the election campaign and certain other factors. A US offer on June 5, 1981, to permit China to purchase additional technology with potential military uses was rejected by the Chinese. The Foreign Ministry commented that "we would rather not buy any US weapon than agree to the continuous US interference in China's internal affairs by selling arms to Taiwan", adding that if the United States continued to sell weapons to Taiwan "we shall be compelled to make a strong response".

The visit which Alexander Haig, the US Secretary of State, made to Beijing on June 14–17, 1981, and which was principally concerned with trade and military relations with China [see above], also covered the Taiwan problem. At a press conference on June 16 after his talks with Chinese leaders, Haig said that he had explained that "unofficial" US relations with Taiwan would continue, "and this was understood" by the Chinese. He had also emphasized "our intent to promote the evolution of our bilateral relations with China on the basis of principles embodied in the joint communiqué on normalization". He had informed the Chinese Government of President Reagan's intention to treat China as "a friendly nation with which the United States is not allied but with which it shares many interests", and to take measures to facilitate an expansion of trade with China. In reply to questions, Haig said that he had discussed the question of arms sales to Taiwan, but refused to give details.

Despite Haig's visit, relations between China and the United States remained strained during the second half of 1981 and the early months of 1982 because of disagreements over the sale of US arms to Taiwan. In consequence, China did not take up Haig's offer on the sale of arms, and the proposed visit by a Chinese Army delegation did not take place. The Chinese Government put forward detailed proposals on Sept. 30, 1981, for the peaceful reunification of Taiwan with China, these being widely regarded as intended to influence the US Administration's attitude on the question of arms sales.

Zhao Ziyang met President Reagan at the Cancún summit conference in Mexico on Oct. 22–23, 1981, and was reported to have warned him that US–Chinese relations would be endangered if the USA persisted in selling arms to Taiwan. Huang Hua visited Washington on Oct. 29–30, 1981, for talks with Haig, during which he was reported to have demanded that the United States should not sell arms to Taiwan more sophisticated than those which it already possessed, that the quantity of deliveries should be reduced yearly, and that the United States should undertake to end arms supplies to Taiwan after a specified date. However, on Dec. 28, 1981, and Jan. 11, 1982, further US arms deals with Taiwan were announced, and it was subsequently revealed that the Administration had refused Chinese demands for a deadline on arms sales to Taiwan.

A Chinese note of March 26, 1982, protested against an immigration law signed by Reagan on Dec. 29 which allowed annually into the United States 20,000 immigrants from China and 20,000 from Taiwan. Beijing said that the law treated Taiwan as an independent state, and demanded that this "mistake" should be corrected.

Relations between China and the United States improved slightly during April and May 1982. Vice-President Bush visited Beijing on May 7–9, when he had talks with Huang Hua, Zhao Ziyang and Deng Xiaoping. He stated on May 8 that it had been agreed that representatives from both sides would continue to hold talks on the question of arms sales to Taiwan. It was reported that Bush had told the Chinese leaders that the United States would not agree to a deadline for ending all arms sales to Taiwan, but that it did not expect to sell arms to Taiwan indefinitely.

This point was echoed in a letter from Reagan to Zhao, dated April 5, 1982, and released on May 9, in which he also welcomed the Chinese peace proposal of Sept. 30, 1981. On the same day a letter from Reagan to Hu Yaobang (who had succeeded Hua Guofeng as party chairman in June 1981) was released, in which he reiterated his commitment to a "one China" policy. However, the United States also gave further indications during the summer of its support for the Taiwan Government.

Following prolonged negotiations through diplomatic channels in Beijing, a joint communiqué was issued by the two Governments on Aug. 17, 1982, stating that "the US Government understands and appreciates the Chinese policy of striving for a peaceful resolution of the Taiwan question, as indicated in China's message to compatriots in Taiwan issued on Jan. 1, 1979, and the nine-point proposal put forward by China on Sept. 30, 1981".

The communiqué continued: "The Government states that it does not seek to carry out a long-term policy of arms sales to Taiwan, that its arms sales to Taiwan will not exceed . . . the level of those supplied . . . since the establishment of diplomatic relations between the United States and China, and that it intends

gradually to reduce its sale of arms to Taiwan, leading . . . to a final resolution."
The two Governments undertook to adopt measures which would make possible a
full settlement of the issue.

The communiqué was interpreted differently by the two sides, being
regarded by the United States as an undertaking by China not to bring
about reunification by force, and by China as an assurance by the United
States to end arms sales to Taiwan within a limited period.

The Chinese on Aug. 21 and Oct. 10, 1982, again criticised expressions
of support for Taiwan by the United States. The controversy coincided
with the opening of consultations between China and the Soviet Union in
October, for the first time since 1979, and Chinese official statements in the
autumn of 1982 suggested that China was moving towards a neutral
position between the Soviet Union and the United States, whose policies
were equally described as "hegemonist"—a term which in recent years had
been reserved for the Soviet Union.

XI: SINO-SOVIET RELATIONS IN THE POST-MAO PERIOD, 1976–82

Chairman Mao's death in September 1976 was followed by a period of reaction and consolidation in China. The supporters of Deng Xiaoping gradually became the dominant grouping in the Chinese Government and important changes were initiated in China's internal policies. The Government's main task of modernizing the Chinese economy required political stability and party discipline. From the late 1970s China's "open-door" policy was pursued more vigorously in order to acquire advanced technology and economic skills. China normalized its relations with the USA on Jan. 1, 1979 [see Chapter X], and made significant progress in developing its contacts with Japan and Western Europe.

These changes were accompanied by a decline in ideological rhetoric condemning the "revisionist" Soviet Union. Soviet hopes for further rapprochement, however, were blocked by continuing Chinese fears of Soviet "hegemonist" intentions. The "three worlds" theory, which dominated Chinese foreign policy statements in the late 1970s, stated that the Soviet Union was the main threat to China's security. During this period, the two countries clashed over their support for opposite sides in the renewed conflict in Indo-China between Vietnam and Kampuchea, and over the Soviet intervention in Afghanistan in December 1979.

In the early 1980s, however, there were signs of an improvement in relations, when the election of Ronald Reagan as President of the USA in 1980 disrupted the comparatively smooth development of Sino-US relations [see Chapter X] and made China more responsive to Soviet wishes to develop bilateral contacts.

Chinese Internal Developments following Mao's Death (September 1976–July 1977)

The death of Chairman Mao on Sept. 9, 1976, brought to a head the conflict between the "radicals" and "moderates" inside the CPC. At first, no faction in the leadership appeared to be dominant, but on Oct. 7 Hua Guofeng was elected by the politburo to succeed Mao as chairman of the party and its military commission. At the same time, the four leading radicals, Zhang Chunqiao, Jiang Qing, Yao Wenyuan, and Wang Hongwen (referred to in the Chinese press as the "gang of four") were arrested on charges of plotting to seize power. The moderates' victory apparently met with little opposition, although troops had to be called in to restore order in a few areas such as the province of Fujian.

In the subsequent months, a campaign was launched denouncing the gang of four. They were charged primarily with conspiring "tirelessly to overthrow a large number of leading cadres in the party, government and army at the central and local levels and usurping party and state leadership". They were criticized for adopting "wrong" policies both during the Cultural Revolution and subsequently when they had impeded China's development and modernization. In later propaganda it was argued that despite their apparent "leftism", they were in fact "rightist" and emphasis was laid on their former association with Marshal Lin Biao. One article in May 1977 alleged that Zhang had become a "follower of Khrushchev's revisionism" in 1954 and had advocated an extreme leftist policy in 1958 to "conceal his counter-revolutionary" nature. In their external dealings they allegedly "fawned on foreigners and maintained illicit foreign relations", involving them in "capitulating to imperialism". The campaign was extended to attack supporters of the gang of four in the provinces. An initial purge in October 1976 was followed by two others in March and October 1977, which resulted in changes in the leadership of many provincial Communist Party organizations.

The gang of four were expelled from the party at a plenary session of the central committee held in Beijing on July 16–21, 1977, which condemned them as "bourgeois careerist conspirators and counter-revolutionary double-dealers". (In January 1981, Zhang and Jiang received death sentences, later commuted to life imprisonment, while Wang was given a life sentence and Yao was sentenced to 20 years.) The same meeting consolidated the position of the moderates by confirming Hua's appointment as chairman of the party and by restoring Deng Xiaoping to the posts from which he had been dismissed in 1976.

Soviet Initiative and Resumption of Polemics (October 1976–April 1977)

Soviet propaganda had consistently attributed the Chinese regime's hostile policy towards the Soviet Union to the influence of Chairman Mao and the "radical" group within the party and had maintained that the "moderate" section of the leadership did not support it. The death of Chairman Mao and the changes in the leadership of the CPC therefore aroused hopes of a rapprochement with China.

Soviet commentators had pointed out that the campaign launched in 1975 against "capitulationists" had attacked advocates of a rapprochement. It was also suggested that the release of a Soviet helicopter crew in December 1975 [see page 148] was intended as a first step towards a more conciliatory policy, but that this process had been reversed by the death of Zhou Enlai in the following month and the resurgence of radical pressure causing the disgrace of Deng Xiaoping. Support for a rapprochement was believed to be particularly strong among the Chinese military leadership. A Tass commentator wrote in February 1976:
"Views in favour of a realistic domestic and foreign policy . . . are gaining currency among the leading personnel. These trends are linked with the position of the so-called moderate or pragmatic line, which is connected with representatives of the administrative and military machine. . . . The course of events in China has disclosed a section of party and government leaders who have not yet compromised themselves by taking action against the 'left' and who show loyalty to Mao Zedong, but whose political records show them to belong to the same category of leading workers of the older and the next generation as the 'moderates'. Hua Guofeng, for example, is named as a representative of this section in the political bureau." Furthermore, a documentary film on China shown on Soviet television on Feb. 3, 1976, had violently attacked Chairman Mao and his wife Jiang Qing but contained no attacks on Zhou.

After Mao's death in September 1976, the Soviet Union made a number of conciliatory gestures with a view to encouraging better relations. The Soviet media suspended all anti-Chinese propaganda and the Soviet Communist Party sent a short message of condolence to the Chinese party which was believed to be the first direct communication between the two parties for several years. This, however, was rejected on Sept. 14 and not published in the Chinese press on the grounds that there were no relations between the two parties (as distinct from the diplomatic relations which continued to exist between the two countries). However, the Chinese press did briefly report that two Soviet Vice-Premiers, Kirill Mazurov and Ivan Arkhipov, and Andrei Gromyko (the Soviet Foreign Minister) had signed a book of condolence at the Chinese embassy in Moscow on Sept. 13.

An article by "I. Alexandrov" published in *Pravda* on Oct. 1, 1976, contained no reference to Chairman Mao, and declared: "Our country is ready to hold talks with China on the settlement of frontier problems without any prior conditions. The Soviet Union has never had and has no economic, territorial or other claims on China. . . . We believe that there are no problems in the relations between our states that cannot be resolved, given mutual desire and a spirit of good-neighbourliness, mutual benefit and consideration for each other's interests." The Soviet Government's message on the Chinese national day was couched in similar friendly terms.

The arrest of Jiang Qing and the other "radical" leaders in October 1976 was welcomed in the Soviet Union. Although the Soviet press abstained from all comment on internal developments in China, the Soviet journalist Viktor Louis, who is believed to reflect official Soviet views, commented in the London *Evening News* on Oct. 12 that "the majority of the leaders hostile to the Soviet Union have been removed from power". In his first public statements on relations with China since Chairman Mao's death, Brezhnev called in the second half of October 1976 for a reconciliation between the two countries.

At a banquet in honour of President Tsedenbal of Mongolia, Brezhnev said on Oct. 18, 1976: "We have of course given particular attention to the problems of Asia, including the most complicated problems. Can they be solved? We answer this question in the affirmative. It is enough to build relations with perseverance step by step, on the principles of good-neighbourliness and real respect for the equality and sovereignty of other states, to look to the future and to carry on a constructive dialogue. Every country which approaches the problem in this way can count on our understanding." President Tsedenbal, whose criticisms of China in the past had often been more marked than those of the Soviet Union, said that "perspectives for the consolidation of peace and security are opening up before the Asian continent".

Addressing the Communist Party's central committee on Oct. 25, 1976, Brezhnev said: "China is the scene of a complex internal political development. At present it is difficult to foresee its political line. But it is already clear that the foreign policy pursued by Beijing for the last 15 years is largely discredited throughout the world. The improvement of our relations with China is our constant concern. We stand firmly by the principles of equality of rights, respect for sovereignty and territorial integrity, non-interference in each other's internal affairs and non-resort to force. In other words, we are ready to normalize our relations with China on a basis of peaceful co-existence. I must emphasize that we consider there are no problems in relations between the USSR and the People's Republic of China which cannot be solved in a spirit of good-neighbourliness. We shall continue to act in this spirit. Everything will depend on the position adopted by the other side."

The changes in the Chinese leadership, however, did not bring about the expected modification in the nature of the anti-Soviet propaganda. A message sent by Brezhnev on Oct. 27, 1976, to congratulate Hua on his appointment as chairman of the CPC was rejected, and an official statement issued by the Chinese Government on Nov. 2 said that there would be no change in China's policy of opposing the "hegemonism" of the two super-powers.

A Chinese Foreign Ministry official told visiting French journalists on Nov. 1, 1976: "If the USSR wants polemics to stop it must admit all its errors since 1960 and change its line. . . . In practice, can there be peace with the USSR? In our opinion that is impossible." *Tass* commented on the same day that "anti-Soviet diatribes" continued in the Chinese press and, referring to China's boycott of the vote to admit Soviet-backed Angola to UNESCO on Nov. 1, 1976, asserted that the Chinese representative had made an "absurd declaration" opposing the admission. These were the first criticisms of China published in the Soviet press since Mao's death, no reports having appeared of violently anti-Soviet speeches by the Chinese representative in the UN General Assembly that autumn.

At a meeting held in Moscow on Nov. 5, 1976, to celebrate the anniversary of the Russian Revolution, Fyodor Kulakov (a member of the Soviet politburo) described the fact that peaceful relations with China had been interrupted for nearly 15 years as "unjustified and unnatural"; the meeting was the first of the kind for 10 years at which the speaker had not attacked China and the Chinese diplomatic representative had not walked out. Li Xiannian, a Chinese Deputy Premier, however, explicitly rejected the Soviet overtures on Nov. 15 in his speech at a banquet in honour of President Bokassa of the Central African Republic. "Social imperialism", he declared, "while continuing to slander and threaten China, has not stopped putting on a show of détente in relations between us, with the aim of blurring the difference in principle between Marxism and revisionism. It has even gone so far as insolently to demand that our country should change its policy. That is wishful thinking and day-dreaming." The Soviet ambassador, Vasily Tolstikov, walked out during his speech.

In late 1976 and early 1977, an attempt to resume Sino-Soviet border negotiations failed [see Chapter XII] and Soviet press reports complained about continuing anti-Soviet polemics by the Chinese. Articles on Dec. 30, 1976, criticized Chairman Hua's "diatribes against social imperialism" at a national agricultural conference held in Beijing in late December, which were seen as indirect attacks on the Soviet Union. A long article in *Pravda* on Feb. 10, 1977, again protested strongly against anti-Soviet attacks, which it said "only play into the hands of the enemies of socialism and the detractors of international détente". Nevertheless, attacks on the Soviet Union in the Chinese press continued unabated and in April 1977 Soviet polemics against China were resumed.

The first public attack on China by a high-ranking Soviet Communist Party leader for several months was made on April 22, 1977, by Mikhail Zimyanin, a member of the party's secretariat, who accused China of "building up international tension" and "allying with the most reactionary forces". An article signed "I. Alexandrov", which was published in *Pravda* on May 14, described the Chinese leaders as publicly advocating "a new world slaughter" and pursuing "expansionist plans" in the Pacific and South-East Asia. A Soviet note of May 19 protested against the anti-Soviet propaganda campaign in China, and complained that "all our moves aimed at establishing a normal situation and favourable premises for improving inter-state relations are being turned against the Soviet Union with the help of demagogic tricks".

Conciliatory Chinese Actions amid Renewed anti-Soviet Polemics (June–November 1977)

Chinese propaganda against the Soviet Union continued in late 1977. The new Soviet constitution approved by the Supreme Soviet on Oct. 7, 1977, was denounced by the *People's Daily* as a "despicable betrayal of Marxism-Leninism". The main thrust of Chinese polemics was directed against the Soviet Union's expansionist foreign policy, especially in Africa, which was depicted as presenting the greatest danger to world peace. These themes were highlighted in Hua Guofeng's report to the 11th CPC congress (held in Beijing on Aug. 12–18, 1977), which laid great emphasis on the "three worlds" theory [see below] and reiterated Chinese attacks on the Soviet regime for its "revisionist" nature.

Hua said: "The Soviet leading clique has betrayed Marxism-Leninism. Restoring capitalism and enforcing fascist dictatorship at home and pushing hegemonism and perpetrating aggression and expansion abroad, it has brought about the degeneration of the Soviet Union, which has become a social-imperialist country. Our debates with the clique on matters of principle will go on for a long time. We will, of course, continue to wage a tit-for-tat struggle against its hegemonism. At the same time, we have always held that China and the Soviet Union should maintain normal state relations on the basis of the five principles of peaceful co-existence. The Soviet leading clique has not shown one iota of good faith about improving the state relations between the two countries. Not only has this clique made it impossible to achieve anything in the negotiations on the Sino-Soviet boundary question, which have been dragging on for eight years now; it has also whipped up one anti-China wave after another to extricate itself from its dilemmas at home and abroad and divert attention by making a feint to the east in order to attack in the west. It has been trying by hook or by crook to force us to change the Marxist-Leninist line laid down by Chairman Mao. This is pure daydreaming. It is the Soviet leading clique, and nobody else, that has led Sino-Soviet state relations up a blind alley. If it really has any desire to improve the state relations between the two countries, this clique should prove it by concrete deeds. . . ."

In earlier passages, Hua accused the Soviet Union of "working overtime to push their global offensive strategy. They want to pocket all Europe, Asia and Africa. Soviet–US contention extends to every corner of the world, but its focus is still Europe. The Soviet Union has massed its troops in Eastern Europe, and at the same time accelerated its plunder of strategic resources and its scramble for strategic bases in Africa and the Middle East, in an attempt to encircle Europe from the flanks by seizing the Persian Gulf in the east, thrusting round the Cape of Good Hope in the south and blocking the main navigation routes of the Atlantic Ocean in the west." Hua said that any policy of détente would "merely abet the expansionist ambitions of the Soviet revisionists" and hasten the outbreak of war, which, he claimed, in the current world situation was "inevitable".

Commenting on Hua's report on Aug. 26, 1977, Tass said: "The congress set the aim to the people of continuing the militarization of the country. . . . This is justified, in the first place, by the fictitious and non-existent 'threat' to China from the Soviet Union. . . . The policy of détente is sharply attacked and the thesis of the 'inevitability of war' is upheld. In other words, the policy of war and the glorification of war continues. . . . Events in the world are explained in such a way as to suit the old Maoist concept of 'three worlds', which, as is known, was used and, going by the report, is still being used to justify Beijing's teaming up with the most reactionary forces in the world for the struggle against the USSR and the world socialist community. . . ."

Chinese actions in late 1977, however, appeared to belie the hostile tone of official Chinese statements. Wang Youping was appointed ambassador in Moscow in June 1977, after the post had been vacant since March 1976. The Chinese Government's message to the Soviet Government on the 60th anniversary of the Russian Revolution on Nov. 7, 1977, stated that "the differences between China and the Soviet Union should not hinder the two countries from maintaining and developing normal state relations on the basis of the five principles of peaceful co-existence", and the Foreign Minister, Huang Hua, attended a reception at the Soviet embassy to mark the occasion; this was believed to be the first visit to the Soviet embassy for such a function by a senior Chinese minister since 1965.

However, a joint editorial published in the *People's Daily*, *Red Flag* and the *Liberation Army Daily* on Nov. 7 was violently hostile in tone: "The Soviet revisionist renegade clique," this editorial declared, "has departed from the road of the October Revolution, betrayed Marxism-Leninism and changed the socialist course of the Soviet Union. This clique has changed the proletarian party founded by Lenin into a fascist party of the bureaucrat-monopoly bourgeoisie. . . . Turning traitor to proletarian internationalism and trying to realize hegemonism with all its might, it has turned the Soviet Union into an imperialist super-power, one of the biggest international exploiters and oppressors and the most dangerous hotbed of a new world war. . . ."

China's "Three Worlds" Theory (1977–78)

Chinese foreign policy statements in 1977–78 were dominated by the "three worlds" theory which analysed the international situation in terms of: the First World consisting of the Soviet Union and the USA, the Third World made up of the developing countries in Africa, Latin America and Asia (including China), and the Second World composed of countries such as Japan, Canada and the European nations. The theory rejected the socialist-bloc conception of a world divided into developed capitalist countries, a socialist camp (including China) and the developing nations. China's alleged "deviation" from this more orthodox interpretation of the Marxist-Leninist theory of international class struggle led to a split between China and Albania in 1977 [see Chapter XIII].

According to Chinese sources, the theory was first formulated by Chairman Mao in conversation with the leader of a third-world country in February 1974. It was first publicly put forward by Deng Xiaoping on April 10, 1974, when addressing the sixth special session of the UN General Assembly, and Zhou Enlai also summarized it in his report to the fourth National People's Congress in January 1975. Little was heard of the theory in the following two years, when attention was focused on internal conflicts within the CPC, but it appeared to be closely associated with the moderate faction. The *People's Daily* alleged on Nov. 1, 1977, that the "gang of four" had "frantically opposed" the theory. Furthermore, it had first begun to figure prominently in the party's propaganda after the arrest of the "gang" in October 1976 and Deng's rehabilitation in 1977. The theory was given great prominence in the summer of 1977, being reaffirmed by Chairman Hua in his reports to the CPC congress in August and the fifth National People's Congress in January 1978.

The theory provided an ideological justification for the main features of the ruling moderate faction's foreign policy, in that it (i) upheld the moderates' contention that China's most important struggle was against the Soviet Union, which posed the greatest threat to world peace; (ii) justified China in seeking allies to counter Soviet world influence, including China's increasingly close ties with the USA and Western Europe; and (iii) buttressed China's independent status by placing China amongst the Third World "non-aligned" countries.

The fullest exposition of the theory appeared on Nov. 1, 1977, in a long article in the *People's Daily* entitled "Chairman Mao's theory of differentiation of the three worlds is a major contribution to Marxism-Leninism", which attempted to establish that the theory had orginated with Chairman Mao and that it was a logical development of the teachings of Marx, Engels, Lenin and Stalin. The article stated that after "a period of great upheaval, great division and great realignment the world's political forces are now faced with a new historical situation". It argued: "With the Khrushchev-Brezhnev clique's complete betrayal of the cause of communism, capitalism was restored in the Soviet Union, and it degenerated and became a social-imperialist country. True, there are China and the other socialist countries, but what was once the socialist camp no longer exists, nor do historical conditions necessitate its formation for a second time".

In the 1960s, continued the article, the Soviet Union developed its economic and military power, becoming "an imperialist super-power that threatened the world as the USA did". On the other hand, "US imperialism" was in "decline", sapped by the Vietnam war and faced with the growing economic power of Western Europe and Japan, so that "many countries in the imperialist camp no longer took their cue from the USA and even openly stood up to it". During the same period, "through hard struggles, most of the colonial and semi-colonial countries in Asia, Africa and Latin America successfully declared independence. . . . China suffered from imperialist oppression for a long time . . . [and] belongs to the Third World". The Third World, the article claimed, was "the main force in the world-wide struggle against the hegemonism of the two super-powers", giving "support and impetus . . . to the workers' movement in the developed countries" which had been undermined by "the Soviet ruling clique's betrayal, the spread of revisionist ideology and the splits in the ranks of the working class".

These changes, the article claimed, had created a world situation of the following sort: "The two imperialist super-powers, the Soviet Union and the United States, constitute the First World. They have become the biggest international exploiters, oppressors and aggressors and the common enemies of the people of the world, and the rivalry between them is bound to lead to a new world war. . . . The socialist countries, the mainstay of the international proletariat, and the oppressed nations, who are the worst exploited and oppressed and who account for the great majority of the population of the world, together form the Third World. . . . The developed countries in between the two worlds constitute the Second World. They oppress and exploit the oppressed nations and are at the same time controlled and bullied by the super-powers. They have a dual character, and stand in contradiction with both the First and the Third World. But they are still a force the Third World can win over or unite with in the struggle against hegemonism. . . ."

The article stressed, however, that of the two super-powers, the Soviet Union was the more "ferocious, the more reckless, the more treacherous and the more dangerous source of world war", listing as reasons: (i) "Soviet social-imperialism is an imperialist power following on the heels of the United States and is therefore more aggressive and adventurous. . . . US imperialism continues to seek world domination, but it has over-reached itself, and all it can do at present is to strive to protect its vested interests and go over to the defensive in its overall strategy. On the other hand . . . the Soviet Union has decided to employ an offensive strategy to encroach on the sovereignty of all other countries, and to weaken and supplant US influence in all parts of the world in its attempt to establish its own world hegemony." (ii) "Because, comparatively speaking, Soviet social-imperialism is inferior in economic strength, it must rely chiefly on its military power and have recourse to threats of war in order to expand. . . ." (iii) "The Soviet bureaucrat monopoly capitalist group has transformed a highly centralized socialist state-owned economy into a state monopoly capitalist economy without its equal in any other imperialist country, and has transformed a state under the dictatorship of the proletariat into a state under fascist dictatorship. It is therefore easier for Soviet social-imperialism to put the entire economy on a military footing and militarize the whole state apparatus. . . ." (iv) "Soviet social-imperialism has come into being as a result of the degeneration of the first socialist country in the world. Therefore, it can exploit Lenin's prestige and flaunt the banner of 'socialism' to bluff and deceive people everywhere."

Soviet Call for Summit Meeting (February 1978)

The Presidium of the Supreme Soviet of the USSR, in a message sent to the standing committee of the Chinese National People's Congress on Feb. 24, 1978 (two days before a session of the Congress opened), proposed that the two countries should issue a joint statement that they would "build their relations on the basis of peaceful co-existence, firmly adhering to the principles of equality, mutual respect for sovereignty and territorial integrity, non-interference in each other's internal affairs and the renunciation of the use of force". The message also suggested that a meeting of representatives of both sides should be held as soon as possible in either Moscow or Beijing "at a sufficiently high level to agree on a mutually acceptable text", and concluded: "For our part, we are also prepared to consider proposals by the People's Republic of China for the normalization of Soviet-Chinese relations". Hua Guofeng replied indirectly to the Soviet message in his report to the National People's Congress on Feb. 26, 1978, saying:

"China and the Soviet Union were once friendly neighbours. The people of the two countries forged a profound friendship in their long revolutionary struggles. The Sino-Soviet debates on matters of principle were provoked by the Soviet leading clique through its betrayal of Marxism-Leninism. The fact that the relations between the two countries have sunk to such a low point today must be traced to the social-imperialist policy pursued by this clique. The debates on matters of principle must go on. At the same time, we have always held that such debates should not impede the maintenance of normal state relations on the basis of the five principles of peaceful co-existence. The Soviet leading clique has expressed its desire to improve Sino-Soviet state relations in its words, but in actuality it stubbornly clings to its policy of hostility towards China. It has gone to the length of arrogantly demanding that we change Chairman Mao's revolutionary line. This is nothing but a pipedream. If the Soviet leading clique really desires to improve the state relations between the two countries, it should prove its sincerity by deeds."

This point was emphasized in the official Chinese reply, delivered on March 9, 1978, which dismissed the Soviet proposed statement of principles as "hollow", "worthless" and not solving any practical problems. To improve Sino-Soviet relations, it declared, steps should be taken to solve the border issue. However, no progress was achieved in subsequent border talks held in Beijing from May to June 1978 [see Chapter XII].

Increased Tension over International Developments
(August 1978–September 1979)

Events in the summer and autumn of 1978 and the early months of 1979 brought renewed tension into Sino-Soviet relations. Hua Guofeng's visits in August 1978 to Romania, Yugoslavia and Iran had aggravated relations. In the same month, China had concluded a treaty of peace and friendship with Japan which had contained an "anti-hegemonist" clause directed implicitly against the Soviet Union, while in December 1978 China and the USA had agreed to establish diplomatic relations and Deng Xiaoping had visited the USA in January 1979 [see Chapter X]. The possible formation of a Pacific alliance by China, Japan and the USA was viewed by the Soviet Union with hostility. China and the Soviet Union had also become involved in the renewed conflict in Indo-China. China's relations with Vietnam had deteriorated during the 1970s, and following the Vietnamese invasion of Kampuchea in December 1978, China had invaded Vietnam in February 1979. The Soviet Union was aligned against China in the conflict, having concluded a treaty of friendship and co-operation with Vietnam in November 1978. [For the background to these disputes, see Chapter XIII.]

As a result of these developments, Sino-Soviet polemics during this period reached a degree of violence and bitterness unparalleled since the border clashes in 1969, and Soviet propaganda began to accuse China of pursuing a "hegemonist" policy—a term which previously had regularly been applied by the Chinese to the foreign policy of the Soviet Union.

Notwithstanding, Ilya Shcherbakov was appointed Soviet ambassador to China on July 22, 1978, in succession to Vasily Tolstikov (who had held this post since 1970) and presented his credentials on Sept. 28, 1978.

Liberalization of Chinese Internal Policies (1978–81)

From 1978 onwards, there was a drastic reversal within China of policies introduced during the Cultural Revolution and later continued up to the arrest in October 1976 of the "gang of four". These changes were associated with the increasingly dominant political figure of Deng Xiaoping, who, after the fall of Hua Guofeng, became the undisputed elder statesman of Chinese politics. Hua had resigned as Prime Minister in September 1980 and was replaced by Zhao Ziyang, an acknowledged supporter of Deng's policies. The resignation allegedly resulted from a central committee directive aimed at preventing the over-concentration of power in one person (Hua being also chairman of the CPC), but it was undoubtedly linked to the serious crisis in the CPC leadership at the end of 1980 and in the early months of 1981, which was resolved by Hua's resignation from the post of party chairman in June 1981 and his replacement by Hu Yaobang, another close associate of Deng.

Hua's demotion partly resulted from the reassessment during this period of Mao Zedong's thought and policies. Hua was criticized in particular for promoting the "two whatevers" policy, that is "we firmly uphold whatever policy decisions Chairman Mao made, and we unswervingly adhere to whatever instructions Chairman Mao gave". This allegedly contributed to Hua committing a number of "left" errors. In the period immediately after Mao's death, the moderate leadership had felt it necessary to reissue policy statements by Mao, such as his speech "On the 10 major relationships" and his "Three directives", which appeared to support the new policies that they were introducing. Subsequently, lip service continued to be paid to the memory of Mao Zedong but he ceased to be the centre of a personality cult and his theories and policies were subjected to increasingly severe criticism.

In June 1981, the CPC central committee adopted a resolution on historical questions which recognized Mao Zedong thought as the "guiding ideology" of the party but asserted that as he grew older Mao's "theoretical and practical mistakes concerning class struggle became increasingly serious, his personal arbitrariness gradually undermined democratic centralism in party life, and the personality cult grew graver and graver", and that this resulted in the "grave" left error of the Cultural Revolution for which Mao was chiefly responsible. This final assessment allowed the mantle of party theoretician and policy-maker to pass to Deng Xiaoping.

The moderates' political influence was further consolidated by continuing purges of supporters of the gang of four, whose leftist tendencies allegedly impeded the implementation of new liberal policies, and the rehabilitation of thousands of people who had been disgraced during the Cultural Revolution or even earlier. This process culminated in the posthumous rehabilitation in February 1980 of Liu Shaoqi, the former President who had been removed from his government and party posts in 1968 as the leading "revisionist" [see Chapter VII]. Emphasis was increasingly placed on political stability, while changes introduced during this period stimulated popular demands for more radical reforms. Posters and unofficial newspapers calling for greater democracy began to appear in Beijing in November 1978. However, a series of peasant demonstrations in Beijing and riots by unemployed young people in Shanghai and other cities in the early months of 1979 led to a reaction and the dissident campaign was suppressed. The period after Hua's fall from power was characterized by the consolidation of party controls and the tightening of ideological guidelines; a streamlining of the administrative machinery and government was announced in December 1981 and subsequent purges attacked both "leftist errors" and "bourgeois liberalism".

Deng Xiaoping and his supporters believed political stability was essential for the successful liberalization of Chinese internal policies. Many policies introduced during the Cultural Revolution were reversed; a session of the National People's Congress in June 1979 abolished the revolutionary committees set up during the Cultural Revolution as organs of local government and replaced them by elected people's congresses. It also adopted a code of criminal law for the first time since the establishment of the People's Republic in 1949 and sought to regularize judicial procedure. The most fundamental changes were made in many aspects of Chinese economic policy from 1978 onwards, which were consolidated and extended in later years. The modernization of the economy and the raising of people's cultural and economic living standards was acknowledged as the major task of the party and government.

An "open door" policy was adopted to acquire equipment and technical assistance from developed countries. From February 1978 loans were accepted from foreign governments and banks, while a law adopted in 1979 permitted foreign companies to establish joint ventures with Chinese companies. In August 1980 regulations were approved for the establishment of special economic zones in south-eastern China in which foreigners and overseas Chinese would be encouraged to invest.

In agriculture and industry, productivity and profit-making were emphasized. To encourage efficiency and initiative industrial enterprises and state farms were given greater control over their operations and finances. To relate wages more closely to output the payment of bonuses and piece rates and the introduction of profit-sharing schemes were encouraged, while the purchase prices paid to communes were increased, their taxes reduced and the tendency to organize them into larger units was reversed. "Sideline production" for private markets was also allowed once state quotas were fulfilled. These reforms were initially accompanied by grave unemployment and inflation and in 1979 a "readjustment" policy was adopted laying less emphasis on heavy industry and more on agriculture and light industry, and later policy statements stressed that enterprises should be organized to respond to the demands of market forces.

Change in China's Ideological Position (May 1979–March 1980)

The transformation of Chinese internal policies was accompanied by a change in Chinese anti-Soviet polemics. For some time after Mao's death, the Chinese press had continued to denounce the Soviet Union's "revisionist" internal policies as well as its "hegemonist" foreign policy. Articles published in 1979 and 1980, however, made it clear that the differences between China and the Soviet Union were to be regarded as concerned not with questions of Marxist ideology but with Soviet "hegemonism". This change of emphasis reflected the following factors:

(1) The fundamental transformation of Chinese foreign policy since 1960, when China had opposed the Soviet view that peaceful co-existence between capitalist and socialist countries was possible and wars between them were no longer inevitable. In recent years, however, China had established close relations with the USA, the West European countries and Japan, whilst Chinese leaders had laid little emphasis on the inevitability of war, stressing instead that a long period of peace was essential for China's economic modernization. Furthermore, whereas in the early 1960s China had violently denounced Yugoslavia as the supreme example of "revisionism", relations between China and Yugoslavia had since the Soviet occupation of Czechoslovakia in 1968 become increasingly close and friendly.

(2) The reassessment of Mao's policies which began in 1978 and which raised the question of the correctness of his attitude to the Soviet Union.

(3) The recent changes in China's own internal policies which made it vulnerable to charges of "revisionism" itself.

An early indication of the Chinese party's readiness to reconsider its views on the Soviet Union appeared in an article published in the *People's Daily* on May 9, 1979, which stated that China had not a monopoly of "authentic socialism", and that each socialist country had a right to pursue its own policy, provided that it adhered to "the universal principles of Marxism-Leninism". "This or that country", the article added, "should not be described as 'socialist', 'revisionist' or 'capitalist' in the name of abstract principles. . . ."

At a conference on contemporary Soviet literature held in Harbin on Sept. 12–21, 1979, a report of which was published on Dec. 20, four views on the nature of Soviet society were put forward. According to the report, most of the delegates held that although the Soviet Union's foreign policy was aggressive and expansionist, its domestic policy was "basically socialist"; "quite a number" described the Soviet Union as "an imperfect and rigid socialist society, with a number of shortcomings", differing from "the open socialism of Yugoslavia and the moderate socialism of Hungary"; "a small number" maintained that it was "a revisionist country"; and some preferred to suspend judgment until further research had been carried out. The report was put on sale in Beijing on March 30, 1980, and sold out within a few days.

The *People's Daily* condemned on April 2, 1980, a series of nine articles attacking the Soviet Union which it had published between Sept. 6, 1963, and July 14, 1964. In these articles, it stated, "the origin and characteristics of revisionism were incorrectly described", and "it was even erroneously suggested that the attitude of a proletarian party in power which was devoting itself to the development of the productive forces was revisionist". As the articles in question contained the fullest exposition of the ideological differences between the Chinese and Soviet Communist parties, this statement constituted an admission that their present differences were concerned not with ideology but purely with policy questions. Also in April 1980, the street in Beijing in which the Soviet embassy stood, which at the beginning of the Cultural Revolution had been renamed "Struggle against Revisionism Street", reverted to its original non-political name.

Hu Yaobang, then general secretary of the Communist Party, told Italian journalists who were accompanying Enrico Berlinguer, the secretary of the Italian Communist Party, on his visit to Beijing on April 15, 1980, that he saw no possibility of talks between the Chinese and Soviet parties, as the Soviet party bullied other parties, interfered in other countries' internal affairs and occupied other countries' territory by force. Deng Xiaoping declared on May 5 that "the Soviet Union is not a socialist country but a social-imperialist country", which pursued a policy of hegemonism and committed aggression against other countries. Both Hu and Deng, however, condemned the Soviet party for its foreign policy, not for its internal policy or its ideology.

The first issue of a magazine entitled *Soviet Literature* was published in Beijing in March 1980. In an introduction the well-known writer Mao Dun said that sectarianism had no place in literature and literary exchanges.

Expiry of Sino-Soviet Treaty of Friendship (April 1980)

The Chinese Government announced on April 3, 1979, that it would not extend its 1950 treaty of friendship, alliance and mutual assistance with the Soviet Union when it expired in a year's time, but offered to negotiate with the Soviet Union on the improvement of relations between the two countries. The treaty, which was signed on Feb. 4, 1950, and came into force on April 1950, provided that it would be valid for 30 years, and would automatically be extended for another five years unless either party gave notice of its intention to denounce the treaty a year before it was due to expire [see Chapter I].

The Chinese announcement said that it had been decided not to extend the treaty "in view of the fact that great changes have taken place in the international situation [a reference to the fact that the treaty provided for joint Sino-Soviet action against possible Japanese aggression] and that the treaty has long ceased to exist except in name, owing to violations for which the Chinese side is not responsible". The Chinese statement continued: "The differences of principle between China and the Soviet Union should not hamper the maintenance and development of their normal state relations on the basis of the five principles of mutual respect for sovereignty and territorial integrity, mutual non-aggression, non-interference in each other's internal affairs, equality and mutual benefit, and peaceful co-existence. To this end, the Chinese Government has proposed to the Soviet Government that negotiations be held between China and the Soviet Union for the solution of outstanding issues and the improvement of relations between the two countries."

An official Soviet statement issued on April 4, 1979, commented that China had rejected in 1971 a Soviet proposal for a treaty renouncing the use of force, and in 1973 a Soviet offer to sign a non-aggression treaty, on the ground that the treaty of alliance made such additional treaties unnecessary. The statement attributed the Chinese leaders' changed attitude towards the treaty to their "hegemonistic aspirations".

A Soviet Note of April 17, 1979, suggested that a document on the principles governing relations between the two countries would provide a suitable basis for an improvement in relations between them, and asked the Chinese Government for its views on the subject and aims of the proposed talks. The Chinese reply (May 5) proposed that wide-ranging talks, independent of negotiations on the frontiers, should be held to resolve questions in dispute between the two countries, and should include the formulation of principles on which their relations should be based, the elimination of obstacles to the normalization of relations and questions concerning scientific, technological and cultural exchanges.

The Soviet Government offered on June 4, 1979, to hold negotiations in July and August of that year in Moscow, at deputy foreign minister level or by specially empowered representatives of the two Governments, and proposed that the two sides should "agree to deny recognition to anyone's claims to special rights or hegemony in world affairs". The Chinese Government suggested on July 16 that a first round of talks at deputy foreign minister level should open in Moscow in September and should be followed by a second round in Beijing, this proposal being accepted by the Soviet Union on July 23.

Preliminary meetings of the two delegations began in Moscow on Sept. 27, 1979, the Soviet delegation being led by Leonid Ilyichev, a Deputy Foreign Minister who had headed the Soviet delegation at the Beijing border talks since 1970, and the Chinese delegation by Wang Youping, who had recently been appointed a Deputy Foreign Minister. Although no agreement was reached on the agenda, it was agreed at the fifth meeting on Oct. 12 to hold the first plenary session. The formal talks began on Oct. 17, the first round concluding with the sixth meeting on Nov. 30, 1979.

No details of the talks were officially published, but *Pravda* revealed on Dec. 8 that the Soviet delegation had submitted a draft declaration on the principles governing relations between the two countries. According to unofficial reports, the

Chinese delegation had been concerned with the question of Chinese security, including the border dispute, and had also asked that the Soviet Union should end its support for Vietnam's "expansionist" policy and reduce its aid to Vietnam. In reply, the Soviet delegation was reported to have made a conditional response to the Chinese border demands [see Chapter XII] and to have stated that Soviet aid to Vietnam was determined by the treaty of friendship and co-operation signed in 1978.

Although the Chinese Government condemned the Soviet intervention in Afghanistan in its public statements and in a Note to the Soviet Union of Dec. 31, 1979, official spokesmen said that as the talks were concerned with bilateral questions they would not be affected by the Afghanistan crisis. On Jan. 19, 1980, however, the Chinese Foreign Ministry issued the following statement: "The Soviet invasion of Afghanistan threatens both world peace and China's security. It has also created new obstacles to the normalization of relations between China and the Soviet Union. In these circumstances it is obviously inappropriate to hold the Sino-Soviet negotiations."

Some commentators suggested that the change in Chinese policy on this question resulted from a visit to Beijing by Dr Harold Brown (then the US Defence Secretary) on Jan. 5–9, 1980 [see page 121], whilst others attributed it to differences of opinion among the Chinese leadership. In support of the latter theory, it was pointed out that a session of the Communist Party central committee held on Feb. 23–29, 1980, greatly strengthened the position of Deng Xiaoping, who was regarded as one of the most intransigent of the Chinese leaders in his attitude towards the Soviet Union.

Some approaches with a view to resuming the talks were apparently made by both sides in the spring of 1980. Yang Shouzheng (formerly ambassador to Mozambique) was appointed Chinese ambassador to the Soviet Union in succession to Wang Youping on Feb. 12. Mikhail Kapitsa, director of the Soviet Foreign Ministry's Far Eastern department and deputy leader of the Soviet delegation to the Moscow talks, arrived in Beijing on March 20, 1980, for what was described as "a private visit at the Soviet ambassador's invitation", and the unofficial "Aug. 1 Radio" reported on April 14 that Chinese delegates had returned to Beijing four days before after privately contacting "Soviet personnel concerned" about improving Sino-Soviet relations.

The "Aug. 1 Radio", which took its name from China's Army Day, had broadcast in Chinese since March 1979, and claimed to speak for the Chinese Army. Its broadcasts, which often criticized the Government's policies and were particularly hostile to Deng Xiaoping, were believed to originate in the Soviet Union.

An article signed "Igor Alexandrov" published in *Pravda* on April 7, 1980, proposed that the talks should be resumed, but a Chinese official spokesman commented on April 10 that the Chinese position on the negotiations "has been publicly announced and remains the same". When the Sino-Soviet treaty of alliance expired on the following day the event was ignored in both the Soviet and the Chinese press.

Stabilization of Relations (February 1981–March 1982)

Speeches in February 1981 and September 1982 by the respective party leaders, Brezhnev and Hu Yaobang, restated their countries' position on Sino-Soviet relations but made no fresh attacks, and there were reports in early 1982 that tentative bilateral contacts had been established.

Brezhnev, in his report to the CPSU congress on Feb. 23, 1981, summarized the current state of Soviet relations with China in a noticeably moderate and conciliatory tone, saying:

"Special mention must be made of China. The social and economic development of the People's Republic of China over the past 20 years is a painful lesson, showing where any distortion of the principles and essence of socialism in home and foreign policy leads. The present Chinese leaders themselves describe the period of the so-called Cultural Revolution in their country as 'a cruel feudal-fascist dictatorship'. We have nothing to add to that assessment. At present changes are under way in China's internal policy. . . . But unfortunately there are no grounds yet to speak of any changes for the better in Beijing's foreign policy. As before, it is aimed at aggravating the international situation, and is aligned with the policy of the imperialist powers. That, of course, will not bring China back to the sound road of development. Imperialists will never be friends of socialism.

"The simple reason behind the readiness of the United States, Japan and a number of NATO countries to expand their military and political ties with China is to use its hostility to the Soviet Union and the socialist community in their own, imperialist interests. . . . If Soviet–Chinese relations are still frozen, the reason for this has nothing to do with our position. The Soviet Union has never wanted, neither does it now want, any confrontation with the People's Republic of China."

Polemics were also largely absent in Hu's report to the 12th CPC congress on Sept. 1, 1982, which described Sino-Soviet relations as having been friendly over a fairly long period but as having "become what they are today because the Soviet Union has pursued a hegemonist policy". While noting that Soviet leaders had expressed the desire to improve relations with China, the report emphasized that deeds rather than words were important, and that Sino-Soviet relations could move towards normalization if the Soviet authorities took practical steps to lift what was described as "their threat to the security of this country".

In a later passage on imperialism, hegemonism and colonialism, the report used the word "hegemonism" to apply not only to Soviet policies but to both superpowers, whose rivalry made the danger of a world war even greater. The USA was also criticized for disrupting the "one China" policy towards Taiwan. This referred to the proposals to upgrade US–Taiwan relations following the election of Ronald Reagan as US President in 1980 [see Chapter X].

The upset in China's relations with the USA over Taiwan coincided with the establishment of contacts between China and the Soviet Union in the first three months of 1982. Beijing radio reported on March 28 that a Chinese group had visited Moscow on Jan. 12–19 for talks on the book trade and had initialled an agreement, and on March 29 that three Chinese economists were visiting Moscow to study the Soviet economy.

Sino-Soviet Economic Relations (1978–82)

The volume of trade under the annual trade and payments agreements between the Soviet Union and China fluctuated sharply during the late 1970s and early 1980s. In 1978 it reached $516,000,000, the highest total since the early 1960s, and in 1979 it was $503,300,000. It fell to about $375,000,000 in 1980 and $200,000,000 in 1981 (compared with trade exchanges totalling over $10,000 million between China and Japan and $5,500 million between China and the United States), but an agreement signed on April 20, 1982, set the value of bilateral trade at $302,000,000. Under the agreement Chinese purchases of Soviet capital goods were to decrease while imports of raw materials were to rise. Another agreement signed on Feb. 6, 1982, provided that Chinese exports to Europe and Iran might cross Soviet territory by rail.

XII: THE BORDER ISSUE, 1969–82

After the serious fighting on the Far Eastern and Central Asian frontiers between March and August 1969 [see Chapter VIII], the Soviet Union and China resumed negotiations on the border issue later in the year. However, the discussions proved inconclusive, and subsequent attempts to settle the overall dispute also failed. Further border incidents took place intermittently.

Stalemated Negotiations (September 1969–August 1974)

Sporadic incidents continued on the islands in the Ussuri (Wusuli) and Amur (Heilong) rivers throughout the spring and summer of 1969, causing a few casualties on each side. Incidents also occurred on the Central Asian border between April and August 1969, culminating in fighting on Aug. 13 which resulted in casualties on both sides. Tension reached such a height that on Aug. 23, 1969, the Chinese Communist Party issued a statement declaring that war might break out at any time. The situation was transformed, however, by the death on Sept. 3, 1969, of President Ho Chi Minh of North Vietnam and by the publication of his political testament, in which he appealed for "the restoration of unity among the fraternal parties". After attending his funeral the Soviet Prime Minister, Alexei Kosygin, flew to Beijing on Sept. 11, where he met Zhou Enlai. As a result of this meeting the two sides agreed to reopen border talks.

The exact terms of the agreement reached between them subsequently became a subject of controversy. According to Soviet sources, it was agreed to take measures to avoid armed conflicts on the border, to settle border questions through negotiations, and to take steps to normalize relations between them, such as the restoration of diplomatic relations at ambassadorial level and the expansion of trade. According to the Chinese version, the two Prime Ministers compared Soviet and Chinese maps, established which parts of the frontier were in dispute, and agreed to withdraw their armed forces from these areas and to conclude an agreement on the preservation of the status quo on the border.

A Chinese statement of Oct. 7, 1969, announcing that it had been agreed to hold talks on the border question said: "The responsibility for the development of the Sino-Soviet boundary question to such an acute state does not all rest with the Chinese side. The Chinese Government has never demanded the return of the territory Tsarist Russia had annexed by means of the unequal treaties. On the contrary, it is the Soviet Government that has persisted in occupying still more Chinese territory in violation of the stipulations of these treaties and, moreover, peremptorily demanded that the Chinese Government recognize such occupation as legal. Precisely because of the Soviet Government's persistence in its expansionist stand, many disputed areas have been created along the Sino-Soviet border, and this has become the root cause of tension on the border. . . ."

The border negotiations opened in Beijing on Oct. 20, 1969, and continued with a number of breaks until July 1973. Although no official statements were issued on the progress of the talks, unofficial reports suggested that a stalemate had been reached at an early stage.

The Hong Kong Communist newspaper *Ta Kung Pao*, sometimes used as a semi-official mouthpiece for the Chinese Government, alleged on Jan. 9, 1970, that the talks had failed to produce any results because the Soviet Union "had refused to put any restraint on its armed forces during the period of the talks, nor had it agreed to the disengagement of the armed forces of both sides in the disputed areas". According to reports both from Moscow and from diplomatic sources in Beijing, the Chinese insisted that the Soviet Union should admit that it had gained much of its Far Eastern territory through "unequal treaties" concluded under the Tsars, and that the discussions should be confined to questions relating to the frontier; however, the Soviet delegation, while apparently offering to hand over certain disputed islands along the Ussuri river (including Damansky/Chenpao), rejected the "unequal treaties" thesis, and also proposed that the talks should be widened to cover diplomatic, trade and cultural relations between the two countries.

The leader of the Soviet delegation, Vasily Kuznetsov, and his deputy, Maj.-Gen. Vadim Matrosov, left for Moscow on Dec. 13, 1969, nominally in order to attend a session of the Supreme Soviet. When Kuznetsov returned to Beijing on Jan. 2, 1970, Gen. Matrosov, who was said to be receiving hospital treatment, was replaced as his deputy by Gen. Viktor Gankovsky.

The Times commented that "Gen. Gankovsky's exact duties are unknown, but he is believed to be commander-in-chief of Soviet frontier guards in the area bordering the Chinese province of Sinkiang [Xinjiang]. Gen. Matrosov holds a similar command in the East Siberia region. The change could therefore mean that the first phase of the talks dealt with problems concerning the Soviet Union's eastern frontiers with China, and that the present talks concern the western frontiers."

Kuznetsov returned to Moscow for health reasons on June 30, 1970, but the negotiations were reported to have continued in his absence. In one of its rare references to the talks, Pravda stated on July 7 that "the Beijing leaders are artificially trying to create a territorial problem by arbitrarily manipulating historical information, or the lack of it", suggesting that the question of the "unequal treaties" was still being debated. Leonid Ilyichev, a Deputy Foreign Minister who had taken part in negotiations with Chinese party leaders in 1963, arrived in Beijing to replace Kuznetsov on Aug. 15, 1970.

Although no incidents were reported from the Sino-Soviet frontier after the opening of the talks, tension continued in the border areas, where the Soviet troops had been greatly reinforced in 1969. Reports in the Soviet press of the military parades held on Nov. 7, 1969, to celebrate the anniversary of the Bolshevik Revolution revealed that a separate military command, known as the Central Asian Military District, had been set up to cover Kazakhstan, Kirghizia and Tajikistan, which border on Xinjiang.

The Soviet delegation on Jan. 15, 1971, repeated its proposal that the two countries should sign a treaty renouncing the use or threat of force against each other. According to unofficial reports, the Chinese rejected this proposal as unnecessary, pointing out that the treaty of alliance of 1950 still remained in force, and also rejected a second Soviet proposal that a declaration reaffirming the validity of the treaty should be issued. During this phase the Soviet negotiators appeared to be willing to concede that most sections of the disputed Amur and Ussuri river boundaries should be defined as running along the "Thalweg" line (i.e. the mid-point of the deepest channel); however, the exclusion from this offer of Heixiazi (an island at the confluence of the two rivers which the Soviet Union regarded as militarily important) rendered it unacceptable to China. [For Sino-Soviet differences over Heixiazi island, see also pages 149–50 below.]

In an interview with Scandinavian journalists, Zhou Enlai said in November 1972: "The Soviet side now maintain that there is no disagreement on the frontier. . . . They now deny that there are any disputed zones. . . . Perhaps they are acting in this way because they are afraid of a chain reaction on the part of certain other countries."

The *Financial Times* commented on the border talks as follows on Dec. 13, 1972: "What little has been said in Beijing and Moscow . . . suggests that the Beijing negotiations are not in fact concerned directly with settlement of the boundary dispute as such but with the creation of conditions which would make it possible for true boundary negotiations to start. . . . The Chinese have proposed a two-part agreement. . . . This would bind themselves and the Russians (i) to maintain the status quo and (ii) to withdraw armed forces from areas in dispute. . . . The Beijing deadlock suggests that both those proposed heads of agreements have become sticking points. Agreement on just what is the status quo or the 'line of actual control' is itself vexed. . . . The Russians apparently suspect that an agreed line of actual control would be presented later by the Chinese as a de facto boundary. . . . The Chinese proposal for withdrawals from disputed territory is, Moscow has made plain, even less acceptable. This proposal looks to withdrawal only of armed forces, the creation of agreed demilitarized areas which would not affect claims to sovereignty. The Russians reject this, primarily, it appears, for strategic reasons. . . ."

Brezhnev revealed on Sept. 24, 1973, that the Soviet Union had again offered in June 1973 to sign a non-aggression pact with China, which would include "undertakings not to attack each other with any type of weapon on land, sea or air and to refrain from threatening to use weapons", and said that the Chinese had not even replied. According to reports from Beijing, China rejected both proposals as pointless unless the Soviet Union carried out the agreement of Sept. 11, 1969, to withdraw its forces from disputed areas. Following the rejection of the second offer, Ilyichev returned to Moscow in July 1973. He was subsequently reported to have resumed his normal duties as a Deputy Foreign Minister, which were not concerned with China.

In a telegram of congratulation to the Soviet Government on the anniversary of the October Revolution, the Chinese Government suggested on Nov. 3, 1973, that the border question should be settled peacefully "by means of negotiations under conditions which exclude any threat". The Soviet Government replied on Nov. 25 repeating its offer to sign a treaty of non-aggression.

While the negotiations were in progress, the Supreme Soviet of the Russian Federation published in March 1973 a decree replacing the Chinese or Manchu names of a number of towns in the Soviet Far East by Russian names. The New China News Agency issued a statement on March 7 bitterly attacking this decision, and claiming that it was intended to suggest that the area had never been Chinese and had been first settled by Russians. By a subsequent decree about 250 rivers and mountains in the area were similarly renamed.

Following Leonid Ilyichev's return to Moscow, border negotiations were suspended for a year. Talks were resumed when Ilyichev returned to Beijing on June 25, 1974. Two months later, however, they were again suspended, and Ilyichev flew back to Moscow on Aug. 19.

Further Exchanges on Non-Aggression Pact (October–December 1974)

In a message of greeting on Oct. 1, 1974, on the 25th anniversary of the Chinese revolution the Soviet Government renewed its offer of a non-aggression pact, in the following terms: "The Soviet Union has been and continues to be a supporter of the normalization of relations with the People's Republic of China and the restoration of friendship with the great Chinese people. These aims are served by the Soviet Union's proposals on, in particular, the conclusion with the People's Republic of China of a treaty on refraining from the use of force and a treaty of non-aggression, and the development of relations in various fields on a mutually beneficial basis."

The Chinese Government replied in a message of greetings on the anniversary of the Russian revolution on Nov. 7, 1974, repeating the proposal that a non-aggression treaty should be accompanied by the withdrawal of all armed forces from the disputed border areas.

"The Chinese Government has frequently proposed that the two parties should conduct negotiations to achieve relations of friendship and good-neighbourliness", the message said. "For this purpose, it is necessary first of all to sign, in accordance with the understanding reached between the Prime Ministers of China and the Soviet Union in September 1969, an agreement, which includes mutual non-aggression and non-use of force against each other, on the maintenance of the status quo on the border, prevention of armed conflict and disengagement of the armed forces of the two sides in the areas of dispute, and then proceed to settle through negotiations the entire boundary question. We have always believed that the normalization of relations between China and the Soviet Union corresponds to the fundamental interests of the two peoples. As in the past, the Chinese Government will bend all efforts to defend the revolutionary friendship between the Chinese and Soviet peoples, and to promote the normalization of relations between the two countries."

The message was broadcast in Russian by the Chinese radio, but was not published in the Beijing press. In Moscow *Pravda* published only a summary of the message, which did not mention the proposals for a non-aggression pact and disengagement, although messages from 25 other countries were printed in full in the same issue.

The Soviet Government's official reply to the message, published on Nov. 26, 1974, said that it favoured talks "without any preliminary conditions" on all questions of Soviet–Chinese relations, including frontier issues, but that the Chinese message, which presented "all kinds of preliminary conditions", did not provide a basis for an understanding. Brezhnev rejected the Chinese proposals on the same day in a speech in Ulan Bator, the capital of Mongolia.

"At first glance", he said, "it would seem that the leaders of the People's Republic of China also come out for normalizing relations with the Soviet Union. The trouble is, however, that their words are divorced from their deeds. Beijing advances as a preliminary condition no more nor less than the demand for withdrawal of Soviet frontier guards from a number of areas of our territory to which the Chinese leaders have now decided to make claims, calling them disputed areas. And Beijing declares outright that it will agree to talks on border questions only after its demand concerning the so-called disputed areas is met. It is quite obvious that such a position is totally unacceptable, and we reject it."

The issue of the Chinese journal *Historical Research* published in December 1974 reaffirmed the Chinese Government's position that China claimed the return not of the territory annexed by Tsarist Russia under the "unequal treaties", which it was prepared to accept as the basis for a settlement, but of territory since occupied by Russia in violation of those treaties, although it was also prepared to consider "adjustments" in the disputed areas as part of a general settlement.

The magazine called on the Soviet Union to reduce its armed forces on the border to their level in "the Khrushchev period" (i.e. before 1964), to end military manoeuvres and "provocations" in the border area and the sending of spies into China, to admit that Russia had seized territory from China by force in the 19th and early 20th centuries, and to conclude a provisional agreement guaranteeing the status quo on the frontiers.

Tension on Central Asian Border (March 1974–February 1976)

A Soviet helicopter with a crew of three frontier guards, which according to Soviet sources had lost its bearings while on its way to pick up a serviceman who was seriously ill, was forced to land in the Chinese frontier province of Xinjiang on March 14, 1974. Although the Soviet Foreign Ministry requested the return of the helicopter and crew on the following day, a Chinese Note of March 23 asserted that it had been carrying neither medical personnel nor medicines, and that documents found on board proved that it had been engaged in espionage; it also alleged that Soviet aircraft had intruded into Xinjiang 61 times since January 1973, and declared that unless the Soviet Government gave guarantees against similar incidents in future it must bear "full responsibility for all the consequences". A Soviet Note of March 28, 1974, completely denied the Chinese allegations, and stated that the only recent incident involving entry into Chinese airspace had occurred in February 1973, when a civilian plane on a regular flight had lost its bearings.

Three further Soviet protests met with no response, and a Soviet request that a representative of the International Committee of the Red Cross should be allowed to visit the helicopter's crew was rejected by China. Chinese officials repeatedly stated that the three men would be put on trial "at a suitable time", but no preparations for their trial were reported.

The incident, unlike the expulsion of five Soviet nationals from China for alleged espionage in January 1974 [see Chapter IX], was made the subject of a propaganda campaign in the Soviet press. *Izvestia* stated on May 15, 1974, that the Soviet Union had proposed in June 1973 that "a meeting between Soviet and Chinese representatives might be organized at any level, including 'the summit'". (The Soviet Union was known to have suggested in June 1973 the signing of a non-aggression pact, but the proposal for a summit meeting had not previously been revealed.) The magazine *Literaturnaya Gazeta* alleged on May 8 that the Chinese had committed "spectacular violations" of the frontier, but said that the Soviet Union had refrained from publicizing them.

A number of unconfirmed reports of armed clashes on the frontiers were received in December 1974. According to one report, about 30 men were killed or wounded in November in a clash between Soviet and Chinese troops on the Mongolian border. President Tsedenbal of Mongolia alleged in an article published in January 1975 in the Soviet magazine *Problems of the Far East* that Chinese troops had violated the border, cut down trees, started forest fires and driven cattle infected with contagious diseases into Mongolian territory.

The three members of the crew of the captured Soviet helicopter were released on Dec. 27, 1975 (i.e. after over 21 months), and returned to Moscow two days later. A Chinese Foreign Ministry statement said that after investigation the public security services considered their story that they had entered China unintentionally to be "credible"—apparently a retraction of the earlier Chinese allegations that the helicopter had been engaged in espionage.

Despite this conciliatory gesture, both countries continued their propaganda campaigns against each other during the weeks following. Beijing radio alleged on Feb. 3 and 12, 1976, that Chinese militia had several times driven out Soviet troops infiltrating into Xinjiang, without giving dates or details; this allegation was categorically denied by the Soviet Union.

Renewed Negotiations (February 1975–February 1977)

Leonid Ilyichev returned to Beijing to resume the border negotiations on Feb. 12, 1975. He left for Moscow on May 5, but other members of the Soviet delegation remained in Beijing. According to unconfirmed reports, an agreement had been reached that the border problem should not be examined in its entirety but item by item, beginning with those on which there was a greater chance of agreement.

The Chinese message of greeting on the anniversary of the Russian revolution sent on Nov. 6, 1975, was much briefer than the previous year's. On the border question it merely stated that it should be settled "in strict accordance with the achieved mutual understanding [i.e. of September 1969] and by taking practical steps through talks based on equality".

A long article in *Pravda* on April 28, 1976, and signed "I. Alexandrov" (a pseudonym used for important policy statements), called for the resumption of border negotiations [see also Chapter IX]. The approach, however, drew no response from the Chinese Government.

The article stated: "Laying unfounded claims to Soviet border territories totalling some 33,000 square kilometres, Beijing is deliberately deadlocking Soviet–Chinese border negotiations that began back in October 1969. The Chinese representatives put forward as a preliminary condition the demand that the Soviet Union recognize all these Soviet territories as 'disputed areas' and lift its control over them. Furthermore, it is declared in the tone of an ultimatum that the delegation is ready to commence a direct examination of the border issues only after its demand regarding the so-called 'disputed areas' has been satisfied. Our position in this matter is clear and precise. The Soviet Union is ready to conduct businesslike and concrete negotiations to settle the border question with China, but without any preliminary conditions. . . . As for the need to verify a number of sections of the Soviet–Chinese border, the USSR is ready to do this on an equal and acceptable basis, and all the problems the Beijing authorities are artifically building up around the settlement of the border issue would be solved in the interests of the USSR and China. . . .

"A package of constructive proposals advanced by the Soviet delegation lies on the table of the Soviet–Chinese border talks. Discussion and implementation of these proposals, which take into account the interests of both sides, could immediately lead the talks out of the blind alley in which they now are. It depends upon the Chinese side whether things will progress in this direction."

Following the death of Mao Zedong on Sept. 9, 1976, an article by "I. Alexandrov" published in *Pravda* on Oct. 1 proposed border negotiations "without any prior conditions" [see also Chapter XI]. Ilyichev returned to Beijing on Nov. 27, 1976, to resume the negotiations (after an absence of 18 months); he had a meeting on Jan. 28, 1977, with Huang Hua, the Chinese Foreign Minister, but subsequently flew back to Moscow on Feb. 28.

Negotiations over Far Eastern Rivers (1970–1977)

Although the Soviet Union and China were unable to reach agreement on the wider border dispute, progress was made on the specific problem of navigation on the Far Eastern rivers. The joint Sino-Soviet commission for navigation on the Far Eastern rivers met in the Chinese town of Heihe from July 10 to Dec. 19, 1970. The commission, which was concerned with purely technical questions, had normally met annually since its establishment in 1951, although no meetings took place in 1967–68. The Tass agency stated on Dec. 19 that the meeting had ended "with the signing of an appropriate protocol", but the New China News Agency stated on Dec. 23 that "no agreement was reached on the questions discussed". Neither statement explained why the commission, which in 1969 had reached an agreement in seven weeks, had continued its discussions for five months.

In a Note of May 23, 1974, the Soviet Foreign Ministry stated that "the Soviet side sees no difficulties in the solving of the question of passage of Chinese vessels through Soviet inland waterways, if China returns to the positions of respect for the sovereign rights and territorial integrity of the Soviet Union".

The Soviet Note referred in particular to the confluence near Khabarovsk of the Amur and Ussuri rivers. At the junction of the rivers lies the triangular island of Heixiazi (with an area of 128 square miles), currently in Soviet occupation but also claimed by China. The island is bounded by the Amur to the north, a narrow watercourse known as the Kazakevich Channel to the south-west and a broader watercourse to the south-east. The Soviet Union held that the two watercourses were arms of the Amur and that its confluence with the Ussuri lay south of Heishatzu, whereas the Chinese maintained that they were arms of the Ussuri and that the confluence was east of the island, at Khabarovsk.

Since 1966 Soviet gunboats had prevented Chinese ships from using the eastern watercourse, which the Soviet Union regarded as an inland waterway, and they were forced to use the Kazakevich Channel, which in summer was too shallow for navigation. The Soviet Note proposed that the two countries should co-operate to deepen it, and that while this was being done Chinese vessels should use the two rivers after giving due notification to the Soviet authorities.

A Chinese Foreign Ministry statement issued on May 30, 1974, which rejected the Soviet offer as "blackmail", claimed that as Heixiazi was Chinese territory the channel, which the Soviet Union regarded as forming the frontier, was a Chinese inland waterway, and that Chinese vessels had the right to use the Amur and the Ussuri up to their confluence, although the Soviet Union had been forcibly obstructing them from doing so since 1966.

The joint commission did not meet again for over three years. Another session took place in Heihe from July 27 to Oct. 6, 1977, during which the two sides reached a limited agreement on navigation on the Amur and Ussuri rivers. This left the Heixiazi question open and provided that Chinese ships might use the eastern watercourse and the Amur when the Kazakevich Channel was not deep enough for navigation.

Sino-Soviet Border Incidents (1977–80)

A number of incidents, in which at least three Chinese and two Soviet citizens were reported to have been killed, occurred during 1977–80 on both the Central Asian and the Far Eastern sectors of the Sino-Soviet border, and Chinese officials accused the Soviet Union of steadily encroaching on Chinese territory in Xinjiang. Details of these accusations are given below.

The Central Asian Border. A Chinese spokesman told foreign correspondents in October 1978 that the Soviet Union had absorbed 185 square miles of territory in the Emin region of northern Xinjiang between 1960 and 1969, and 1,080 square miles in the Ili river region of western Xinjiang between 1972 and July 1977, expelling Kirghiz and Uzbek herdsmen and blocking access with barbed wire barriers; out of 3,686 square miles in dispute between the two countries, he added, the Soviet Union occupied 3,475 square miles. Another Chinese official said on Sept. 29, 1979, however, that 20 areas along the Xinjiang border were in dispute, varying in size from 390 to 11,600 square miles, and that in some of these areas the Russians were moving into Chinese territory "like a silkworm devouring a mulberry tree leaf by leaf".

According to Chinese sources, six "armed Soviet spies" crossed the Xinjiang border early in July 1977, of whom one was killed in a clash with local militia, another committed suicide and four escaped. Soviet sources described the men as opium smugglers. Two Soviet border guards were reported to have penetrated into Chinese territory on Aug. 5, killed a Kazakh shepherd and wounded and kidnapped another, who was handed over to the Chinese authorities 10 days later.

A tense situation developed on the Xinjiang border in February and March 1979 during the Chinese invasion of Vietnam. Both sides strengthened their forces in the area; children and old people were evacuated from Ili, Tacheng and other towns near the border; and normal contacts at boundary posts to settle local disputes were suspended for a period.

A Soviet verbal Note of July 17, 1979, alleged that on the previous day four Chinese servicemen had crossed into Soviet territory in the Tacheng area, one being killed and another wounded and taken prisoner in a clash with Soviet border guards. A Chinese Note of July 24, however, maintained that about 20 Soviet border guards had opened fire, killing one Chinese and wounding another, and had then crossed the border and carried them into Soviet territory. The Chinese who had been captured was handed over on Feb. 14, 1980.

The Far Eastern Border. A Chinese Note of May 11, 1978, stated that about 30 Soviet troops had crossed the Ussuri river on May 9, landed on the Chinese side and wounded a number of Chinese. The Soviet Foreign Ministry apologized on the following day, stating that Soviet border guards had mistaken the Chinese bank for a Soviet island while pursuing an armed criminal by night, but denied that they had molested Chinese citizens. The Chinese Foreign Ministry rejected this explanation on May 17, maintaining that the incident had occurred in daylight and repeating its allegation that a number of Chinese had been fired on and wounded.

An incident of which the two sides gave completely opposed versions occurred on the Argun river frontier on Oct. 5, 1980. A Chinese Note of the following day alleged that four Soviet armed personnel had landed on the Chinese bank, kidnapped a herdsman, shot him dead when he tried to resist, and fired on Chinese border guards (who returned the fire), killing one of them. A Soviet Note of Oct. 9 asserted that Chinese border guards had fired on three unarmed Soviet citizens who were fishing from a boat and killed one of them. No subsequent deaths were reported, although Chinese officials in Harbin said in February 1982 that over 100 minor incidents had occurred in 1981.

A number of trials of alleged Soviet spies were reported from Heilongjiang province in 1980 and 1981. A Chinese who had killed a policeman while resisting arrest was found guilty of spying for the Soviet Union at Mudanjiang on July 20, 1980, and executed on Aug. 16. A Soviet citizen said to have been arrested in 1974 was found guilty of espionage at Beian Zhen on July 20, 1980, and sentenced to seven years' imprisonment, no explanation being given why his trial had been so long delayed. It was announced on Aug. 4, 1981, that a Chinese had recently been convicted at Yichun of spying for the Soviet Union and executed.

Talks Interrupted by International Developments (May 1978–January 1980)

The Presidium of the Supreme Soviet of the USSR proposed on Feb. 24, 1978, that the Soviet Union and China should issue a joint statement that they would develop their relations on the basis of peaceful co-existence and mutual respect for territorial integrity. Hua Guofeng replied indirectly in his report to the National People's Congress on Feb. 26 [see also page 134].

In his speech, Hua set out China's demands in the border dispute as follows: "First of all, in accordance with the understanding reached between the Premiers of the two countries in 1969, [the Soviet Union] should sign an agreement on maintaining the status quo on the borders, averting armed clashes and disengaging the armed forces of both sides in the disputed border areas, and then enter into negotiations on resolving the boundary question. . . . It should also withdraw its armed forces from the People's Republic of Mongolia and the Sino-Soviet borders, so that the situation there will revert to what it was in the early 1960s."

The official Chinese reply to the Soviet message, delivered on March 9, 1978, accused the Soviet Government of being unwilling to implement the understanding between the Soviet and Chinese Prime Ministers of September 1969, and even of denying its existence. If the Soviet Union wished to improve relations with China, said the reply, it should sign an agreement on the maintenance of the status quo on the border, proceed to settle the boundary question though negotiations, and withdraw its armed forces from Mongolia and from the Sino-Soviet border.

The Mongolian Government, in a Note of April 12, 1978, to China, stated that Soviet troops were stationed in its territory at its own request because of "Chinese expansionist aspirations", and would remain there as long as a "Chinese threat" continued.

The border negotiations, which had been suspended since February 1977, were resumed in Beijing on May 4, 1978. No progress was achieved, however, and the talks were again suspended in June. During the second half of 1978 and early 1979, developments in various areas revived tension in Sino-Soviet relations giving rise to bitter polemics and inhibiting the holding of further discussions on the border dispute. The Soviet Government had disapproved of the recent marked improvement in China's relations with Japan and the USA, while in Indo-China, the Soviet Union and China had become embroiled on opposite sides in the conflict between Kampuchea and Vietnam. [For further details of these developments, see Chapters XI and XIII.]

Renewed contacts between the Soviet Union and China during spring and summer 1979 led to negotiations in the autumn on the improvement of their relations. Preliminary meetings began in Moscow on Sept. 27 and formal talks continued until Nov. 30, 1979.

According to unofficial reports, the Chinese delegation asked that the Soviet forces on the Chinese border should be reduced to their 1964 level, in both numbers and equipment, and that Soviet troops should be withdrawn from Mongolia and the areas claimed by China. The Soviet delegation was reported to have replied that any reduction of the Soviet forces would be conditional on a corresponding reduction of the Chinese forces on the border.

Following the entry of Soviet military forces into Afghanistan at the end of December 1979, the Chinese Government decided that it was "inappropriate" to continue the negotiations and no further talks on the improvement of relations were held until October 1982. Border negotiations were also suspended.

Chinese Initiative on Border Issue (June 1981)

Proposals for a settlement of the border question were put forward in an article by Li Huichuan, deputy leader of the Chinese delegation to the 1979 Moscow talks, which appeared in the *People's Daily* on June 17, 1981.

Li stated that the Sino-Soviet border had been determined by a series of "unequal treaties imposed on China by Tsarist Russian imperialism", under which Russia had annexed over 1,500,000 square kilometres of Chinese territory (about 580,000 square miles), an area three times the size of France, and that after the Russian Revolution the Soviet Government in 1920 had declared these treaties null and void. A Sino-Soviet agreement of 1924 had provided that the border would be redemarcated and that meanwhile the status quo would be maintained, but no agreement had been reached at talks held in 1926, with the result that "the Sino-Soviet border issue remains unsettled to this day".

The Chinese Government, he continued, was prepared to take the existing treaties, "unequal" though they were, as the basis for determining the border line. Articles in the Soviet press, however, maintained that the present border had not only been delimited by the treaties, but had been "formed historically" and was "actually guarded" by Soviet troops, and the Soviet Government demanded that the "historically formed" and "actually defended" boundary line, which went far beyond that delimited by the treaties, should be taken as the basis for solving all boundary questions.

In conclusion, Li laid down the following conditions for a settlement: (i) The "unequal" nature of the treaties should be recognized. (ii) The boundary question should be settled through peaceful negotiations on the basis of the treaties. (iii) Any territory occupied by either side in violation of the treaties must be returned, although adjustments might be made in these areas in the interests of the local inhabitants. (iv) A new treaty should be signed and the boundary line surveyed and demarcated. (v) Pending the reaching of a settlement the status quo should be maintained, armed conflicts should be avoided, the two countries' forces should withdraw from or refrain from entering all disputed areas (i.e. those at which the boundary line was drawn in a different way on the maps exchanged during the boundary negotiations in 1964), and an agreement on the maintenance of the status quo should be signed.

The article was published on the day that Alexander Haig, the then US Secretary of State, left Beijing after talks at which no agreement was reached on the question of US sales of weapons to Taiwan, and was widely regarded as a warning to the United States that China might seek to improve her relations with the Soviet Union [see also Chapter X]. A few days later Li Xiannian (a vice-chairman of the Communist Party) told a West German delegation that China wanted to resume negotiations on the normalization of relations, but that the talks must deal with the withdrawal of Soviet troops from the Chinese border and from Afghanistan.

A new source of friction arose during the summer of 1981, when the Soviet Union signed a border agreement with Afghanistan, which recognized the Soviet claim to territory which was also claimed by China [for further details, see Chapter XIII].

Soviet Approaches (September 1981–March 1982)

In a Note of Sept. 25, 1981, the Soviet Government proposed that border negotiations should be resumed in Moscow. A Chinese official spokesman said on Dec. 29 that China had recently replied to the proposal, emphasizing that as previous negotiations had been unsuccessful adequate preparations should be made before they could be resumed. Sergei Tikhvinsky, deputy leader of the Soviet delegation to the Moscow talks, was reported to have arrived in Beijing on Jan. 14, 1982, for 10 days of secret talks with Chinese Foreign Ministry officials.

In an interview with the Italian Communist newspaper L'Unità published on Jan. 8, 1982, Li Xiannian said that both countries claimed 80,000 to 90,000 square kilometres of territory which were occupied by Soviet troops, and that the issues of withdrawal of Soviet troops from Afghanistan and of Vietnamese troops from Kampuchea and the Soviet troops on the Chinese border and in Mongolia would also have to be discussed at future talks. China favoured normalization of relations on the basis of the five principles of peaceful coexistence, he added, but "not a relationship like that between father and son".

The Soviet Government again proposed on Feb. 1, 1982, that the border talks should be resumed, although a Foreign Ministry spokesman said on

154 CHINA AND THE SOVIET UNION

Feb. 23 that the Soviet Union did not intend to discuss "territorial questions". In a major speech on Sino-Soviet relations delivered in Tashkent on March 24, 1982, President Brezhnev repeated the Soviet offer to reopen border negotiations. He stressed that the Soviet Union had no territorial claims on China and said that the Soviet Union was ready to continue talks on "existing border questions" and "possible measures to strengthen mutual trust" in the border area.

Although contacts between the two countries increased during the spring and summer of 1982, border negotiations were not formally resumed. Between 1982 and 1984, discussions on a possible settlement of the border dispute were subsumed within talks on an overall improvement of Sino-Soviet relations [see Chapter XIV].

Sino-Mongolian Relations (1969–84)—Maintenance of Mongolian Support for Soviet Union

Due to its position between China and the Soviet Union, Mongolia was drawn into the Sino-Soviet controversy, and in particular into the border dispute between the two powers. Mongolia maintained close and stable relations with the Soviet Union, and had thus had poor relations with China since the early 1960s. A central problem was the stationing of a large number of Soviet troops on the Sino-Mongolian border under a Mongolian-Soviet treaty of friendship, co-operation and mutual aid signed on Jan. 15, 1966.

Diplomatic relations between Mongolia and China were frozen in 1964 as a result of Mongolia's support for the Soviet Union in the Sino-Soviet ideological conflict. Relations reached a particularly low point in mid-1967, following the expulsion of Chinese teachers from Ulan Bator (the Mongolian capital), mass Chinese demonstrations outside the Mongolian embassy in Beijing, and an attack on the embassy in August. Diplomatic relations between the two countries were, however, normalized in 1971, with the arrival of a new Chinese ambassador to Mongolia on Aug. 20 and of a new Mongolian ambassador to China on Dec. 14, 1971.

From early 1978, the Chinese Government made the withdrawal of Soviet troops from Mongolia one of its key demands in exchanges on the border issue with the Soviet Union. The demand was made by Hua Guofeng in a speech on Feb. 26, 1978, and in an official Chinese reply on March 9 to a Soviet initiative [see page 151 above]. The Mongolian Government, in a Note of April 12 to China, stated that Soviet troops were stationed in its territory at its own request because of "Chinese expansionist aspirations", and would remain there as long as a "Chinese threat" continued.

Sino-Mongolian relations deteriorated after 1978 because of the Chinese demands. Friction was also caused by the expulsion from Mongolia in March and June 1979 of Chinese accused of "premeditated and organized crimes" and the initiation of proceedings against others charged with "embezzlement, opium cultivation and inferior work". Early in December 1979 *Unen*, the daily newspaper of the Mongolian People's Revolutionary Party (MPRP), claimed that some Chinese in Mongolia (among a local Chinese population of about 7,000) had confessed to collecting military and economic information in Mongolia on orders from Beijing and in order to cultivate anti-social nationalistic sentiments among morally unstable individuals. The Chinese school in Ulan Bator was also attacked as a breeding-ground for Chinese "chauvinism", and its director had been convicted of a number of serious crimes.

A Chinese diplomat was expelled from Ulan Bator in June 1980 after being accused of espionage. The Soviet news agency Tass subsequently reported on Sept. 2, 1980, that six Chinese residents had also been expelled for committing "illegal acts" which involved the violation of individual liberties.

President Tsedenbal, reporting on May 26, 1981, to the 18th congress of the MPRP, stressed the close relations between Mongolia and the Soviet Union, noting the significance of Soviet aid in strengthening Mongolia's defences and stating again that the Soviet troops were in Mongolia "at the request of our country".

Tsedenbal remarked that relations with China had deteriorated because the Chinese leaders "have distorted the principles of socialism, grossly violated the norms of intergovernmental relations and replaced them with policies and actions of great-power hegemonism, threats and dictates". He said that "the present Chinese leadership ranks with the forces of imperialist reaction", adding that Mongolia would continue to wage "an uncompromising struggle against China's actions", which constituted "an increasing threat to universal peace."

Further forcible expulsions of Chinese from Mongolia occurred in June 1982 and between March and June 1983, when a "certain number" (according to the Mongolian Government) of Chinese were also required to transfer from Ulan Bator (where most of them lived) to farms in the north of the country. The Chinese government protested against these actions by Mongolia.

Reports in August 1983 suggested that the number of expulsions had fallen after consultations between the Mongolian and Chinese Governments, but in September Chinese sources asserted that Chinese residents were still being expelled at a rate of at least 100 per day, and a statement by Mangalyn Dugersuren, the Foreign Minister, who said that only 200-300 of the Chinese residents were working, led to fears that the whole Chinese community could be expelled.

Diplomatic sources alleged that the expulsions were an attempt by the Mongolian Government to influence the second phase of talks on the normalization of relations between China and the Soviet Union [see Chapter XIV] and were linked to its opposition to the Chinese Government's demand for the withdrawal of Soviet military units from Mongolia.

An article in *Unen* of May 1983 attacked this Chinese demand as "an act of blatant interference in our country's internal affairs, an attempt to solve issues directly affecting the interests of the Mongolian people behind their backs", and asserted that Soviet troops were stationed in Mongolia temporarily, at the request of the Mongolian Government. Reiterating long-standing Mongolian concerns over China's alleged expansionist policies, Dugersuren reportedly said in August 1983 that China had long been trying to destroy Mongolia's independence and to annex the country, and asserted that "according to some sources, almost half the entire

[Chinese] armed forces are concentrated on the Chinese–Mongolian border". Meanwhile from Feb. 15 to March 15, 1983, when mass defence work tasks were traditionally promoted, a campaign of "reporting to the Marshal" (President Tsedenbal) was undertaken, aimed at improving the defence of Mongolia's borders.

XIII: CONTINUING INTERNATIONAL RIVALRIES, 1970–84

During the 1970s and early 1980s the Sino-Soviet split made itself felt more widely than previously through direct rivalry between the two Communist powers in certain regions of the world. The effect was strongest in Asia, where geo-strategic considerations led both countries into military action in neighbouring states in 1979. China suspected the Soviet Union of seeking to encircle it; this led to Chinese hostility towards India (especially in 1971–2) and Vietnam after 1978, since both had close links with the Soviet Union. The Soviet military presence in Afghanistan after 1979 aroused Chinese concern for the same reason. The Soviet Union feared the possibility of a Sino-Japanese alliance, and the two rivals vied for preferential relations with Japan.

Further afield China challenged Soviet influence more at a political and diplomatic level. Emerging from the isolation of the Cultural Revolution, it developed its contacts outside Asia. In Western Europe especially, China sought co-operation in modernizing its economy and counter-balancing Soviet power. During the 1970s China also developed a more pragmatic attitude towards other Communist states, which gained it useful contacts in Yugoslavia and Romania. International rivalry between China and the Soviet Union had an increasing effect on the world Communist movement, contributing to its growing fragmentation.

Indo-Pakistan War and its Aftermath (1971–July 1972)

During the crisis over East Pakistan (later Bangladesh) which led to the Indo-Pakistan War of December 1971, the Soviet Union and China took opposite sides. This arose from the longstanding identification of the Soviet Union with India and of China with Pakistan. Relations between China and India had been marked by hostility since before the Border War of 1962, and the Chinese remained suspicious of potential Indian encouragement for opposition in Tibet. For the Soviet Union, India represented a powerful supporter in South Asia, while China maintained its influence in the region through friendship with Pakistan.

The crisis in East Pakistan developed during 1971 over demands for full autonomy for the province. Fighting between East Pakistan rebels and the Pakistan army continued for much of the year, causing an exodus of over 9,000,000 refugees to neighbouring India. This imposed a severe strain on the Indian economy, and the crisis led to confrontation between India and Pakistan. Finally Indian forces entered East Pakistan in late November, swiftly taking control of the province. A ceasefire was concluded on Dec. 17.

As the crisis developed during 1971, China and the Soviet Union stated on a number of occasions their full support for Pakistan and India respectively. The Soviet Union blamed the Pakistani Government for allowing the situation to deteriorate, while China accused India of interfering in Pakistan's internal affairs. The Chinese drew a parallel between events in East Pakistan and the Tibetan rebellion of 1959, which India was alleged to have incited.

The initial Chinese reaction to the entry of Indian forces into East Pakistan was restrained, but this soon gave way to expressions of support for Pakistan and denunciations of the Indian action. Li Xiannian, a Deputy Premier, declared on Nov. 29, 1971, that "the Indian Government, supported and encouraged by social imperialism [i.e. the Soviet Union], has been carrying out subversive activities and military provocations against East Pakistan", and reaffirmed China's support for Pakistan in its "just struggle against foreign aggression".

In a statement issued by Tass on Dec. 5, 1971, the Soviet Government attributed the responsibility for the war to Pakistan, because of its failure to "take measures for a political settlement in East Pakistan". The statement called "for the speediest ending of the bloodshed, and for a political settlement in East Pakistan on the basis of respect for the lawful rights and interests of its people".

An Indian External Affairs Ministry spokesman stated on Dec. 4, 1971, that India had invoked Article 9 of the Indo-Soviet Treaty of Peace, Friendship and Co-operation, which provided for consultations in the event of an attack or threatened attack upon either party.

The *People's Daily* on Dec. 6, 1971, again attacked India in the strongest terms, repeating the allegations of Indian complicity in the 1959 rebellion in Tibet. After comparing "the gangster's logic of the Indian expansionists" to the policy of the Japanese in China in the 1930s, and Bangladesh to the Japanese puppet state of Manchukuo, it declared that "the Indian reactionaries are rampant to such an extent because they have the support of social imperialism" (i.e. the Soviet Union).

In reply to such Chinese attacks on the Soviet Union, *Pravda* accused China on Dec. 9, 1971, of provoking the war. "On the one hand", *Pravda* declared, "the Maoists tried by every means to worm their way into East Pakistan, and with the help of their agents preached a 'people's war' there. On the other they proclaimed their support for the military regime in Pakistan, trying to turn it into an instrument of their chauvinist great-power line in Asia. They are profoundly indifferent to the Pakistani people's real national interests, and regard Pakistan as just a puppet in their filthy game on the international scene. . . ."

The UN Security Council debated the war on Dec. 4–5, 1971. Huang Hua, the Chinese delegate, called on the Council to "condemn the aggressive acts of the Indian Government". A resolution calling for a ceasefire and the immediate withdrawal of armed personnel to their own sides of the border was vetoed by the Soviet delegate, Yakov Malik, who rejected the resolution as one-sided. He stated that it equated India, which was not to blame for the crisis, with Pakistan, whose actions had led to the fighting.

Further attempts in the Security Council on Dec. 5–6, 1971, to agree on a resolution were unsuccessful, as the Soviet Union was not prepared to accept a resolution which did not refer to the political situation in East Pakistan, and the US and China would not accept one which did. A feature of the Security Council's debates was the bitter exchange which took place between the Chinese and Soviet representatives. Huang Hua, for example, asserted on Dec. 6 that "the Soviet social imperialists are carrying out aggression, subversion and expansion everywhere", to which Malik retorted: "The Chinese representative, with his vicious pathological slander against the Soviet Union, is aspiring to the role of the imperialists' court jester."

The Security Council finally decided on Dec. 6, 1971, to refer the question to the General Assembly, which met the next day. A group of countries (of which only Italy was directly allied to either super-power) presented a resolution calling for a ceasefire and the withdrawal of forces by both sides. Malik again rejected this motion, suggesting that "a mere ceasefire between the armed forces of India and Pakistan would in practice mean the continuation of reprisals and terror by the Pakistan authorities"; the Pakistan Government must also "end the bloodshed and promptly and unconditionally recognize the will of the East Pakistani population". Jiao Guanhua, the Chinese delegate, asserted that "the Indian Government is an outright aggressor" and that "the Soviet Government is the boss behind the Indian aggressors", and declared that "the UN must strongly condemn India's aggression against Pakistan and thoroughly expose the shameless support given by the Soviet social imperialists to the Indian aggressors". The resolution was passed, with the Soviet Union and its allies (except for Romania) voting against.

The Security Council met again on Dec. 12–13, 1971. The US delegate moved a resolution virtually identical to that adopted by the General Assembly on Dec. 7. This was opposed by Yakov Malik, who again stated that the resolution ignored the main cause of the fighting. During the course of the debate, Malik proposed that a Bangladeshi (East Pakistani) representative, Justice Abu Sayeed Chowdhury, should be allowed to address the Council. Malik had first raised this suggestion in the Security Council on Dec. 4, but had agreed then that the matter required further consultation. On both occasions, Huang Hua objected (stating on Dec. 4 that participation of the Bangladeshi representative would be tantamount to interfering in Pakistan's domestic affairs). As a result, Justice Chowdhury did not address the Council.

The Chinese Government on Dec. 16, 1971, issued a new statement violently attacking Indian and Soviet policies. After accusing the Indian forces of "most brutal atrocities" in East Pakistan, the statement remarked that India was planning to "swallow up" the province and "destroy Pakistan as a whole". It also asserted that the purpose of Soviet policies was "further to strengthen its control over India and thereby to proceed to contend with the other super-power for hegemony in the whole of the South Asian subcontinent and the Indian Ocean, and at the same time to foster India and turn it into a sub-super-power on the South Asian subcontinent as its assistant and partner in committing aggression against Asia".

Zhou Enlai made a similar attack on India and the Soviet Union on Dec. 17, 1971, accusing India inter alia of having "massacred" the people of East Pakistan. *Pravda* retorted on Dec. 22 with an article alleging that China had urged the United States to send its warships into the Indian Ocean, and accusing Zhou Enlai of being a main instigator of China's anti-Soviet policies.

Following the conclusion of a ceasefire in East Pakistan, the Security Council met again on Dec. 22, 1971, when a compromise resolution was put forward. This called for strict observance of the ceasefire, and the withdrawal of all armed forces as soon as practicable to their respective territories. The resolution was adopted by 13 votes to none, with the Soviet Union abstaining. China, while voting for the resolution, expressed dissatisfaction with it.

The Bangladesh government-in-exile established itself in Dacca on Dec. 22, 1971 (having originally declared independence on March 26). The Soviet Union recognized the new state on Jan. 24, 1972, and immediately began to provide it with economic assistance. China did not recognize Bangladesh until Aug. 31, 1975.

Relations with Japan (1972–83)

Both China and the Soviet Union had an interest in gaining the favour of Japan, an increasingly powerful economic and political neighbour. The Chinese wished to enlist Japanese support to counter the growing Soviet strength in the Pacific, while the Soviet Union wanted to prevent Japan from joining China in an anti-Soviet alliance. The situation was complicated by territorial disputes, especially between the Soviet Union and Japan. For its part, Japan attempted to maintain a balance in its dealings with China and the Soviet Union.

The Soviet–Japanese territorial dispute concerned a number of islands off the north-east coast of Japan, occupied by the Soviet Union in the closing stages of World War II. The islands in question were the Habomai group, Shikotan, Etorofu and Kunashiri, all regarded by Japan as integral parts of its national territory. The islands lie at the southern end of the Kurile island chain, and are important both strategically and as fishing centres. Although the two countries normalized their diplomatic relations in 1956, the dispute over the islands has prevented the conclusion of a formal peace treaty.

The Soviet Union and Japan held ministerial meetings intermittently to discuss the problem of the "Northern Territories", as the Japanese call the islands under dispute. Although no real progress was made in the talks, this did not stop the two countries from signing a number of agreements between June 1974 and July 1975 for the joint development of natural resources in Siberia and the Soviet Far East.

Japan had also been discussing the signing of a treaty of peace and friendship with China, since the establishment of diplomatic relations between the two states in September 1972. Oleg Troyanovsky, the Soviet ambassador in Tokyo, was early in February 1975 reported to have suggested that the conclusion of such a treaty would entail "an unfortunate reaction" on Soviet–Japanese relations. He was also said to have repeated an earlier Soviet proposal to postpone the conclusion of a peace treaty and to sign instead a treaty of "friendship and goodwill", as proposed by Andrei Gromyko during a visit by Kiichi Miyazawa, the Japanese Foreign Minister, to Moscow in mid-January 1975. This suggestion was raised again in mid-February by Leonid Brezhnev in a letter to Takeo Miki, the Japanese Prime Minister. However, the Japanese rejected the proposal on the grounds that a friendship treaty would virtually shelve the issue of Japan's claim to the disputed islands.

The Japanese Government persisted with its avowed aim of concluding a treaty of peace and friendship with China. The Soviet Government on June 18, 1975, published a statement cautioning Japan against allowing itself "to be drawn, in one form or another, into the orbit of Chinese policy", and adding: "It is in the joint interest of Japan and the Soviet Union to administer a deserved rebuff to all attempts by third powers . . . which seek to prevent an improvement in Soviet–Japanese relations."

The Japanese Foreign Ministry replied on June 19, 1975, that the proposed peace treaty with China was "not directed against any third country". Miki declared on the same day: "We have no particular country in view, as for instance the Soviet Union, while negotiating with Beijing. The anti-hegemony clause [in any agreement with China] is nothing but the expression of a universally accepted principle of peace."

It was reported in mid-September 1975 that Miyazawa had been strongly warned again by Gromyko against signing a treaty with China embodying the "anti-hegemony clause". The Japanese Foreign Minister indicated reservations about the clause, but he said that China still insisted on its inclusion in a Sino-Japanese treaty. The issue of the "anti-hegemony clause" remained a prominent question in Sino-Japanese negotiations over the next two years.

Obstacles to the signing of a peace treaty between China and Japan appeared to arise between April and June 1978 over two issues—Japan's sovereignty over the uninhabited Senkaku Islands, part of the Ryukyu Islands but claimed both by China and Taiwan, and the exchange of documents of ratification between Japan and South Korea on an agreement on the development of the continental shelf between them. The first problem emerged when a Chinese fishing fleet began operations on April 12, 1978, in the territorial waters of the Senkaku Islands; following Japanese representations to the Chinese Government, officials in Beijing stressed that the incident was "an accidental affair" and indicated that China would seek to avoid a recurrence of any conflicts over the islands. By mid-August 1978 it was being suggested that China had practically recognized Japan's control over the Senkaku Islands.

With regard to the Japanese–South Korean agreement on the continental shelf, the Chinese Government reiterated on May 10, 1978, its previous statement of June 13, 1977, that the agreement infringed China's sovereignty over its continental shelf in the East China Sea. The exchange of ratification documents between Japan and South Korea on June 22, 1978, led to strong protests by China. The issue remained unresolved, but did not prevent the conclusion of a Sino-Japanese peace treaty within two months.

The Sino-Japanese treaty was signed in Beijing on Aug. 12, 1978, by Huang Hua and Sunao Sonoda, the Chinese and Japanese Foreign Ministers respectively. Article II of the treaty stated: "The contracting parties declare that neither of them should seek hegemony in the Asia–Pacific region or in any other region and that each is opposed to efforts by any other country or group of countries to establish such hegemony." Article IV stated: "The present treaty shall not affect the position of either contracting party regarding its relations with third countries." The Chinese had objected to the inclusion of a sentence stating that the "anti-hegemony clause" was not directed at any particular third country.

The Soviet Union reacted strongly to the signing of the treaty. Tass remarked on Aug. 13, 1978, that Japan had yielded to Beijing's "diktat" and that it was taking the risk of being involved in China's "hegemonistic policy". The Soviet Union had warned Japan before the treaty was signed of the possible consequences for their relations.

Relations between China and Japan improved greatly during 1978–80 following the signing of the treaty of peace and friendship. As a result of an eight-year trade agreement signed by the two countries on Feb. 16, 1978, a number of economic co-operation agreements were concluded. These included industrial development schemes in China and oil exploration off the China coast. In return for Japanese equipment and loans, China was to supply Japan with coal and oil.

The intensification of economic links between China and Japan was accompanied by increased ministerial contacts which often took place at an unprecedentedly high level. During these visits, as well as discussing bilateral economic relations, the Chinese and Japanese leaders consulted on international developments of mutual concern, particularly the Soviet build-up in the Pacific, the Soviet involvement in Afghanistan after December 1979, and developments in Indo-China. While the two countries agreed about developments in the Pacific and Afghanistan, Japan did not join in condemnation of the Vietnamese campaigns in Kampuchea after December 1978, and it protested against China's military action against Vietnam in February and March 1979.

During 1978–79 the Soviet Union and Japan made no further progress in negotiations towards a peace treaty or towards a settlement of the "Northern Territories" dispute. Japan claimed that the Soviet Pacific fleet was being steadily reinforced and that the Soviet Union was building up its forces on the disputed islands. The Soviet Union rejected Japanese complaints over this build-up, and on Sept. 2, 1980, the Novosti news agency referred to Japan's recent "dangerous alliance with American and Chinese hegemonists on the basis of nationalism and anti-Sovietism".

Despite these difficulties, the Soviet Union and Japan agreed in this period on a number of joint development projects relating to mineral resources on and around Sakhalin and in Siberia. Mutual trade also increased up to 1980, but was then affected by Japanese sanctions applied in response to the entry of Soviet forces into Afghanistan. China's economic co-operation with Japan was also affected in 1980, due to the re-orientation of Chinese development plans. During a visit to Japan by Hua Guofeng on May 27–June 1, Gu Mu (a Deputy Premier) indicated that China might have to cut some joint projects and lower its agreed oil deliveries to Japan. The Japanese strongly expressed disappointment over the cancellation of contracts, but on Feb. 13, 1981, Gu Mu apologised for the "troublesome problems" caused by China's decisions, and said that Japan would be indemnified against any losses arising as a result.

Following the imposition of martial law in Poland on Dec. 13, 1981, the Japanese Government joined the United States and its allies in imposing certain sanctions on the Soviet Union during February 1982. Japan also joined the Western countries in protesting strongly against the shooting-down of a Korean airliner off Sakhalin by a Soviet fighter on the night of

Aug. 31–Sept. 1, 1983. Japan's relations with China were affected in mid-1982 by a controversy over the official revision of Japanese school history textbooks, which minimized Japanese atrocities on the Asian mainland during the 1930s and 1940s. Following vigorous Chinese protests, Japan agreed to amend the texts.

Conflict in Indo-China (1975–84)

During the late 1970s, Indo-China became one of the foremost areas of confrontation between China and the Soviet Union as a result of the hostility between China and Vietnam. The latter maintained an armed presence in neighbouring Kampuchea and Laos, and was supported by the Soviet Union. China suspected Vietnam of aiming to control all of Indo-China, encouraged by the Soviet Union, and saw this as evidence of Soviet expansionism and as a threat to its security. The Soviet Union accused China of deliberately prolonging conflict in Indo-China for its own ends, including the exacerbation of international tension.

Following the Communist victories in South Vietnam and Kampuchea during April 1975, relations between Vietnam and China soon began to deteriorate. Vietnam inclined increasingly towards the Soviet Union, while Kampuchea revealed sympathy for China in the Sino-Soviet controversy. Sino-Vietnamese relations were also complicated by an unsettled dispute over the Paracel and Spratly Islands, situated in the South China Sea. At the same time, relations between Vietnam and Kampuchea worsened after 1975, leading to intermittent border clashes. By 1977 this had led to serious fighting, and on Dec. 31 of that year Kampuchea broke off diplomatic relations with Vietnam. China supported Kampuchea, and the Soviet Union and its allies backed Vietnam; both powers accused each other of having hegemonistic aims in the region.

During early 1978 Sino-Vietnamese relations rapidly worsened. Vietnamese economic policy and the regional situation caused insecurity among the Chinese minority in Vietnam, which numbered about 1,500,000. Encouraged by the authorities, over 160,000 fled to China during mid-1978. China protested against Vietnamese pressure on the Chinese minority. During April 1978 border clashes between the two countries were reported, and incidents on the Sino-Vietnamese border occurred increasingly frequently after August. Chinese economic aid to Vietnam was ended on July 3, 1978, four days after Vietnam had been admitted to Comecon. On Nov. 3 the Soviet Union and Vietnam signed a treaty of friendship and co-operation, as well as six economic agreements. These developments and the fighting on the Kampuchean border contributed to a rise in tension between China and the Soviet Union during the course of the year.

Fighting on the Vietnamese–Kampuchean border continued during 1978, and finally on Dec. 25 Vietnamese troops invaded Kampuchea. Phnom Penh, the Kampuchean capital, fell on Jan. 7, 1979, and the following day a "People's Revolutionary Council", with Heng Samrin as President, was set up by Kampuchean exiles who had been leading an armed campaign against the Khmer Rouge regime since 1975. Vietnam and the Soviet bloc recognized the new regime, whereas China denounced the Vietnamese invasion and Heng Samrin's Government, asserting on Jan. 14, 1979, that "the Vietnamese aggressors" were "aided and abetted by Soviet social-imperialism". There were unconfirmed reports during February 1979 of Chinese supplies to the Khmers Rouges through Thailand.

The UN Security Council debated the crisis on Jan. 11–15, 1979. The Soviet Union vetoed a resolution calling for the withdrawal of foreign forces from Kampuchea. During the debate the Chinese representative, Zhen Zhu, said that the Soviet Union was using Vietnam as its "Asian Cuba" in a drive for worldwide hegemony; Oleg Troyanovsky, the Soviet representative, accused the Khmers Rouges under Pol Pot of committing "open genocide" in the construction of a "Maoist society", and of aggression against Vietnam and Thailand.

Clashes on the Sino-Vietnamese border continued during early 1979. On Feb. 17 China invaded Vietnam, claiming it was undertaking a limited counter-attack in self-defence after repeated Vietnamese provocations. The Chinese troops occupied a number of towns in the border area, but after suffering heavy casualties began to withdraw on March 5, completing their evacuation by March 16, 1979. Inconclusive border negotiations between the two countries took place later in the spring.

Although the Soviet Union indicated that it would not intervene in the war so long as its scale remained limited, Soviet criticism of the Chinese invasion was stern. An article published in *Pravda* on Feb. 28, 1979, accused China of treating South-East Asia as its sphere of influence. China, it alleged, had offered to send troops to North Vietnam during the war with the United States, while obstructing the delivery of Soviet military aid; brought the Pol Pot regime to power in Kampuchea; had "planned in detail the wholesale annihilation of the Kampuchean people" as a step to "Chinese assimilation of . . . Kampuchea and its transformation into an important Chinese bridgehead for the encirclement of 'disobedient' Vietnam, offering also direct access to Malaysia, Thailand and Indonesia"; and had ordered the Pol Pot regime to attack Vietnam, in order to "make Vietnam fight on two fronts at once".

The article also suggested an element of encouragement of China by the United States, adding that "Beijing does not deny the connexion between the timing of the aggression, the conclusion of the Sino-Japanese treaty and the 'normalization' of Sino-American relations. . .". In a speech on March 2, 1979, Brezhnev condemned China's policy as "the most serious threat to peace in the whole world" and referred to "the danger of any forms of connivance with that policy", but did not directly mention the United States in this context.

A debate on the situation in South-East Asia began in the Security Council on Feb. 23, 1979. Deadlock ensued due to Soviet insistence on vetoing any resolution which did not specifically condemn China, while Zhen Zhu threatened the Chinese veto against any resolution which did, and also sought to include the Vietnamese occupation of Kampuchea in the debate. After further consultations, the Council on March 16 debated a motion which "deeply regretted" the invasion of Vietnam and Kampuchea and called for the withdrawal of foreign troops from both countries. Oleg Troyanovsky vetoed the resolution, since it did not contain a "clear-cut condemnation of Chinese aggression" and put the "aggressor on the same footing as its victim". Zhen Zhu voted for the resolution, although he criticized it for not condemning Vietnam sufficiently and for regretting China's "just action" which had now been completed by the withdrawal of Chinese forces.

The events of 1978 and early 1979 had a decisive effect on China's relations with Laos, which had come under full Communist control in 1975. Up to 1978 Laos attempted to remain neutral in the disputes dividing the region and in the Sino-Soviet controversy. However, the Lao regime was unable to maintain this position; it recognized the Heng Samrin Government in Kampuchea and called for the withdrawal of Chinese forces from Vietnam after the invasion. Accordingly, relations between Laos and China became increasingly strained from March 1979 onwards, and led to a number of incidents on their common border.

In late April 1979 the presence of Vietnamese troops in Laos was admitted officially for the first time. Nguyen Duy Trinh, the Vietnamese Foreign Minister, said on April 29 that the troops were stationed there at the Lao Government's request, in accordance with the treaty of friendship and co-operation signed by the two countries in July 1977. Further border incidents between Laos and China occurred in 1981, and there were reports that China was assisting Lao groups opposed to the regime.

From 1979 onwards Vietnam continued to maintain armed forces in Kampuchea in an attempt to quell resistance to the Heng Samrin Government by the Khmers Rouges and other groups. China kept up its insistence on the withdrawal of Vietnamese troops as a condition for the improvement of Sino-Vietnamese relations. Soviet economic assistance to Vietnam increased steadily. Border clashes between China and Vietnam occurred at intervals; peaks in Chinese shelling tended to coincide with Vietnamese offensives in Kampuchea.

The Vietnamese military presence in Kampuchea became one of the central issues dividing China and the Soviet Union. China demanded the withdrawal of Soviet support and aid from Vietnam as one of the three conditions for an improvement in Sino-Soviet relations. Chinese leaders also expressed concern about the possibility that the Soviet navy would use Vietnamese ports. The Soviet Union refused to discuss the issue of Kampuchea, maintaining that this was a question affecting a third country, and that Soviet aid to Vietnam was determined by the 1978 treaty of friendship.

Soviet Intervention in Afghanistan (1978–84)

A coup d'état in Afghanistan in April 1978 brought to power a revolutionary socialist regime which developed close relations with the Soviet Union, leading to the signing of an Afghan–Soviet treaty of friendship and co-operation in December 1978. The Soviet Union sent military aid and advisers to Afghanistan to help the regime combat Moslem resistance groups, which challenged government authority through much of the country. In addition, the Soviet Union supplied extensive economic assistance. The growing Soviet influence in Afghanistan caused concern in China, which feared that the security of its western border would be endangered. The subsequent entry of Soviet forces into Afghanistan at the end of 1979 turned the country into one of the focal points of the Sino-Soviet conflict.

During 1978 and 1979 the Afghan and Soviet authorities repeatedly accused China of giving aid to the Moslem rebels. These allegations were rebutted by China on June 21, 1979, in a protest note to the Afghan chargé d'affaires in Beijing. The Chinese Government subsequently accused the Soviet Union of intending to expand its sphere of influence in the Afghan-Pakistani region.

President Nur Mohammad Taraki, the Afghan leader, was overthrown by a rival faction led by Hafizullah Amin in September 1979. Under Amin the internal situation, and relations with the Soviet Union, deteriorated. Amin was in turn removed at the end of December and executed, being replaced by Babrak Karmal. The change of regime was accompanied by the entry into Afghanistan of 4,000–5,000 Soviet troops on Dec. 25–26, 1979. The Soviet Union maintained that the Afghan Government had invited it to send troops under the treaty of friendship in the face of provocation from Afghanistan's external enemies. One of the apparent reasons for the Soviet action was to provide military support for the Afghan armed forces in their campaign against the Moslem resistance fighters. By the end of January 1980 the Soviet forces had risen to an estimated 85,000, and were deployed throughout the country with hundreds of tanks.

The Chinese Government on Dec. 29 called the Soviet move "another grave international incident following the Soviet armed occupation of Czechoslovakia in 1968", the first large-scale Soviet military intervention in a third-world country, and a "threat to peace and security in Asia and the whole world". This time, the Soviet Union had "unmasked itself by trampling underfoot all international norms" and could no longer pass itself off as an "angel championing world peace". A formal Note of protest was delivered to the Soviet Union by China on Dec. 31, 1979.

The *People's Daily* on Jan. 1 accused the Soviet Union not only of gaining an "iron grip" on Afghanistan but also of seeking a "stepping stone for a southward thrust towards Pakistan and the whole subcontinent", adding that there would be "no peace from South Asia to the Horn of Africa with 45,000 Soviet soldiers in strategic Afghanistan".

The Chinese Foreign Minister, Huang Hua, was in Pakistan from Jan. 18 to 23, 1980, on an official visit, stating on his arrival in Islamabad that developments in Afghanistan had added new significance to his visit. At the conclusion of the visit, Hua told a press conference that his talks with the Pakistan Government had been mainly concerned with Afghanistan and he called on the world, "above all the USA, Western Europe and Japan", to give "real support to Afghanistan's neighbours in order to counter the Soviet power".

Hua said that China felt that the Soviet invasion was another step towards the gulf oilfields with the aim of isolating the United States and the West; the industrial powers and other peace-loving nations must work out a joint strategy over Afghanistan and must avoid a third world war by being aware of Soviet expansionism. According to the Lahore Urdu-language daily *Nawa-i-Waqt*, China had offered to give Pakistan full military and economic support in the face of the Soviet military intervention in Afghanistan. *Pravda* had claimed on Jan. 9, 1980, that China was sending large arms supplies into Pakistan over the Karakoram

Highway (which linked the two countries). However, the Pakistani authorities stated on Jan. 22 that no agreements for military aid had been concluded with China.

The Chinese Foreign Ministry announced on Jan. 19, 1980, that negotiations on the normalization of relations with the Soviet Union (the first phase of which had taken place during the previous autumn—see page 139) had been suspended due to the Soviet intervention in Afghanistan. From this point on the Soviet presence in the country constituted one of the main obstacles to the resumption of border negotiations and a general improvement in Sino-Soviet relations.

An Afghan-Soviet border agreement signed on June 16, 1981, provoked strong Chinese reactions. The agreement related to the Wakhan Salient, a mountainous, sparsely populated but strategically important tongue of Afghan territory which ran north-east from the main part of Afghanistan to the Chinese border, passing between the Soviet Union in the north and Pakistan in the south [see map on page 88].

No exact details of the agreement were released, but Kabul radio said on June 17, 1981, that it regulated the local boundary between Afghanistan and the Soviet Union. During the next two months Soviet troops began a massive occupation of the salient, and by mid-August it was reported that they had expelled the 2,000–3,000 Afghan residents, that they had closed the border with Pakistan and manned it with Soviet officers, and that they had set up extensive military bases in the region.

The Chinese Ministry of Foreign Affairs on July 22, 1981, issued a statement complaining essentially that the Soviet Union had no right to conclude with a third country (i.e. Afghanistan) a border treaty involving this line, since the land immediately to the north of the border was not the rightful territory of the Soviet Union, but had in fact for some 90 years been in dispute between China and Russia (subsequently the Soviet Union). The treaty was, it said, therefore "illegal and invalid", although it stressed also that China had no outstanding territorial disputes with Afghanistan itself, having signed on Nov. 22, 1963, a border agreement regulating its 43-mile border with Afghanistan along the extreme eastern edge of the Wakhan Salient.

China's case against the Soviet Union rested on an 1884 protocol "concerning the Chinese-Russian border in the region of Kashgar" (or, as the New China News Agency termed it on Aug. 31, 1981, the "Sino-Russian Kashgar boundary treaty"). The agreement, which had been reached after a prolonged period of Russian incursions into and encroachments on the traditional Chinese territories of central Asia, had specified that from the Uz-Bel mountain pass "the Russian boundary turns to the south-west and the Chinese boundary runs due south"; Russia had, according to the Chinese, nevertheless in 1892 illegally occupied some 20,000 square kilometres of Chinese territory, and had subsequently attempted to legitimize this invasion by describing an 1894 Chinese-Russian exchange of notes on the issue as constituting a border agreement (an account rejected by China since, it said, in the 1894 exchange of notes the two sides had agreed to differ over the sovereignty of the territory in question but had decided to maintain the positions which they then held, pending a permanent settlement).

Tass responded on Aug. 11, 1981, by asserting that the newly-signed border treaty between Afghanistan and the Soviet Union was a bilateral affair involving no third countries, and accused China of "inventing", by "falsifying history", a dispute over a matter which had been finally settled by the 1894 exchange of notes. "The [1894] line is still in existence", said the report, "and there is no other line".

The New China News Agency claimed on Aug. 24, 1981, that the Soviet troops had installed ballistic missiles in the Wakhan Salient. Mrs Jeane Kirkpatrick, the US permanent representative to the UN, claimed on Nov. 18, 1981, that the Soviet Union had carried out a "de facto annexation" of the salient, and that the treaty of June 16 included the accession by Afghanistan to the formal Soviet annexation of the area.

The Chinese Government continued to maintain a strongly hostile position towards the Soviet Union with regard to the Afghan crisis. The withdrawal of Soviet forces from Afghanistan was among China's three basic demands put forward in negotiations on the differences between the two powers. The Soviet Union, however, insisted that its presence in Afghanistan was a matter affecting only the internal security of a third country, which could not, therefore, be discussed with China.

The East European Connexion (1969–84)

After 1969 China sought to use the East European states as a means of political pressure on the Soviet Union. Earlier ideological objections to the Yugoslav regime were played down, and good relations with Yugoslavia, and with President Ceausescu's Romania, were cultivated assiduously. The root of these links was the common opposition of all three states to the invasion of Czechoslovakia in 1968 [see page 84]. Between 1968 and 1971 a rapprochement in Sino-Yugoslav relations took place, and on Aug. 17, 1970, diplomatic contacts (kept at chargé d'affaires level only since 1958) were restored to ambassadorial level. At the same time China maintained good relations with Romania, which had shown further signs of independence in foreign policy and had openly disagreed with the Soviet Union.

From the late 1960s the Chinese press ceased attacking Yugoslav "revisionism", and now restricted its criticism to states loyally supporting the Soviet Union. The workers' riots in the Polish Baltic cities in mid-December 1970 were applauded by the *People's Daily* on Dec. 22, 1970, leading to an accusation by *Pravda* of "unpardonable interference" in Poland's internal affairs by China.

It was reported on April 26, 1971, that Romania had been acting as a diplomatic channel between China and the United States, following Ceausescu's visit to the USA the previous October. On June 1–9, 1971, he paid an official visit to China, accompanied by the Romanian Prime Minister, Ion Gheorghe Maurer, meeting Chairman Mao and Zhou Enlai for talks.

At a banquet on June 1, 1971, Zhou praised Romania's resistance to "foreign pressure" and "big-power chauvinism", in reply to which Ceausescu appealed by implication for the ending of the Sino-Soviet dispute and said that Romania was trying to overcome difficulties "existing between the socialist countries and between the Communist parties". The joint communiqué issued at the end of the visit reaffirmed Chinese support for Romania's independent foreign policy, while

Romania noted that "no thorough settlement of important international questions is possible" without China, also stating its approval of the normalization of relations between China and capitalist states.

Mirko Tepavac, the Yugoslav Foreign Minister, led a delegation which visited Beijing on June 9–15, 1971. At the start of the visit, Li Xiannian (a Deputy Premier and a member of the CPC politburo) praised Yugoslavia's independence and its "struggles against the interference, subversion and threats of aggression by the super-powers".

Tepavac's visit to China coincided with a period of increased tension in relations between Yugoslavia and the Soviet bloc. The Yugoslav Government was reported to have made a verbal protest to the Soviet ambassador at the beginning of June 1971 against the activities in Moscow of Yugoslav "Cominformists" who had taken refuge in the Soviet Union after the break between Yugoslavia and the Cominform in 1948. Yugoslav sources also suggested that the Soviet Government was encouraging the activities of extreme right-wing Croat nationalists in Western Europe.

Relations between Romania and the rest of the Soviet bloc became extremely strained in August 1971, following Ceausescu's visit to China and the announcement on July 15 of President Nixon's forthcoming visit to China, which was viewed with deep suspicion in Moscow as an attempt to bring pressure on the Soviet Union. The Communist Party leaders of the Soviet bloc, excluding Romania, met in the Crimea on Aug. 2, 1971, and approved a communiqué condemning "right-wing and left-wing opportunism"—terms applied in Soviet parlance respectively to the policies of Romania and Yugoslavia and that of China. The Crimea meeting was followed by a violent campaign against Romania in the Soviet, Polish, Czechoslovak and Hungarian press.

Both the Romanian and the Yugoslav leadership rejected charges that their developing contacts with China were creating an anti-Soviet axis in the Balkans. The Soviet ambassador to Romania, V. I. Drozdenko, had a meeting with Ceausescu on Aug. 18, 1971, at which he was unofficially reported to have delivered a Soviet note accusing Romania of organizing an anti-Soviet bloc in the region under Chinese and US patronage, and demanding an end to such activities. However, Ceausescu continued to assert Romania's independence in foreign policy and to reject the idea of a centrally-controlled world Communist movement. A Chinese military delegation, led by Gen. Li Desheng (director of the army's political department and an alternate member of the politburo), visited Romania on Aug. 22–31, 1978. During the visist Gen. Li restated China's support for Romania's independent policy.

Soviet pressure on Yugoslavia also continued during the summer of 1971. President Tito was reported to have received a message from Brezhnev on Aug. 18 (the same day as the Soviet note to Romania) expressing misgivings over Yugoslavia's increasingly friendly relations with China, and the manoeuvres in Hungary and the proposed manoeuvres in Bulgaria were regarded as a gesture directed against Yugoslavia as well as Romania. However, Soviet–Yugoslav relations improved during September 1971, leading to a visit by Brezhnev on Sept. 22–25.

Yugoslavia continued to build up its links with China during the mid-1970s, while maintaining regular contacts with the Soviet leadership. Inter-party relations were restored between the CPC and the League of Communists of Yugoslavia in March 1978, and Sino-Yugoslav trade rose rapidly.

Hua Guofeng visited Romania and Yugoslavia during August 1978, the first visit to Europe by a chairman of the CPC since Mao's visit to Moscow in 1957. Hua's visit to Romania (on Aug. 16–21, 1978) coincided with the 10th anniversary of the invasion of Czechoslovakia. Speaking on Aug. 16, Hua declared that "imperialism and hegemonism, reaching out everywhere in Asia, Africa, Latin America and Europe, have kept carrying out infiltration, subversion, aggression and expansion against other countries". However, his speech was regarded as moderate in tone, and it was reported that the Chinese visitors had been asked by the Romanian Government to refrain from allusions which the Soviet Union might find offensive. A press communiqué on the talks issued on Aug. 18 (which was reported to have caused some disagreement between the two sides) condemned "any form of domination and diktat", but did not mention the controversial word "hegemonism". Nevertheless, the Soviet press denounced the visit, and on Aug. 24 *Pravda* attacked "Beijing's aggressiveness", stating that "only those who put blinkers over their eyes can fail to see this".

In a speech on the first day of his visit to Yugoslavia, Hua repeated his charge that the USSR and the USA were competing for world domination, as well as speaking approvingly of Yugoslavia's policies of self-management and non-alignment. He pointed to the role of the non-aligned movement [to which Yugoslavia belonged] in the "struggle of the world's people against imperialism, colonialism and hegemonism", and accused "some people" of "doing their utmost to undermine the unity of the non-aligned movement, change its orientation and subordinate it to their own hegemonist aims". *Pravda* implicitly criticized the Yugoslavs for not dissociating themselves from Hua's remarks.

Romania and Yugoslavia maintained a neutral stance towards the Vietnamese–Kampuchean conflict during 1978, but they attacked the Vietnamese invasion of Kampuchea in December and thereafter kept up their opposition to the Vietnamese military presence in Kampuchea. Romania also differed with its Warsaw Pact partners at a summit in Moscow on Nov. 22–23, 1978, when Ceausescu refused to raise Romania's defence spending by 3 per cent or to integrate the Romanian forces into a unified Warsaw Pact command. Both Yugoslavia and Romania strongly criticized the Soviet military intervention in Afghanistan in December 1979.

China maintained its close relations with Yugoslavia and Romania between 1978 and 1984, and a number of visits by party and government leaders were made in both directions. In May 1983 Hu Yaobang, the CPC general secretary, visited Romania and Yugoslavia. Although he praised Yugoslav non-alignment, he did not refer directly to the Soviet Union nor did he attack hegemonism. His moderate tone (compared with that of Hua Guofeng in 1978) was linked by observers with the Sino-Soviet negotiations then in progress.

Following Hu's departure from Yugoslavia on May 15, 1983, Qian Qichen (the Deputy Foreign Minister and chief Chinese representative at the Sino-Soviet talks, who had been accompanying Hu) went on to visit Hungary, Poland and East Germany. This was regarded as a sign that China wanted better relations with all the East European states. In early 1982 China had refrained from condemning the imposition of martial law in Poland on Dec. 13, 1981, and instead of joining the West in raising sanctions against Poland as a response, China signed a trade agreement with Poland in early February 1982.

Wu Xueqian, the Chinese Foreign Minister, stated on March 28, 1984, during a visit to Yugoslavia, that the two countries had "identical points of view on numerous international questions" and "many similarities in the internal development of their socialist societies".

During the 1970s China's rapprochement with Yugoslavia and the improvement in its relations with the USA and other capitalist states lost it the support of Albania, its only ally in Eastern Europe since the early 1960s. Albania began criticizing the Chinese "three worlds" theory in mid-1977, and gradually its attacks on Chinese policy sharpened until July 11, 1978, when China announced the termination of all economic aid to Albania. The Albanians continued thereafter to denounce China. Trade links between the two countries were resumed during 1983, but Albania did not modify its political criticism of China.

Relations with West European States (1969–84)

During the years after 1969, the relations of China and the Soviet Union with Western Europe resembled the pattern of their dealings with the United States. After its hostility to the West during the Cultural Revolution, China decided to cultivate the West European countries as a counterweight to the Soviet Union and as a partner in economic and technical co-operation. Economic considerations similarly influenced the Soviet Union in seeking to encourage détente in Europe, as well as the desire to lessen tension in the continent. The latter aim was seen as being in part prompted by the continuing confrontation between the Soviet Union and China; the maintenance of strong defences on two fronts placed a heavy strain on the Soviet economy, and the Soviet leaders were concerned about the possibility of attack from two directions.

Détente was effectively pioneered by the Soviet Union and France during the 1960s, while Charles de Gaulle was President of France. The two countries held a number of governmental meetings at the highest level, developed trade and economic co-operation, and signed a series of agreements in various fields. Following the October 1969 election of a Social Democratic Government in West Germany, with Willy Brandt as Chancellor, a similar process began. During the 1970s the Soviet Union further improved its relations with the remaining West European states, leading to a general increase in trade and technical exchange and a temporary decrease in tension.

China's rapprochement with Western Europe began with limited gestures such as the release of European nationals imprisoned by the Chinese during the Cultural Revolution, and the restoration of direct telephone links. China and the United Kingdom on March 13, 1972, established full diplomatic relations at ambassadorial level, after an interval of 22 years (during which period the two countries had been represented by chargés d'affaires in each other's capitals). The United Kingdom acknowledged that Taiwan was a province of China, and withdrew its consulate from Taiwan immediately. Diplomatic relations between China and West Germany were established on Oct. 11, 1972, during a visit to Beijing by Walter Scheel, the West German Foreign Minister.

Both the Soviet Union and China developed contacts with the European Community during the mid-1970s—the Soviet Union through Comecon, which built up closer relations with the EEC in negotiations between autumn 1974 and early 1976. The Chinese ambassador to Belgium, Li Lianbi, was on Sept. 15, 1975, accredited as China's ambassador to the European Community. China thus became the second Communist country (the other being Yugoslavia) to have taken up official accreditation with the Community.

European Community (the official publication of the London office of the European Commission) observed that "in 1969 the EEC was still being variously portrayed by Beijing as the 'centre of imperialist contradictions' and 'an American machination'. By 1971, however, the Community, on the verge of its enlargement, had become 'a factor of equilibrium between the super-powers' for a China whose cardinal strategic tenet was—and remains—rejection of a bipolar world [i.e. dominated by the Soviet Union and the United States]."

A five-year non-preferential trade agreement was signed by the EEC and China on April 3, 1978. Further negotiations between the EEC and Comecon also took place during 1977–78, although serious obstacles prevented these contacts from producing any substantive result.

James Callaghan, the British Prime Minister, on Jan. 16, 1979, stated that the West wanted to develop closer relations with China, although not at the expense of détente with the Soviet Union. In fact, relations between the Soviet Union and the West were already deteriorating by this point, with a growth in mutual suspicion. Callaghan mentioned the United Kingdom's plans to sell 80 Harrier fighter jets to China. At the same time China was also negotiating for the purchase of substantial supplies of military equipment from France, with which it signed a major trade agreement on Dec. 4, 1978.

The Soviet news agency Tass on Jan. 24, 1979, confirmed earlier reports that President Brezhnev had sent several personal warnings to Callaghan that the sale of Harrier jets to China would seriously damage UK-Soviet relations. According to Tass the Soviet leader had asserted inter alia that "military deliveries can hardly be put in the framework of ordinary trade"; that such sales "cannot but affect the interests of other states, especially those bordering on the one which is being armed"; and that "contributing towards militarization means complicating the resolution of international problems and undermining the fundamentals of confidence among states". Similar warnings were understood to have been forwarded to France and Italy (also a potential supplier of arms to China).

During a tour of Western Europe, including visits to France, West Germany, the United Kingdom and Italy, from Oct. 15 to Nov. 6, 1979, Hua Guofeng attacked the Soviet Union sharply several times. He prefaced his departure with a press conference for West European journalists on Oct. 6, when he emphasized that China was not against détente, but was against "hegemonism" and the "policies of aggression and expansion", adding: "With the hegemonists engaged in expansion and aggression, it is impossible to have détente even if you desire it. There has been no détente in the world in the past year, particularly in the Middle East, in Africa, in the Red Sea and the Gulf area, in South Asia and in Indo-China. . . . While opposing hegemonism, we also want to caution people against following a policy of appeasement."

Beginning his tour in France, Hua (who was accompanied by Huang Hua, the Foreign Minister, and Yu Qiuli, a Deputy Premier and Chairman of the State Planning Commission) had talks with President Giscard d'Estaing. On Oct. 18, 1979, Hua gave a press conference at which he gave his views on relations with the Soviet Union.

He said that although agreements between the Western countries and the Soviet Union "might serve some purpose", it was more important to "take effective action and wage a tit-for-tat struggle against acts of expansion and aggression". The Soviet forces enjoyed a strong superiority over those of Western Europe in both conventional and nuclear weapons, and China wished Europe to strengthen its co-operation and its defences, as a strong and united Europe would be in the interests of world peace. He maintained that the Soviet Union supported Vietnam's attempts to establish an Indo-Chinese federation as part of its global strategy, in order to link up its military deployment in South-East Asia with that in the Red Sea, the Persian Gulf and the Indian Ocean.

During his visit to West Germany on Oct. 21–28, 1979, Hua expressed his support for German reunification, and he repeated his call for "all the peace-loving countries and peoples in the world" to unite against "hegemonist aggression and expansion". In the UK (where he stayed until Nov. 3) Hua was still more outspoken in his attacks on the Soviet Union than he had been earlier in the tour. He praised Margaret Thatcher, the British Prime Minister, stating that she "had unequivocally identified the source of the war danger and called for effective counter-measures". On Oct. 31 Hua remarked that growing Anglo–Chinese collaboration "may be a source of irritation to some people". He again attacked "some people seeking world hegemony" in a speech at a luncheon given by the Governor of the Bank of England on Nov. 1, 1979.

While in Italy (which he visited on Nov. 3–6) Hua met Enrico Berlinguer, the secretary of the Italian Communist Party (which disagreed frequently with the Soviet Communist Party) as well as Francesco Cossiga, the Italian Prime Minister. During the Italian and other stages of the Chinese delegation's tour of Western Europe, a number of economic and other agreements were signed. On several occasions Hua made clear China's wish to expand trade and economic co-operation with Western Europe. Politically, the aim of the tour was—according to remarks made by Hua in the UK on Nov. 2—not the formation of an alliance, but an exchange of views on problems of common concern.

The worsening climate in East-West relations after December 1979 (when the NATO countries decided on the deployment of US intermediate-range nuclear missiles in Western Europe, and the Soviet Union sent its forces into Afghanistan) presented fertile ground for increased dialogue between China and Western Europe. At the same time, China was interested in balancing its links with the USA and Japan, both for political reasons and in order to promote competition among Western countries and companies for trade with China.

Zhao Ziyang, the Chinese Prime Minister, travelled in Western Europe from May 30 to June 16, 1984, visiting France, Belgium, Sweden, Denmark, Norway and Italy. On the eve of his departure he said that China would "always support the efforts of Western Europe to become strong and powerful". Addressing the French Parliament on May 30, Zhao urged the super-powers to "adopt an attitude of restraint, to stop deploying new nuclear weapons, to conduct serious talks and to make due efforts towards drastically reducing nuclear weapons". He said that the task of containing the two super-powers would be greatly helped by a "closer co-operation between China with its independent policy and a Europe that is the master of its own destiny". During his tour of Western Europe, a further series of economic agreements between China and European states were signed.

XIV: THE POST-BREZHNEV PERIOD, 1982–84

Bilateral contacts between China and the Soviet Union developed steadily following the death of Leonid Brezhnev in November 1982 and the succession of Yury Andropov to the Soviet leadership. Trading links were extended and cultural and sporting exchanges became more frequent, while talks at deputy foreign minister level were held biannually (beginning in October 1982) to discuss the normalization of relations. However, these talks made no progress towards resolving outstanding issues, as China continued to insist on wide-ranging safeguards for Chinese security including: a Soviet withdrawal from Afghanistan, the ending of Soviet support for Vietnam, as well as the reduction of Soviet forces on the Chinese border. The Soviet negotiators, on the other hand, wished to restrict talks to purely bilateral issues.

Following the deterioration in China's relations with the United States in the early 1980s [see Chapter X], the Beijing Government appeared to be moving towards a neutral position between the two super-powers; Chinese foreign policy statements during this period stressed China's independent and non-aligned position. When China's relations with the United States improved in late 1983, the Chinese leadership dissociated itself from US anti-Soviet rhetoric. Other Chinese actions, however, exacerbated Sino-Soviet relations, such as the development of its relations with East and West European states and with Japan, as strategic counterweights to the two super-powers. Moreover, renewed conflict on the Sino-Vietnamese border in the first half of 1984 also provoked strong Soviet protests against alleged Chinese aggression.

Furthermore, Konstantin Chernenko, who succeeded Andropov following the latter's death in February 1984, adopted a more hard-line policy towards China. This appeared to be part of a wider trend in Soviet policy seen in a number of prevailing circumstances, including: the continuing impasse over restarting East-West talks on reducing intermediate-range nuclear missiles in Europe (discontinued by the Soviet Union in November 1983); the launching of a major new Soviet offensive in early 1984 in Afghanistan; and the Soviet boycott of the Los Angeles Olympic Games in July 1984.

These developments slowed the early momentum toward improved Sino-Soviet relations, but did not halt it. Qian Qichen, the Chinese Deputy Foreign Minister, visited Moscow in July 1984.

Brezhnev's Tashkent Speech (March 1982)

In a speech in Tashkent on March 24, 1982, President Brezhnev, besides repeating the offer made in the Soviet Note of Feb. 1 that year to reopen border talks [see page 153], made an appeal for normalization of relations which the *Financial Times* described as "the most emphatic conciliatory gesture since the dispute over the border between the two nations took them to the brink of war in 1969".

"The principled position of our party and Soviet state on the matter of Soviet-Chinese relations", President Brezhnev said, "was set forth clearly in the decisions of the 25th and 26th CPSU congresses [see Chapters VII and XI respectively]. I would like here to recall additionally the following things:

"First, despite the fact that we have openly criticized, and continue to criticize, many aspects of the policy (especially the foreign policy) of the Chinese leadership as being at variance with socialist principles and standards, we have never tried to interfere in the internal life of the PRC [People's Republic of China]. We have not denied and do not deny now the existence of a socialist system in China. Beijing's lining up with the policy of the imperialists in the world arena, however, is of course contrary to the interests of socialism.

"Second, we have never supported, and do not support now in any form, the so-called 'concept of two Chinas', but have fully recognized, and continue to recognize, the PRC's sovereignty over Taiwan island.

"Third, there has not been and there is no threat to the PRC from the Soviet Union. We have not had and do not have any territorial claims on the PRC, and we are ready at any time to continue talks on existing border questions for the purpose of reaching mutually acceptable decisions. We are also ready to discuss the matter of possible measures to strengthen mutual trust in the Soviet-Chinese border area.

"Fourth, we remember well the time when the Soviet Union and People's China were united by bonds of friendship and comradely co-operation. We have never considered as normal the state of hostility and estrangement between our countries. We are prepared to come to terms, without any preliminary conditions, on measures acceptable to both sides to improve Soviet–Chinese relations on the bases of mutual respect for each other's interests, non-interference in each other's affairs and mutual benefit—and certainly not to the detriment of third countries. This refers to economic, scientific and cultural as well as political relations, as the two sides become ready for these or other specific steps in any of these spheres. . . ."

A Chinese Foreign Ministry spokesman commented on President Brezhnev's speech on March 26, 1982: "We firmly reject the attacks on China contained in the remarks. What we attach importance to are actual deeds of the Soviet Union in Sino-Soviet relations and international affairs."

Obstacles to Improved Relations (May–September 1982)

The first contacts between the two countries' Foreign Ministries after President Brezhnev's Tashkent speech of March 1982 occurred during a visit to Beijing on May 13–21, 1982, by Mikhail Kapitsa, director of the Soviet Foreign Ministry's Far Eastern Department (subsequently appointed a Deputy Foreign Minister in December 1982). Although the visit was officially described as a private one at the invitation of the Soviet ambassador, Kapitsa had a number of meetings with Qian Qichen, a Deputy Foreign Minister, and Yu Hongliang, director of the Chinese Foreign Ministry's Soviet and East European Department. According to unofficial reports Yu Hongliang visited Moscow in August 1982 to discuss arrangements for the resumption of talks on the disputed Sino-Soviet border, which a Chinese Foreign Ministry spokesman said on Sept. 15 should be resumed once adequate preparations had been completed.

Contacts between the two countries had increased during the spring and summer of 1982. Two Chinese scientists attended an international symposium held in Dushanbe (the capital of Soviet Tajikistan) in April; Soviet athletes took part in sporting events in Beijing in June and September, for the first time since 1966; and two Soviet economists visited Beijing in July.

The steps towards re-establishing bilateral talks were not accompanied, however, by any greater flexibility in the positions held by the two countries, which had deadlocked previous talks. The three major obstacles to improved relations were repeatedly identified by Chinese spokesmen as (i) the deployment of large numbers of Soviet troops on the Chinese border and in Mongolia, (ii) the Soviet intervention in Afghanistan and (iii) Soviet support for the Vietnamese occupation of Kampuchea. Chinese spokesmen alleged that 1,000,000 Soviet troops were stationed on or near the border; Japanese military sources, however, estimated the strength of the two countries' forces in the frontier areas at 450,000 Soviet and 1,500,000 Chinese troops. The Soviet negotiators, however, said that the talks should be confined to bilateral issues and should not cover issues affecting third countries. These positions were reiterated in policy statements made during this period.

An article published in *Pravda* on May 20, 1982, while Kapitsa was in Beijing, said that the Soviet Union made no territorial or other claims on China, and was ready to continue border talks at any time. It criticized, however, Chinese demands for "renunciation of support and assistance to the Mongolian People's Republic, the countries of Indo-China and Afghanistan, unilateral withdrawal of the armed forces of the Soviet Union from the border with the People's Republic of China and recognition of China's 'rights' to vast areas of the USSR", and commented that "the piling up of all sorts of preliminary conditions bordering on ultimatums in no way testifies to a desire on the part of the Chinese side to find a way out of the blind alley in which Soviet–Chinese relations are at the moment". The article was signed "Igor Alexandrov", the pseudonym used for semi-official policy statements.

Hu Yaobang, who was elected as CPC general secretary on Sept. 12, 1982 (the post of chairman having been abolished), repeated demands for a reduction of Soviet forces on the Chinese border, the ending of Soviet support for the Vietnamese occupation of Kampuchea and the withdrawal of Soviet troops from Afghanistan, in his report to the 12th party congress on Sept. 1, 1982, and accused both the Soviet Union and the United States of "hegemonism". The new party constitution adopted by the congress, however, omitted references to "the hegemonism of the two super-powers" and to Soviet "modern revisionism" contained in the previous constitution.

The issue of *Beijing Review* for Aug. 8, 1982, had previously said that "as the Soviet Union is on the offensive and the United States on the defensive in their contention, the major threat to world peace comes from the Soviet Union".

President Brezhnev said in a speech in Baku on Sept. 26, 1982, that "we would deem it very important to achieve a normalization, a gradual improvement of relations between the USSR and the People's Republic of China on a basis which I would describe as that of common sense, mutual respect and mutual advantage". During talks with Zenko Suzuki (then the Japanese Prime Minister), who was visiting China, however, the Chinese Prime Minister, Zhao Ziyang, said on the following day that the establishment of contacts between the Soviet Union and China was not easy and would take time, and that the Soviet Union must take measures to remove the threats to China's security presented by the deployment of Soviet troops on the frontier and in Mongolia, Soviet support for the Vietnamese invasion of Kampuchea and the occupation of Afghanistan. He added that China had no desire to "play the Soviet card against the United States or the American card against the USSR", and that there could be no question of "allowing anyone to play the Chinese card".

Consultations at Deputy Foreign Minister Level (October 1982)

Talks at deputy foreign minister level (officially described as "consultations") opened in Beijing on Oct. 5, 1982, and concluded on Oct. 21. The Soviet delegation was led by Leonid Ilyichev, who had headed the Soviet delegation at the Beijing border talks of 1970–78 [see Chapter X] and the Moscow talks of 1979 [see Chapter XI], and the Chinese delegation by Qian Qichen.

As it had been agreed not to reveal the content of the talks, no official statement or communiqué was issued. Wang Bingnan, president of the Chinese People's Association for Friendship with Foreign Countries, however, said in Tokyo on Oct. 7 that China had demanded the withdrawal of 600,000 troops from the border, and other statements by Chinese leaders indicated that the questions of Kampuchea and Afghanistan had also been raised. The Soviet delegation, on the other hand, was believed to have attempted to confine the talks to strictly bilateral matters such as trade and economic and cultural exchanges. Both sides agreed to continue the consultations alternately in Moscow and Beijing.

Brezhnev's Death (November 1982) and Renewed Polemics

The death of President Brezhnev on Nov. 10, 1982, provided a further impetus to the gradual rapprochement between the two countries. Huang Hua, the Chinese Foreign Minister, flew to Moscow on Nov. 14 to represent China at the funeral on Nov. 15 and also met the Soviet Foreign Minister, Andrei Gromyko. Huang was the highest-ranking Chinese minister to visit Moscow since the visit in 1964 by Zhou Enlai, then Prime Minister; his meeting with Gromyko was the highest-level meeting between Chinese and Soviet ministers since that between Zhou and Alexei Kosygin, then the Soviet Prime Minister, in Beijing in 1969 [see page 143].

After the funeral, Yury Andropov held a brief reception at which he met the leaders of numerous foreign delegations; much the longest of his conversations was with Huang Hua. Following Huang's meeting with Gromyko, Tass reported that the Soviet Foreign Minister had stressed "that the Soviet leadership attaches great significance to normalization of relations with the People's Republic of China, and that it will continue to strive for the switching of these relations onto the lines of good-neighbourliness"; for his part, Huang had reportedly expressed a hope "that through the joint efforts of both countries relations between them will be gradually normalized". Both men (according to the same Tass report) had agreed "that a political dialogue between the Soviet Union and the People's Republic of China should be continued". On returning to Beijing on Nov. 18, 1982, Huang said that he and Gromyko had "discussed ways of removing obstacles" to the consultations between their deputies, and that he was "optimistic" about the prospects for them.

Viktor Afanasyev, the editor of *Pravda*, told Japanese journalists in Tokyo on Nov. 16, 1982, that "the two sides might promise each other a reduction of military forces in border areas". He also stated that the Soviet troops would eventually withdraw from Afghanistan; the Soviet Union, he added, did not intend to establish a Soviet-type regime there, and wanted Afghanistan to be a non-aligned country maintaining good-neighbourly relations with the USSR. His remarks apparently referred to the proposals for "removing obstacles" put forward by Gromyko.

Andropov, who succeeded Brezhnev as general secretary of the Soviet Communist Party and subsequently as President, said on Nov. 22, 1982, that the Soviet Union wanted to "improve relations with all socialist nations", including "our great neighbour, the People's Republic of China". The Chinese Foreign Ministry commented on Nov. 25 that it had "noted" his statement, and hoped to see the new Soviet leadership "make a new effort in eliminating the obstacles hindering the normalization of relations".

In a message of greeting to the Soviet Government on the 60th anniversary of the founding of the USSR (in 1922), the Chinese Government said: "China sincerely hopes that the relations between the two countries will be normalized step by step and a good-neighbourly relationship established. The two sides should jointly work for the realization of this goal through negotiations, concrete actions and removal of obstacles." The message was published in *Pravda* on Dec. 26, 1982, but did not appear in Beijing until two days later, and then only as a report by the English-language service of the New China News Agency.

Pierre Bauby, political secretary of the French Marxist-Leninist Communist Party (a Maoist organization), who had recently returned from Beijing, stated in Paris on Jan. 5, 1983, that China had sent the Soviet Union proposals for a settlement of the Kampuchean problem, which would "enable the Kampuchean people to decide in full independence on the future of a neutral and non-aligned Kampuchea, improve relations between the different countries of the region and re-establish peace there".

Attacks on Soviet policies meanwhile continued to appear in the Chinese press, though less frequently than in the past. The *People's Daily* accused the Soviet Union on Dec. 1, 1982, of "hegemonist ambitions of a long-term occupation of Afghanistan and proceeding south", and declared on Dec. 27 that "the Soviet aggression against Afghanistan is a major step in the Soviet global strategy for world domination". An article on the situation on the Sino-Soviet border, however, which appeared in December 1982 in the official monthly magazine *Observation Post*, stated: "Over the past six months or so the border has seemed quieter than before, military exercises by the Soviet Army have been held less frequently, and disputes involving [each other's] foreign nationals have stood a better chance of being solved fairly reasonably. . . ."

In the first attack on China in the Soviet press for more than six months, the weekly journal *New Times* accused the Chinese Government on Jan. 14, 1983, of putting forward claims to 1,500,000 square kilometres of Soviet territory, which it alleged had been annexed by the Russian Tsars under "unequal treaties", and declared that "a genuine striving to improve and normalize Soviet–Chinese relations presupposes clear and unconditional renunciation of territorial claims on each other". The article was distributed in advance of publication by the official Tass agency. The Chinese reply, published in the *People's Daily* on Jan. 23, 1983, accused *New Times* of defending "Tsarist aggression against China", which had been condemned by Marx, Engels and Lenin, and stated: "China has no territorial claims whatsoever on the Soviet Union, nor does it demand the return of territories ceded to Tsarist Russia under a series of unequal treaties, but stands for an overall solution to the border issue through peaceful negotiations by taking into consideration the actual conditions, and on the basis of the above-mentioned treaties. . . ."

Second Round of Talks (March 1983)

A second round of talks between delegations headed by Leonid Ilyichev and Qian Qichen took place in Moscow from March 1 to 15, 1983. According to Chinese sources, the Soviet delegation proposed the signing of a non-aggression pact and measures to restore confidence on the frontier, but refused to discuss Afghanistan or Kampuchea on the ground that these questions involved third countries. The Chinese delegation, on the other hand, held that the signing of such a pact would have little meaning unless the three main obstacles to normal relations were all removed.

After visiting Uzbekistan, Qian met Gromyko on March 21, 1983. A Tass statement on the meeting said that the Soviet side had "expressed its readiness to examine ways towards the normalization of relations with the People's Republic of China and the existing possibilities for gradual broadening of bilateral ties and contacts, which would promote a general improvement of relations". On returning to Beijing Qian said on March 22 that there had been no new developments, but that the consultations had been "useful". A Chinese Foreign Ministry spokesman said on March 31 that it had been agreed in principle to revive student exchanges, beginning with 10 students from each country.

Polemics, however, were resumed by both sides in the following months. During a visit to New Zealand Zhao Ziyang expressed concern on April 15, 1983, at the increased build-up of the Soviet naval presence in the Pacific, and particularly the Soviet ability to use Vietnamese ports. The Soviet Government newspaper *Izvestia* accused Chinese leaders on April 19 of hindering the normalization of relations by repeating Western "fabrications" about an alleged Soviet military threat. Hu Yaobang said in an interview on May 5 that Indo-China was the main obstacle to the normalization of relations, and that China was determined to struggle against global or local hegemonism.

Further Bilateral Contacts (July–September 1983)

Despite these polemics, cultural and sporting exchanges between the two countries continued to increase. Chinese delegations took part in the Moscow film festival in July 1983 and the Moscow book fair in September, for the first time for many years, and a Soviet football team arrived in Beijing on Aug. 11. A spokesman for the China Tourism Administration said that the Soviet Intourist organization would be represented at a forthcoming international conference on tourism in Beijing, and that Soviet tourists had been visiting China since 1981.

Soviet and Chinese statements in the late summer of 1983 were noticeably warmer in tone. President Andropov called on Aug. 26 for an expansion of trade, the development of bilateral exchanges and a relaxation of tensions on the border, and said that the Soviet Union was ready for a political dialogue with China on problems of strengthening peace and international security, which both countries needed in order to accomplish major long-term economic tasks. Welcoming his appeal, President Li Xiannian said on Sept. 2, 1983, that although obstacles to the normalization of relations still existed, China sincerely hoped that they would be removed, so that the two countries could develop "normal state relations on the basis of the five principles of peaceful coexistence". An article published on Sept. 1 in the official Chinese magazine *World Knowledge* said that the Sino-Soviet treaty of friendship and alliance (allowed to lapse by China in 1980—see page 138) had benefited both countries, promoted world peace and thwarted the "US imperialists", who were "propping up the Japanese militarists".

Mikhail Kapitsa arrived in Beijing on Sept. 8, 1983, for talks with Qian Qichen, and also met Wu Xueqian on Sept. 15. (Huang Hua, who was suffering from ill-health, had been replaced as Foreign Minister by Wu on Nov. 19, 1982.) Whereas his previous visits had been described as private ones as the guest of the Soviet ambassador, the New China News Agency emphasized that Kapitsa had come as the guest of Qian Qichen.

Soviet sources stated that Kapitsa and Qian had found a number of "points of convergence" in Soviet and Chinese foreign policies, but Chinese sources said that Kapitsa had been told that no fundamental improvement in relations could occur until the three main obstacles were removed, although China remained ready to reciprocate movement on any of them. According to Japanese reports, it was agreed to expand exchanges of students and tourists and cultural and sporting contacts, and to study a possible resumption of Soviet technical co-operation in the modernization of China. On leaving for Moscow on Sept. 16, 1983, Kapitsa described the talks as "businesslike", and said that "we have opened a new channel of contact, this time on international affairs".

During Kapitsa's visit to Beijing, China was among four countries which abstained on Sept. 12, 1983, on the draft United Nations Security Council resolution (vetoed by the USSR) which deplored the destruction of the South Korean airliner shot down by a Soviet fighter aircraft on Sept. 1, after it had flown into Soviet airspace.

Third Round of Talks (October 1983) and Further Polemics

A third round of talks between Ilyichev and Qian which opened in Beijing on Oct. 6, 1983, made no apparent progress in overcoming China's "three obstacles" to improved relations. These had been extended to include the question of Soviet SS-20 missiles sited on China's Far Eastern borders. At a news briefing on Oct. 5 Qi Huaiyuan, director of the information department at the Chinese Foreign Ministry, said that there was no fixed schedule or timetable for the talks, and also stated, in reply to a question, that the matter of the deployment of SS-20s along the border should be included within the "three obstacles", as China hoped that the Soviet Union would reduce its troops along the border "including conventional and nuclear weapons".

When commenting earlier on the US–Soviet talks being conducted in Geneva on reduction of intermediate-range nuclear forces in Europe *The People's Daily* had said on Sept. 17, 1983: "The Soviet Union has already deployed large numbers of SS-20 missiles in its Asian region, and these pose a very serious threat to China and other Asian countries. If, as it says, the Soviet Union really hopes to reduce the danger of nuclear war, the missiles which it has deployed in the Asian region must also be greatly reduced. One of the three main obstacles to the development of Sino-Soviet relations which China has called on the Soviet Union to remove is that of reducing military forces in the Sino-Soviet and Sino-Mongolian border regions, and this naturally includes missiles. . . ." (There were an estimated 108 such missiles deployed by the Soviet Union in its Far Eastern territories and Soviet officials at the talks had said that some of the missiles removed from the European theatre would be redeployed in the Soviet Far East.)

At the end of Ilyichev's visit to Beijing a communiqué was issued on Oct. 30, 1983, stating that the talks had been useful and that a fourth round would be held in Moscow in March 1984. Sources indicated that agreement was reached on increasing trade and low-level technological exchanges and strengthening cultural and sporting links, but that the Chinese delegation had dismissed a Soviet proposal that the Vietnamese problem should be discussed in a separate forum.

On the anniversary of the Soviet October Revolution, a goodwill message was sent from the Chinese leadership to the Soviet people calling for "friendly relations"; the message was published at the top of a list of greetings in *Pravda* on Nov. 7, 1983.

Wu Xueqian, in a major policy statement on Dec. 7, 1983, to the Standing Committee of the National People's Congress, said that talks on normalizing relations with the Soviet Union had made no headway because of Moscow's refusal to discuss the "three obstacles". This deadlock resulted in a growing number of attacks in the Soviet and Chinese media on each other's policies. Soviet criticism became particularly intense in late 1983 when Sino-Japanese relations improved with the visit to Tokyo on Nov. 23–26 by Wu and Hu Yaobang.

Following a visit to Vietnam in late October 1983 by Geidar Aliyev (a Soviet First Deputy Premier), Xinhua on Nov. 3 attacked the Soviet use of military bases in Vietnam, saying that the Soviet Union "had moved its outposts in the Asian and Pacific region southward by more than 2,000 nautical miles" and that this threatened "the security of all the countries" in the region and also "international sea-lanes". An article in the Soviet newspaper *Izvestia* (signed A. Petrov, a pseudonym used for high-level Soviet statements) criticized a statement made by Wu during his Japanese visit which referred to the responsibility of "the two nuclear super-powers" for the nuclear arms race. "Is it really permissible", *Izvestia* asked, "to ignore the true sources of the growing military danger whose roots lie in the adventurism of the most reactionary circles of imperialism and to attempt in the guise of impartiality to distort the peace-loving aims of the Soviet Union?" On the same day *Pravda* criticized Wu's "astonishing" support for Japan's claim to the Soviet-held islands off northern Japan which Tokyo regarded as part of its national territory but which had been occupied by the Soviet Union since 1945 [see pages 105 and 160]. It quoted a pro-Soviet statement made in 1950 on this issue by Zhou Enlai, the then Chinese Prime Minister, and described Wu's statement as "interference in the affairs of other countries" and a "manifestation of hegemonism".

Soviet polemics against China were renewed in early 1984, partly in response to the improvement in Sino-US relations related to Zhao Ziyang's visit to Washington in January of that year. *Izvestia* on Jan. 3 attacked Xinhua (the official Chinese news agency) for publishing what it described as anti-Soviet lies about Soviet policy in Afghanistan, while *Krasnaya Zvezda* (the Soviet army newspaper) criticized China for seeing a military threat only from the Soviet Union and ignoring the US military build-up. During Zhao's visit to the USA, the Soviet media accused China of adopting a pro-US stance on the issue of nuclear arms.

The improvement in Sino-US relations had begun in late 1983. The joint communiqué on reducing US arms sales to Taiwan concluded in August 1982 [see Chapter X] had not prevented controversy over this question continuing for several months. A number of other issues had contributed to cool relations in early 1983, including the decision in April to grant political asylum in the United States to the Chinese tennis player Hu Na, which had led to China cancelling all official cultural and athletic exchanges with the United States. US–Chinese relations had improved, however, after a visit to Beijing by Malcolm Baldridge, the US Secretary of Commerce, who informed the Chinese Government that restrictions on the export of high technology would be relaxed. The latter measures were instituted in June 1983, paving the way for the successful visits of Caspar Weinberger (the US Secretary of Defence) to China in September 1983 and of Zhao to Washington in January 1984.

Andropov's Death (February 1984)—Consequences for Sino-Soviet Relations

In a press interview on Jan. 24, 1984, Hu Yaobang made a renewed appeal for a rapprochement with the Soviet Union. Calling for greater flexibility on the part of Soviet negotiators, he said that the "possibility" for an improvement in relations still existed and that "it is also our hope". The Chinese initiative was pursued following the death of President Andropov on Feb. 9, 1984.

Wan Li, a Deputy Premier and the highest-ranking Chinese figure to visit Moscow for 20 years, represented China at the funeral. At a brief reception for foreign leaders held after the funeral, Konstantin Chernenko (who was later appointed to replace Andropov) spoke only briefly to Wan, who later held a meeting with Geidar Aliyev.

In subsequent developments, Deng Xiaoping reportedly said on Feb. 22, 1984, that "radical changes" in Sino-Soviet relations were unlikely while the "three obstacles" remained, but maintained that this "must not stop us from improving and developing ties in certain other areas". On March 9, 1984, the newspaper *China Daily* announced that Wang Bingnan, president of the Chinese People's Association for Friendship with Foreign Countries, would visit the Soviet Union later in 1984.

Fourth Round of Talks (March 1984)

Speculation that the improved climate of relations would produce a breakthrough, in the fourth round of talks scheduled for March 1984 in Moscow, was countered by Chinese and Soviet statements in early March. Wan Li said on March 2 that he did not think that "the policies of a country will change with the death of a single person". In a speech on the same day, Chernenko rejected the Chinese call to break the deadlock, saying that the Soviet Union could not make agreements to the detriment of a third country. The Soviet news agency Tass published, at the beginning of March 1984, a Mongolian government statement rejecting Chinese demands for the withdrawal of Soviet troops from its territory. The presence of these troops, the statement said, was a "purely domestic matter" posing no threat to Chinese security.

The fourth round of talks between delegations headed by Qian Qichen and Leonid Ilyichev took place in Moscow on March 12–27, 1984. No apparent progress was made on the main issues but a joint statement noted beneficial links in sports, trade and culture. Western diplomats said that China was keen to emphasize points of contact, to show a balance between the two super-powers on the eve of President Reagan's visit to China [see below]. Tass reported on March 27 that the talks had taken place in a frank and calm atmosphere and would resume in October 1984.

During the talks Qian met with the Soviet Foreign Minister Andrei Gromyko on March 23, 1984. Tass reported that they discussed international problems and the need for a positive dialogue between China and the Soviet Union, and that Gromyko expressed his hope for a further improvement in relations.

President Reagan's Visit to China (April 1984)

President Reagan visited China from April 26 to May 1, 1984, in his first trip to a Communist country and the first visit to China by a US President since the establishment of formal diplomatic relations in 1979 [see page 118]. The trip represented a further step in the recent improvement in Sino-US relations on the basis of pledges to continue co-operation in all fields. Four protocols were signed, including an agreement to resume cultural exchanges (called off in April 1983—see above), and a tax treaty preventing the double taxation of Chinese and US companies operating in the other country. A pact on nuclear co-operation was also initialled. Talks between President Reagan and Chinese leaders, however, underlined the independent direction of Chinese foreign policy.

Zhao criticized US policy on disarmament as well as the US stance in Central America, the Middle East and Korea (where US troops were stationed in South Korea), while Deng Xiaoping stressed that the Taiwan issue still "overshadowed" China's relations with the United States. Furthermore, President Reagan's remarks criticizing the Soviet Union (and extolling the benefits of capitalism) were censored in the Chinese media on two occasions. A Chinese Foreign Ministry spokesman explained that it was "inappropriate" for the Chinese media to publicize the comments by President Reagan on a third country.

In particular, Chinese television broadcasts covering a speech made by President Reagan on April 27, 1984, deleted his comments alluding to the Soviet threat to China's borders, the occupation of Afghanistan, the "crushing" of Kampuchea and the shooting down of a South Korean airliner by a Soviet fighter in 1983. The Chinese authorities also censored remarks made by the US President during an interview for Chinese television on April 28 which referred obliquely to the Soviet threat; the USA, said Reagan in that interview, had "no troops massed" on the Chinese border.

Soviet criticism of China's "military and economic co-operation" with the USA was stepped up during the visit, although plans had been announced on April 25, 1984, for a visit to China in May by Ivan Arkhipov, a Soviet

First Deputy Premier [see below]. Moreover, it was reported that a Chinese friendship delegation then travelling in Eastern Europe would travel to Moscow—the first such visit for 20 years.

In a long commentary on April 24, 1984, Tass described an identity of views between the USA and China on "Japanese militarism", Afghanistan, Kampuchea and Vietnam, and complained about recent Chinese "anti-Soviet" statements which failed to condemn the USA's "militaristic policy". It said that the USA was seeking to penetrate and dominate China economically through capital investment and the sale of technology for weapons and it criticized China for co-operating with "imperialist" countries. On April 29 Tass denounced President Reagan for his "calumnious" attacks on the Soviet Union and for attempting to draw China into an anti-Soviet alliance. Following President Reagan's departure, Tass criticized Chinese leaders on May 3 for allowing themselves to be used in tacitly or even openly supporting US policies and asserted that Beijing was taking positions that "hinder the normalization of Sino-Soviet relations".

Further polemics were engendered by Gen. Zhang Aiping's visit to the USA in June 1984, when it was announced on June 14 that "an agreement in principle" had been reached for the sale of anti-tank and anti-aircraft weapons to China. A commentary released by the Soviet press on June 6, 1984, warned that "if Sino-US military co-operation poses a threat to the Soviet Union, its friends and allies, Moscow will undoubtedly find an adequate answer to any menace". It also warned the US administration that China would exploit it, and that it should take care in selling weapons to China which could pose a military threat to the USA and the Soviet Union.

Postponement of Soviet Deputy Premier's Visit to China (May 1984)

Ivan Arkhipov, a Soviet Deputy Premier and prospectively the most senior official to visit China for 15 years, was due to arrive in Beijing on May 10, 1984, for trade talks; Tass announced on May 9, however, that the visit had been postponed "by mutual agreement". Qi Huaiyuan, a spokesman for the Chinese Foreign Ministry, said on the same day that the trip had been called off as it was "not fully prepared" and that no new date for the visit had been set. Zhou Ziyang, in the first official comment on the cancellation of the visit, said on May 23 that it would not affect talks on improving relations. Earlier, on May 18, Wu Xueqian had said that it was "no use for the Soviet Union to resort to various excuses to evade a discussion" of the three Chinese obstacles to improved relations.

Some Western commentators viewed the development as underlining Soviet disapproval over growing Sino-US ties, although it appeared more directly linked to the recent increase in tension between China and Vietnam. On April 28, 1984, China launched a series of attacks on the Vietnamese border, described as the heaviest since China's February 1979 invasion, and on May 1 China's southern fleet carried out manoeuvres which on one occasion appeared to threaten the Vietnamese-held Spratly Islands [for China's dispute with Vietnam over these islands, see page 163]. Soviet criticism of Chinese policy culminated on June 18, 1984, in President Chernenko's first direct condemnation of China for its "hostile actions" in Indo-China. In reply China intensified its anti-Soviet rhetoric, comparing

Soviet activities in Afghanistan to "Nazi atrocities" and denouncing Soviet support for Vietnam.

In earlier exchanges, Tass accused China in May 1984 of invading Vietnamese territory and committing serious "armed provocations" which were reprehensible and short-sighted. Xinhua on May 5 rejected the criticism, maintaining that Moscow had distorted facts to cover up Vietnamese aggression and was supporting Vietnamese invasions into Chinese territory.

Nevertheless, it was announced in Beijing on June 20, 1984, that Qian Qichen was to visit Moscow as the official guest of Mikhail Kapitsa, who had extended the invitation during his visit to China in late 1983. During his stay commencing on July 2, Qian had a meeting with Gromyko, described by Tass as part of "consultations on international issues", where he reiterated China's three preconditions for the normalization of relations. On his return from Moscow, Qian said that the talks had been "useful".

Sino-Soviet Economic Relations (1982–84)

A trade and payments agreement for 1983, under which the volume of trade between the two countries was expected to rise from $300,000,000 in 1982 to $800,000,000, was signed in Moscow on March 10, 1983, by the Soviet and Chinese Deputy Ministers of Foreign Trade. Under the agreement China would export meat, tea, edible oils, textiles and minerals, and would import machinery, lorries, non-ferrous metals, fertilizers and timber.

Following negotiations in Khabarovsk (in the Soviet Far East) in October 1982, two agreements were signed on April 10, 1983, on local trade between Heilongjiang province and the Soviet Far East and between Inner Mongolia and Siberia, under which China would barter edible oils, pork, grain spirit and textiles for timber, cement, glass and consumer goods. Cross-border trade had stopped in 1966 because of a dispute over payments, and had been officially suspended in 1969. Chinese sources stated on June 5 that China and the Soviet Union had agreed to open two crossing posts on the border of the Xinjiang autonomous region from July 1, 1983, to facilitate state-to-state trade exchanges.

The lack of progress in the normalization talks delayed the opening of the border crossings until Nov. 16, 1983, when a first delivery of Soviet lorries was made to the Chinese frontier town of Korgas in Xinjiang province. Xinhua reported the same day that Turugart, a town in southern Xinjiang, would also be reopened.

A trade and payments agreement for 1984, under which the annual value of trade between the two countries was expected to rise from $800,000,000 to $1,200 million, was signed in Beijing on Feb. 10, 1984, by the Soviet and Chinese Deputy Ministers of Trade.

There were reports that China was seeking to increase imports of Soviet technology, partly in order to replace the old equipment of industrial plants set up with Soviet aid in the 1950s, and partly to diversify its sources of foreign technology, preventing it from becoming dependent on one country. On April 12, 1984, while on a visit to Japan, Fang Yi (director of China's Scientific and Technological Commission) said that the Soviet Union had offered to sell nuclear reactors to China "unconditionally".

In other developments, on March 20, 1984, a Soviet passenger ship berthed at Shanghai for the first time since the 1960s, while the Soviet Union participated for the first time in 20 years in an international exhibition of medical equipment held in China in early 1984. A spokesman for the Chinese Ministry of Railways said on April 20, 1984, that China planned to expand rail links with the Soviet Union in Heilongjiang province and Inner Mongolia.

Improvement of Relations from September 1984—Soviet Deputy Premier's Visit to Beijing—Signature of Trade and Co-operation Agreements (December 1984)

During July and August 1984 official Chinese sources on several occasions accused the Soviet leadership of intensifying its anti-Chinese disposition. However, Sino-Soviet relations entered a new positive phase in September as a result of meetings in New York between Andrei Gromyko and his Chinese counterpart. This impetus to better relations was maintained in the following months, enabling the postponed Beijing visit of Soviet Deputy Premier Arkhipov to be reinstated in December 1984.

The talks between Gromyko and Wu Xueqian at the Chinese and Soviet UN missions in New York on Sept. 21–22, 1984, were the highest-level formal contacts between the two sides since September 1969. The discussions were described as frank and useful by both sides, following which the Soviet Government sent a relatively warm message to the Chinese President on Sept. 30 on the occasion of the 35th anniversary of the foundation of the People's Republic. During the second half of October Soviet Deputy Foreign Minister Leonid Ilyichev was in Beijing for talks with the Chinese leadership, and although the two sides remained seriously divided on three critical issues (the Soviet troop presence on the Chinese border, the Soviet intervention in Afghanistan and Soviet support for the Vietnamese involvement in Kampuchea) the Chinese side announced in early November that the Arkhipov visit would take place before the year's end.

Ivan Arkhipov arrived in Beijing on Dec. 21, 1984, to become the highest-ranking Soviet leader to visit China since 1969. He met the Chinese Prime Minister, Zhao Ziyang, in the course of his stay, which concluded with the signature on Dec. 28 by Arkhipov and his counterpart Yao Yilin of three agreements. These were (i) an agreement on economic and technical co-operation, (ii) an agreement on scientific and technological co-operation and (iii) an agreement to establish a Sino-Soviet committee for promoting trade and scientific and technological co-operation. According to authoritative reports, it was also agreed in principle during Arkhipov's visit that the volume of trade exchanges between the two countries should increase to a value of some $1,800 million in 1985 and that the two sides would seek to conclude a longer-term trade agreement covering the period 1986–90.

The outcome of Arkhipov's trip to Beijing indicated that China and the Soviet Union had moved to a greater degree of normalization in their relations than at any time since the 1969 border clashes. At the same time there appeared to be little prospect of the wheel turning full circle to restore the era of close friendship and co-operation of the early 1950s. Even during Arkhipov's visit the underlying tensions in Sino-Soviet relations were displayed in a commentary by the New China News Agency which not only dwelt upon the economic problems currently being experienced (it claimed) by the Soviet Union and other Comecon countries but also disclosed that China had recently strengthened its military defences along its border with the Soviet Union. In other words, the underlying geo-political rivalry and mutual suspicion of the two great powers of Asia, rooted in historical and territorial factors rather than in differences over ideological interpretation, had not been dissipated by the signature of three trade and co-operation agreements.

SELECT BIBLIOGRAPHY

CLEMENS, W.C., *The Arms Race and Sino-Soviet Relations*, Hoover Institution Studies (Stanford University), 1968

CLUBB, O.E., *China and Russia*, Colombia University Press (New York), 1971

CRANKSHAW, EDWARD, *The New Cold War: Moscow v. Peking*, Penguin Books, 1963

DOOLIN, D.J., *Territorial Claims in the Sino-Soviet Conflict*, Hoover Institution Studies (Stanford University), 1965

ELLISON, HERBERT J. (ed.), *The Sino-Soviet Conflict*, University of Washington Press (Seattle), 1982

GARTHOFF, R.L. (ed.), *Sino-Soviet Military Relations*, Praeger/Pall Mall Press, 1967

GELMAN, HARRY, *The Soviet Union and China*, The Rand Corporation (Santa Monica), 1980

GELMAN, HARRY, *The Soviet Far East Build-up and Soviet Risk-taking against China*, The Rand Corporation (Santa Monica), 1982

GINSBURG, G., and PINKELE, F.A., *The Sino-Soviet Territorial Dispute 1949–64*, Praeger (New York), 1978

GITTINGS, JOHN, *Survey of the Sino-Soviet Dispute: A Commentary and Extracts from the Recent Polemics*, Oxford University Press (for RIIA), 1969

GRIFFITHS, W.E., *Sino-Soviet Relations 1964–65*, MITP, 1967

GRIFFITHS, W.E., *Sino-Soviet Rift*, Allen & Unwin, 1964

HALPERIN, M.H. (ed.), *Sino-Soviet Relations and Arms Control*, MITP, 1967

HINTON, HAROLD C., *The Sino-Soviet Confrontation: Implications for the Future*, Crane Russak (New York), 1979

HOUSTON, J.V.D., *Russia and China*, R. Hale, 1960

JACKSON, W.A.D., *The Russo-Chinese Borderlands* (2nd ed.), Van Nostrand, 1968

JACOBSEN, C.G., *Sino-Soviet Relations since Mao*, Praeger (New York), 1981

LABEDZ, LEOPOLD, and URBAN, G., (eds.), *The Sino-Soviet Conflict*, The Bodley Head, 1965

LEVINE, D.C., *The Rift: The Sino-Soviet Conflict*, Harris-Wolfe, 1968

LIEBERTHAL, K.G., *Sino-Soviet Conflict in the 1970s: Its Evolution and Implications for the Strategic Triangle*, The Rand Corporation (Santa Monica), 1978

ROBINSON, T.W., *The Sino-Soviet Border Dispute: Background, Developments and the March 1969 Clashes*, The Rand Corporation (Santa Monica), 1970

ROBINSON, T.W., *The Border Negotiations and the Future of Sino-Soviet-American Relations*, The Rand Corporation (Santa Monica), 1971

RUPEN, R.A., and FARRELL, R. (eds.), *Vietnam and the Sino-Soviet Dispute*, Praeger (New York), 1967

SALISBURY, HARRISON E., *The Coming War between Russia and China,* Secker & Warburg/Pan Books, 1969

TAI SUNG AN, *The Sino-Soviet Territorial Dispute,* Westminster Press, 1973

TSIEN HUA TSUI, *The Sino-Soviet Border Dispute in the 1970s,* Mosaic Press (Ontario), 1983

TUNG, WILLIAM L., *China and the Foreign Powers: The Impact of and Reaction to Unequal Treaties,* Oceana Publications (New York), 1970

WATSON, F., *The Frontiers of China,* Praeger (New York), 1966

WEI, H., *China and Soviet Russia,* Van Nostrand, 1956

WHITING, ALLEN S., *Soviet Policies in China 1917–24,* Colombia University Press (New York), 1957

WU, A.K., *China and the Soviet Union,* Kennicat, 1968

ZAGORIA, D.S., *Sino-Soviet Conflict 1956–61,* Princeton, 1962

INDEX